W

"The Thir ond"

In the Peninsular and other Campaigns

BY

HARRY ROSS-LEWIN

OF ROSS HILL, CO. CLARE

EDITED BY

JOHN WARDELL, M.A.

READER IN MODERN HISTORY IN THE UNIVERSITY OF DUBLIN, AND
PROFESSOR OF JURISPRUDENCE AND POLITICAL ECONOMY
IN THE QUEEN'S COLLEGE, GALWAY

DUBLIN
HODGES, FIGGIS & CO., Ltd.
PUBLISHERS TO THE UNIVERSITY
LONDON: SIMPKIN, MARSHALL & CO., Ltd.
MCMIV

TO
H. R-L. M.

PREFACE

THESE Memoirs originally appeared in the year 1834.[1] I have ventured to reprint them in the hope that they may prove of some interest to those who care to read of the deeds done by our soldiery in the days when England saved Europe. I have omitted all description of the scenery, curiosities, &c., of the various places visited by the author, and have preserved only such portions of his remarks on manners and customs as tend to illustrate, either the state of the army, or social life in the Ireland of those days. In connection with the latter, I have been careful to include Major Ross-Lewin's account of the treatment dealt out to the '98 rebels, and of the suppression of the rising under Emmet.

The greater part of the third volume has been laid aside, and the reader will find those portions of it only which deal with the conduct of that petty tyrant, Sir Thomas Maitland, and with the infamous system of espionage adopted by the then military authorities.

I have of set purpose introduced much genealogical matter in the notes, and this for two reasons. First, I wish in some measure to show the injustice of the charge so frequently brought by historians

---

[1] Published by Bentley, 3 vols., 973 pp., under the title, *The Life of a Soldier, by a Field Officer*.

of the Nationalist school that the Cromwellian officers were *canaille*. Secondly, there can be little doubt that Mr. Wyndham's Act will expatriate many of the gentle families of the south, and this slight record may have some interest for Irish readers.

The somewhat lengthy description of Waterloo has been retained, inasmuch as it won the approval of the "Duke" himself.

I take this opportunity of expressing my thanks to Mr. Oman, Fellow of All Souls, and Deputy (Chichele) Professor of Modern History in the University of Oxford, to whom I stand indebted for much kind advice. I also wish to acknowledge the kindness of Mr. E. A. Little, M.A., LL.D., who has read over and corrected my proof sheets. I also have to thank the Committee of the United Service Club, Stephen's Green, Dublin, who most kindly permitted me to make use of their library.

JOHN WARDELL.

TRINITY COLLEGE, DUBLIN.

CONTENTS

CHAPTER I

CONTENTS

CHAPTER V

CHAPTER VI

CHAPTER VII

CHAPTER VIII

CHAPTER IX

CONTENTS xi

CHAPTER X

CHAPTER XV

CHAPTER XVI

CHAPTER XVII

CHAPTER XVIII

INTRODUCTION

AT the beginning of the last century the family to which Major Ross-Lewin belonged was well known in the south of Ireland. It was famous alike for the beauty of its women and the wit and bravery of its men. The Lewins were of that strong Anglo-Irish breed which has given so many gallant soldiers to the British service, and which has been repaid by the constant ingratitude of successive British Governments. The first of them to settle in the County Clare appears to have been an officer in the service of William of Orange, who probably lost his life during the campaigns of 1689–91. His son, in accordance with the will of one of his mother's relatives,[1] assumed the additional surname of Rosse,

[1] George Rosse of Fortfergus, born in 1621, formerly a Lieutenant of Horse under Cromwell. He was son of John Rosse of York, by his wife, daughter of John Harrison of Bishop Auckland, Co. Durham. During the Protectorate he was one of the trustees of the Thomond estates, was High Sheriff for the county in 1664, and Dinely mentions him as residing at Liskalogue, or Fortfergus, in 1680. His horses and arms were seized by Tyrconnell in 1689. He died May 19, 1700, and was buried in his "chapple of Clondegad." His seal bears the arms of the ancient and once powerful Rosses of Yorkshire, and impales those of Crofton of Moate, of which family his first wife was a member. The shield on his tomb displays the water-bougets of Rosse impaling the lions of Norton. His second wife was probably a daughter of Desuny Norton, a Cromwellian officer who had settled in the Co. Clare. The Harrisons occupied a good position in Yorkshire and Durham, and intermarried with many of the old northern families. Thomas Harrison was Lord Mayor of York in 1592 and 1595, while his son John filled that office in 1612. His son Robert of Bishop Auckland was ancestor to the Harrisons of Garruragh, in Clare, and father of the "Dame Barbara Lewin" of George Rosse's will.

and, as John Rosse-Lewin [1] of Fortfergus, was High Sheriff of Clare in the year 1724. He had issue by his wife, " Mistress Elizabeth Hastings," [2] a son, Harrison Rosse-Lewin, High Sheriff in 1755, who married Hannah, daughter of John Westropp [3] of Lismehane, Co. Clare, and sister to Ralph Westropp of Attyflin, Co. Limerick. George Ross-Lewin of Ross Hill, second son of this marriage, entered the

---

[1] See Froude, *The English in Ireland*, vol. i. p. 424.

[2] Said to be a near relative of the Marquess of Hastings. I rather think she was of the Daylesford family. The portrait of her mother, "Lady Hastings," is in the possession of Canon Ross-Lewin.

[3] According to a sixteenth century pedigree, preserved at Attyflin, the Westropps descend from John de Westhorpe of the Pickeringlythe, in northern Lincolnshire, who lived in the time of King John. Certain it is that every step of their pedigree can be proved from the year 1345. In later years their chief residence was Cornborough Manor in Yorkshire. Like the Rosses, Harrisons, Nortons, and others, they settled in Ireland during the Protectorate. They have given many High Sheriffs to the counties of Clare, Limerick, and Cork, while the following members of the family have served in the army and navy :—Amos, Captain R.N. (Trafalgar) ; Berkeley, Colonel ——, 1770 ; Dawson, Leland ; Edward, Lieut.-Col. 29th, 1860 ; George Ralph Collier, Major-General, 1850–91 ; George Ralph Collier, Major I.S.C. and 83rd, 1878–1903 ; George William, Lieut. 11th ; George O'Callaghan, Captain Irish Rifles, 1882–89 ; John, Captain 66th and 5th, 1774–78 ; John, Ensign 36th, 1778 ; John Parsons, General, 1822–77 ; John Massy, Captain 12th Lancers, 1882–88 ; John Thomas, Lieut. 49th and 65th, 1813–39 ; James Edward, Major-General, 1843–70 ; Henry (Bruen ?), Captain 7th Dragoon Guards, 1800–10, Lieut. 9th Dragoons, 1799–1800 ; Henry Bruen, Lieut. 51st, 1845–47 ; Lionel John, Captain 58th and 95th, 1805–19 ; Lionel Beecher, —— ; Michael Roberts, Lieut. 63rd, 1767–68 ; Michael Lionel, Lieut. 58th, 1839–42 ; Michael Dudley Seymour, Lieut. Irish Rifles, 1888–93 ; Palmes (lost an arm at Trafalgar), Brevet Lieut.-Colonel R.M.L.I., 1779–1827 ; Poole, Captain Royal Irish Artillery, 1794 ; Ralph, Lieut. 12th Light Dragoons and 51st (killed at Badajoz), 1805–12 ; Ralph, 68th, 1846 ; Richard, Lieut. 5th Foot, 1774–78 (killed in America) ; Roberts Michael, Colonel Poona Horse, and Major-General, 1841–75 ; Walter Mountiford, Captain 76th, 1847-57 ; William Keiley, Lieut.-Colonel Durham Light Infantry, 1860–81 ; Henry C. E., Major Manchester Regt., 1883–1903 ; Richard, Lieut. R.A., 1892–95 ; Robert, Captain 66th and 106th, 1857–65 ; Simpson H., Lieut. Gloucester Regt., 1887.

army as a cornet in the 14th Light Dragoons. The
junior officers of this regiment, a set of gay young
bachelors, had decreed that whosoever of them
should commit matrimony must retire from the
service. Cornet Ross-Lewin, one of the strongest
advocates of this measure, was the first to pay the
penalty. He met his cousin, Anne Lewin,[1] of Cloghans, in 1777, and resigned his commission! Henry,
his second son, but eventual heir, was born in 1778.
He joined the Limerick Militia at the age of fifteen,
and on November 4, 1795, obtained a commission
as ensign in the 32nd Foot. In 1796–97 he took
part in the expedition to the West Indies, when, his

[1] The Lewins of Cloghans, Co. Mayo, who bear the same arms and are
traditionally of the same stock as their namesakes of Clare, trace their
descent from Captain James Lewin, who served under Sir Richard Bingham
in 1586. He and his descendants obtained large grants of land in Munster
and Connaught. Thomas Lewin of Croom, Co. Limerick, sold his property
in that county to Thady Quin, ancestor of the Earl of Dunraven, and
settled at Cloghans in 1663. The present representative of the family is
Frederick Thomas Lewin, D.L., of Castlegrove, Co. Galway, and of Cloghans, Co. Mayo, who has served the office of High Sheriff for both counties.

These families have never been able to boast of large numbers, yet
many of their sons have held commissions in one or other of the services.
Of the Lewins of Cloghans and Oakfield, Henry, a cavalry officer, killed
at Fontenoy; James, a Captain in the 30th, 1805–17; Thomas, Lieut.
30th, 1815–17; James St. George, Lieut. 61st, 1844–46; Carrique
(wounded at Waterloo), 71st Highland Light Infantry, 1809–22; Arthur,
D.S.O., Captain 8th King's Own Liverpool.

The Ross-Lewins of Fortfergus, Ross Hill, and Cornfield Manor, rivalled
in this respect their relatives of Mayo. George, Cornet 14th Light Dragoons, 1771–78; Ralph, Captain 5th Foot, and on the Staff, 1781–1810;
John, Lieut. 69th, 1795–96; Henry, Major 32nd, 1794–1822; Thomas,
Lieut. 32nd, 1804–22; George William, Royal Navy and 17th Light
Dragoons, 1804–10; William, Lieut. 1st West India Regiment, 1806;
Henry, Lieut. 70th, 1810; Edward (killed at San Sebastian), Lieut. 9th,
1808–13; John (killed at Inkerman), Lieut. 30th, 1847–54; George Harrison, Henry Hastings, Richard, and Robert O'Donelan, were chaplains
in the Royal Navy.

regiment having lost thirty-two officers, he was
promoted to the rank of Lieutenant. In 1803 he
witnessed the outbreak under Emmet, and in the
following year was chosen as Adjutant to the "light
company" battalion, commanded by Colonel Colman
of the Guards. In 1805 he became a Captain in the
first battalion of the 32nd, his marriage taking place
next year. His wife was Anne, daughter of William
Burnet[1] of Eyrecourt, by his wife, sister to Hyacinth

---

[1] A cadet of the Burnets, Barts., of Leys. The Donelans, of Rossdon-
nelan, Co. Roscommon, and of Ballydonelan Castle, Co. Galway, were a
branch of the royal clan O'Melaghlin of Meath. They are thus referred to
in a poem by O'Dugan, who died in 1372 :—

> " Princes of Hy Fiairtie of great victories,
> They are the O'Flynns and O'Donnellans ;
> O'Haire rules over Fiacre Finn,
> Who never flinched from battle or conflict.

.   .   .   .   .   .

> Noble the blood and achievements
> Of the O'Donellans of handsome form ;
> Rushing to battle like a torrent
> Come the fair-haired sons of Clan Breasil."

Their chief residence, the Black Castle of Ballydonelan, was burned
down in 1407, and the oldest part of the present house dates from 1412, in
which year Tully, chief of the clan, built for himself a stone keep.   His
great-grandson, Melaghlin, who died in 1548, was father of the well-known
Nehemias of Ballydonelan, chief of his clan and Archbishop of Tuam. He
married Elizabeth, granddaughter of O'Donel, Celtic Prince and English
Earl, of Tyrconnel. Two of his sons, one of them Sir James, were Fellows
of Trinity College, Dublin. His descendant, Colonel Melaghlin, sur-
named "of Aughrim," fought gallantly for James II.   This chief was
wounded at Aughrim, and his brother, Major James, was slain at Piedmont
when in the French army.   John, of Ballydonelan, son of Melaghlin, was
father to Edmond of Hillswood and Kinvara, and great-grandfather to
Mrs. Ross-Lewin. The penal laws do not seem to have been enforced in
Co. Galway, for in old letters Donelan is described as habitually driving
a six-horse coach with outriders. After the surrender of Limerick, the
Donelans became loyal subjects of the British crown, and many gentlemen
of the name fought for the Hanoverians. Prominent amongst them was

Donelan, of Hillswood and Kinvara Castle, Co.
Galway. I have seen a letter written by Sir Charles
Napier, in which, speaking of Mrs. Ross-Lewin, he
says that " her great beauty is only equalled by her

Nehemiah, who died in 1787, when Governor of Carrickfergus. At
Fontenoy he is stated to have been the only officer of his division (? corps)
who escaped with his life, and " *though wounded in ten parts of his body
brought off the colours of his corps,* which were almost shot to rags."
Malachi Donelan, a Captain R.N., served under Nelson, Collingwood,
Duckworth, and Cochrane. He greatly distinguished himself on several
occasions, and was awarded the Greenwich Hospital Pension in 1858.
Charles Donelan, who led the 48th Foot at Talavera, was a nephew of
Edmond of Hillswood, and is mentioned as follows by Napier (*Battles
of the Peninsula,* 1861 edition, p. 40) when describing the crisis of the
combat :—" At this time Hill's and Campbell's divisions stood fast on each
extremity of the line, yet the centre of the British was absolutely broken,
and victory inclined towards the French, when suddenly Colonel Donelan
was seen advancing with the 48th through the midst of the disordered
masses. It seemed as if this regiment must be carried away with the
retiring crowds, but *wheeling back by companies,* it let them pass through
the intervals, and then resuming its proud and beautiful line struck against
the right of the pursuing enemy, plying such a destructive musketry and
closing with such a firm countenance that his forward movement was checked.
The Guards and Germans then rallied, a brigade of light cavalry came up
from the second line at a trot, the artillery battered the flanks without
intermission, the French wavered, and the battle was restored." Soon
after this Colonel Donelan fell mortally wounded. Raising himself with
difficulty on his arm, he called, in a voice clearly heard above the roar of
musketry and the shoutings of the men—he called, I say, to one of his
majors, and as if on parade requested that " he would do him the honour
of taking command of the regiment." Then, summoning the remnants of
his rapidly failing strength, he raised his cocked hat and waved on to
victory the corps of which he was so proud.
Wellington in his despatches says : " The battle was certainly saved by
the advance, position, and steady conduct of the 48th Regiment." Professor Oman, while pointing out that the 3rd Brigade deserves a share of
the credit, remarks, " If the 48th had been carried away in the general
backward movement, the day would have been lost."—*History of the
Peninsular War,* vol. ii. p. 542.
Ballydonelan Castle was sold during the famine of 1848, and the clan is
now represented by O'Conor Donelan of Sylane, Co. Galway, head of a
cadet branch which descends from Sir James Donelan, F.T.C.D., Lord
Chief Justice *temp.* Charles I.

b

marvellous intelligence." She was indeed a very talented woman, and in addition to the usual ladylike accomplishments of the day, was well versed in several languages. She survived until the year 1876, preserving to the last the "grand manner" of the eighteenth century. The eldest son of this marriage, a wrangler and M.A. of Cambridge, was well known throughout the British navy as the "Fighting Chaplain."

In 1807 Captain Ross-Lewin took part in the siege and capture of Copenhagen, while in the ensuing year he fought at Roleia and Vimiera. He next witnessed the taking of Flushing, and the storming of the forts at Salamanca. In the general action that followed this last exploit he received a severe wound, which to the end of his life proved a continual source of trouble. He next served at the unsuccessful siege of Burgos, and took part in the retreat from that town. He saw something of the siege of Badajos, fought at Orthes, and, as a field officer of the 5th Division, was in the thick of the fighting at Quatre Bras and Waterloo. He is said to have distinguished himself by his remarkable coolness during the course of the latter action. The last shot he saw fired in anger was in the Ionian rising of 1820.

His younger brother, Thomas Ross-Lewin, had entered the army in 1807 as an ensign in the 32nd. As one of the officers of the light company,[1] he saw much desperate fighting. "Cavalry," he was wont

---

[1] "He was," says one who wrote at the time of his death, "always a light company officer, active and indefatigable, alert and lively."

to say, " were always fatal to me ; " and indeed he
bore marks of more than one encounter with the
" arme blanche," tokens received at Sarrozin,[1]
Pampeluna,[2] and Waterloo. In the latter action
*Ponsonby's Union Brigade charged over him as he lay
wounded on the ground.* I have heard it said that he
would have been smothered but for the efforts of
two grenadiers of the 32nd, who pulled him out of
the mud. The marks of this adventure never left
him, and those who knew him well have informed
me that at first sight his appearance was most extraordinary. His aquiline and somewhat large nose had
suffered terribly from frostbite and exposure to the
weather. It boasted all the colours of the rainbow,
and in addition to this, was deeply pitted and scarred
with gravel from the field of Waterloo ; for he happened to have fallen on his face just as the Union
Brigade charged past the 32nd. Children especially
shrank from such an apparition ; but his sweet and
kindly nature, in which he resembled his less battered
brother, soon put them at their ease, and the Major
and the Captain (there is no lower rank in Ireland !)
were the idols of the younger generation for miles
around. He retired about the year 1822, and in
1848 received the Peninsula War Medal, with eight
clasps.[3] This decoration he would never wear, for
he contended that he was entitled to nine bars. He

[1] *Query* Sauroren? but there may have been a skirmish at Castel
Sarrazin in Spain.

[2] Hart's *Army List* says : " Severely wounded at Pampeluna and Waterloo." He bore the reputation of being a singularly brave but reckless
officer.

[3] Roleia, Vimiera, Corunna, Salamanca, Pyrenees, Nivelle, Nive,
Orthes.

died in 1853 at his house of Rossmount, and the county paper commenting on his death refers to him as "a kind-hearted and gallant soldier of the old army."

Major Ross-Lewin retired from the army shortly after his brother, and, on his father's death, resided at Ross Hill. As an active magistrate he was largely instrumental in preserving order amongst the disaffected in his part of Ireland. For this he received the special thanks of the authorities at Dublin Castle, and yet never forfeited the attachment and esteem of his tenantry.

Ross Hill was indeed attacked in one of the then numerous raids for arms, but it was in no spirit of personal animosity, and the peasantry were the first to tell the tale of the polite reception accorded to the "bhoys" by the Major. "If you want my arms," said he, in response to the demands of the assailants, "you have only to come and take them. I can promise you a right warm welcome." The fact that he could not be " blandandthered " into acts of weakness won for him the respect of the shrewd peasantry of Clare. His unwearying interest in the condition of his poorer neighbours was universally recognised, while his courteous manners and ready generosity endeared him to all. The peasantry always believed that from the Major they would receive nothing but justice tempered by mercy. He himself used frequently to say that his knowledge of Irish had enabled him to save many prisoners from the tender mercies of the " interpreters," who too often misrepresented the evidence given at the Sessions.

He had a horror of duelling, but his courage was undoubted. On one occasion, when a parade-ground soldier, an English officer of dragoons, presumed on the pacific character of the county magistrate, he received a lesson which we may believe he never forgot. Major Ross-Lewin died in the year 1843. His death left his country poorer by the loss of a brave and courteous, if somewhat punctilious, gentleman of the old school.

JOHN WARDELL.

THE 32ND REGIMENT AT WATERLOO

(From Dalton's *Roll-Call;* Swiney's *Historical Records.*)

K. = Killed.   w. = Wounded.   Q. B. = Quatre Bras.   W. = Waterloo.
†=Wounded in Peninsula.   [In all probability many other officers of the corps had been hit during the Peninsular campaigns, but I have only been able to identify those marked.]

Brevet Lieut.-Col. John Hicks.
Major Felix Calvert.
Brevet-Major Charles Haines.
†   ,,   Henry Ross-Lewin.
†   ,,   William H. Toole, w. W.
Captain John Crowe, w. W.
    ,,   Jaques Boyse, K.   ⎫
    ,,   Thos. Cassan, K. ⎬ Q. B.
    ,,   Edward Whitty, K. ⎭
    ,,   Hugh Harrison, w.
    ,,   Charles Wallett, w. Q. B.
Lieut. Henry Wm. Brookes, w. Q. B.
    ,,   David Davies (Adjutant).
    ,,   George Barr, w. Q. B.
    ,,   Michael Wm. Meighan, w. Q. B.
    ,,   Samuel Hill Lawrence, w. Q. B.
    ,,   Theobald Butler.
†   ,,   John Boase, w. Q. B.
†   ,,   Thos. Ross-Lewin, w. W.
†   ,,   Henry Butterworth.
    ,,   John Shaw M'Cullock.

Lieut. Jas. Robt. Colthurst, w. W.
†   ,,   Jas. Robinson, w. Q. B.
    ,,   Robt. Tresilian Belcher.
    ,,   James FitzGerald, w. Q. B.
    ,,   Thos. J. Horan, w. W.
    ,,   Edward Stephens, w. Q. B.
    ,,   Henry Quill, w. Q. B.
    ,,   Jonathan Jagoe, w. W.
    ,,   George Small.
Ensign Jasper Lucas.
    ,,   James M'Conchy, w. Q. B.
    ,,   Henry Metcalfe, w.
    ,,   John Birtwhistle, w.
    ,,   Alexander Stewart, w. Q. B.
    ,,   George Brown.
    ,,   William Bennett, w.
    ,,   Chas. R. K. Dallas, w. Q. B.

Non-Combatant. {
   Paymaster Thos. Hart.
   Quartermaster William Stevens.
   Surgeon William Buchanan.
   Assistant-Surgeon Rynd Lawder.
        ,,   Hugh M'Clintock.

SERVICES OF THE 32ND IN THE PENINSULA AND FLANDERS

Battle of Roleia, August 17th, 1807.
    ,,   Vimiera, August 21st, 1807.
    ,,   Corunna, January 16th, 1809.
Expedition to Walcheren and siege of Flushing.
Storming of the Salamanca Forts, June, 1812.
Battle of Salamanca, July 22nd, 1812.
Siege of and retreat from Burgos, 1812.

Blockade of Pampeluna and battles in the Pyrenees, 1813.

Combat at Maya, October 7th, 1813.

Battle of the Nivelle, November 10th, 1813.

    ,,   Nive, December 12th, 1813.

    ,,   Orthes, January 27th, 1814.

    ,,   Quatre Bras, June 15th, 1815.

    ,,   Waterloo, June 18th, 1815.

WITH THE "THIRTY-SECOND" IN THE PENINSULA

CHAPTER I

My military career begins with an ensigncy in a militia regiment —The raising of the corps—Its first mutiny—The route comes down—Second mutiny—March out of town—Quarters at Cork —Fight between our men and another Irish corps—Marched to Granard—I leave the militia.

In his younger days my father was a cavalry officer, but left the service soon after his marriage ; from him, among other qualities, I inherited a predilection for the profession of arms, which began to manifest itself some time before the memorable event of the donning of my first jacket and trousers. Whenever I happened to be reported absent without leave, during my father's sojourn in any garrison town, the domestics sent in search of me invariably directed their steps to the barracks, well knowing that they might be sure to find me there, watching with unwearied attention the progress of the drill, and endeavouring to imitate with my mimic gun the various motions of the manual and platoon exercise. At first, indeed, I was occasionally much chagrined by the surliness of the sentries, who would refuse to let me pass the gate ;

A

but, as my acquaintance with the world grew older,
I learned the persuasive power of a bribe, and, by
making to the soldiers well-timed presents of smart
canes, which are so indispensable to the complete
equipment of an orderly, I secured the *entrée* to the
barrack-yard.

In the year 1793 I began my military career by
entering a southern city regiment of Irish militia with
the rank of ensign.[1] In those days commissions were
given to more juvenile aspirants for military glory
than are now permitted to hold them ; and I had
barely completed my third lustrum when I wore, or
rather, as an old brother-in-arms afterwards said, was
tied to a sword for the first time.

The Irish are a people naturally fond of the care-
less, chequered, errant life of a soldier ; and, as one
proof of it, my corps was raised voluntarily in a single
day. A large quantity of cockades were provided,
not alone for the men, but also for the colonel's
friends ; a number of dinner parties were given in
honour of the occasion ; and the festivities concluded
with a grand ball in the evening. The next morning
our one-day-old regiment assembled, as ordered, in
front of their colonel's house, and that officer directed
that a shilling should be given to each man wherewith
to drink his health ; but, as his servants proceeded
to distribute the money, a general cry arose that the
colonel wanted to put them off with a shilling in lieu
of the guinea which, on being called out, each was
entitled to receive. All attempts at explanation proved

[1] The 13th or Limerick City Militia. His friend Hugh, afterwards
Viscount, Gough entered the regiment at this time, aged *thirteen*.

perfectly unavailing; never were men so deaf to
reason; they tore the cockades from their hats, as
well as from the dresses of the ladies and gentlemen;
trampled under foot these now valueless insignia; and
gave disagreeable proof of the strength of their lungs
by vociferating in full chorus, that we were all officers
and none soldiers. They were not yet amenable to
military law, so that the only check they received was
from sundry applications of the lieutenant-colonel's
whip, which he laid on with great spirit whenever he
fell in with a group of his refractory men dancing on
their cockades.

In a few days, however, the matter was better understood. The corps was called out, and then became
subject to military discipline; not a man was absent,
and considerable concern for their past conduct, which
had made their officers look so foolish, was clearly
observable in the air and bearing of all; the drill proceeded regularly under non-commissioned officers of
the line; undress clothing, blue jackets, white trousers,
and forage caps came down from Dublin, and with it
the route.

Early in the morning of the day fixed for our
marching out of town, the commanding officer gave
directions that half the regiment should proceed to
the town-house for the arms, and that every man
of the party should bring from it two stand to the
barrack-square, the place of muster. Instantly it ran
through the ranks that each private was to be forced
to carry two firelocks during the whole march; and
a scene of confusion and anarchy, not inferior to
that of the cockades, was momentarily expected to

be enacted—"H—ll to the one toe," they exclaimed, "will we move out of this, only with one gun. The d—l a leg will we stir!" But at length the meaning of the order was satisfactorily explained, and then, running into the opposite extreme, several were heard to declare that for such a distance each individual would cheerfully carry an arm chest.

The arms were brought accordingly and distributed; the band of the 34th moved to the right of the line; with some difficulty I drew from its retentive sheath the rusty sword which I had borrowed for the occasion, as our officers' appointments had not yet arrived; and, highly pleased with my warlike appearance, I fell in with my company. "Precisely at my age," thought I, "did the great Marlborough first unsheath his sword on parade with his regiment." True, his sword was not rusty, and his regiment of Guards was most probably superior to mine of raw militia, but no such humiliating reflections crossed my mind at that moment. In a few minutes the whole body moved off in file, for Dundas had not yet appeared: it was then that military pride took possession of me—I marched along exultingly, looking up to the peopled windows, and nodding courteously to my old partners at the dancing school, amid the silent acknowledgments of the waving kerchiefs of those peerless damsels. Human happiness had reached its height—when, lo! my ear was suddenly assailed by the well-known accents of a voice, inquiring whether anybody knew where Master Harry was to be found, and the next instant my progress was arrested by our greasy kitchen-maid, who stood in melting mood before me. She blubbered out that since my departure the female portion of my family were all in tears, and that I had forgotten a pair of stockings; and she forthwith proceeded to thrust these useful articles into my pocket. Oh! it was with sore indignation that I snatched at and flung them away, and, while my tormentor stood gazing in mute amazement, hastened to resume my place on the march, but so completely crestfallen that even my favourite quickstep of Garryowen, which the band had just begun to play, failed to restore my lost equanimity.

In progress of time we were quartered in Cork. The Tipperary and Louth regiments had been there before us, and had had some desperate fighting, as one corps was called southern and the other northern; of course they were immediately separated. We, like the Tipperary, were also placed in garrison with a northern regiment, which, by the way, was the finest body of infantry that I have yet seen in our service; but we could not agree.

One day, while some of our officers were walking with me on the Grand Parade, we were told that both the militia regiments were hard at work tearing up the pavement and pelting at each other. We ran at once to the barracks, which then stood on either side of the Bandon road, and found that the report was too true, for both corps were outside their gates and hotly engaged. In the attempt to put a stop to the affray, one of our officers had a narrow escape from being killed by the bayonet of a northern; I received a blow of a

stone on the hip, which broke the hilt of my sword ;
several of the men were also hurt. At length our
regiment, being the weaker, fell back to the barracks,
and, seizing their arms, began to fire on their opponents from the upper windows that commanded
the road. An attempt made to close the barrack-
gates proved ineffectual, owing to the quantity of
stones that had been thrown in, and blocked up
the way. The northern regiment, imitating ours,
rushed into their barracks to arm themselves, but
in the meantime their officers succeeded in shutting
their gates, and keeping them in. Our corps seemed
to be sorely disappointed, when they saw themselves
thus debarred of an opportunity of redeeming their
credit after the change of weapons ; as they maintained that, though less numerous, they were more
"handy at their arms" than their opponents.

General Stuart soon arrived to inquire into this
unfortunate affair, and the consequence was, that
we were ordered to get under arms instantly, and
marched off to Mallow, receiving, as we passed, a
volley of stones, discharged by the northerns from
behind their barrack-wall. We were followed out
of town for some distance by the whole mob of
Cork, who naturally sided with the southerns. About
the middle of the night, to their no small surprise, the
good people of Mallow were roused from their peaceful slumbers by our band playing up "the Rakes"
through the town, and we received there a route for
Granard.

At Clogheen we found the Thirty-third regiment,
which was then under orders to embark for the West

Indies;[1] they were commanded by the Honourable Colonel Wellesley. He happened to be standing near the bridge while we were marching over, and I, wishing to come off with flying colours, unfurled mine; but, unluckily, the wind was very high, I was blown out of the ranks toward the future Duke of Wellington, and, before I could stop myself, my sacred charge was wrapped round him, and his hat knocked off. How little idea had I then that I should yet be under his command in many a well-contested field !

While we were still some miles from Mullingar our county regiment, which was stationed there, paid us the compliment of coming out to meet us, and, certainly, our interview was most hearty, and truly Irish; both corps mingled together, embracing and making every demonstration of joy; the preservation of order was altogether impracticable, and we entered Mullingar *en masse.* Then the festive scene that ensued sets description at defiance ! Parades, or anything like discipline, were quite out of the question; nothing but mirth and revelry was thought of; the first two days we dined with our friends; on the third they were entertained by us; and on the fourth we marched out of Mullingar, just as we had entered it, in a most unmilitary disarray, the embracings being repeated on taking leave.

Our stay at Granard had not been of long continuance when I secretly resolved to leave the militia. One day we invited the ninth dragoons to dine with

[1] The 33rd sailed with Admiral Christian's fleet for the West Indies; but, being obliged by contrary winds to put back, their destination was altered, and they were sent out to India.

us, and our chief aim was to floor the cavalry, according to the custom of those Gothic days of hard drinking. A young cornet was the first to fall under the table; he was quickly followed by me. We were carried into an adjoining room, and thrown on a bed in a state of insensibility. We wore our best uniforms, and found at daylight that they could never be mounted again; but this was of no consequence to me, as since that morning I have never worn a militia uniform.

Having changed my red coat for a plain one, I set off for Ballymahon on foot without apprising any one of my intentions. The distance was seventeen miles, and, while performing my journey, the reflections with which my mind was occupied were far from being agreeable. I had stolen out of the inn before its other inmates had risen, and, in taking my departure so unceremoniously, I felt that I should draw down upon me the censure of the colonel, from whom I had received particular marks of favour, as well as of the other officers, who, I may say, formed a band of brothers, and of whom some were my near relatives. This reflection caused me much pain; still the resolution to which I had come I firmly determined never to break, and by making any of my brother officers acquainted with it I should only have incurred the certainty of offending them in a greater degree, by rejecting the advice which they would think my youth and inexperience required, and which I knew would be to abandon my purpose. I also sincerely regretted the necessity that existed for my leaving a corps of which the officers were so much my friends,

and the men, though once the most unruly of Irishmen, then in so high a state of discipline and efficiency
as to reflect the utmost credit on those who had
exerted themselves unceasingly to inspire them with
that soldier-like sense of duty, and that consciousness
of superiority over most other regiments, which stood
them in such good stead during the subsequent insurrection.[1] Under such circumstances, I entered the
village of Ballymahon in melancholy mood, and
being unable to procure a horse there, had to walk
on to Clogheen. Thence I proceeded on a hired
hack to Menagh, and the next morning continued
my journey on foot to Castle Connell, where I surprised my father's family, who passed the summer
in that village, while discussing the important meal
of breakfast.

[1] Colonel Gough (Lord Gough's father) speaks of them as his "gallant
Garryaon Boys, a braver, or more loyal, or a more divoted set of
fellows to their officers never carried firelocks."—*Life of Viscount Gough*,
by Robert S. Rait, 1903.

CHAPTER II

Reasons for leaving the militia—Join the expedition for the West Indies at Cork—The fleet sails—Storm—Put our commanding officer in Coventry—Anchor in Carlisle Bay—Bumboats—Court-martial—Capture of a transport by the French—Sir Ralph Abercrombie—Missing ships arrive—Notice of rising in St. Domingo — Expedition sails from Barbadoes — The voyage—Anchor off the Mole.

THE reasons which induced me to leave the militia also prevented my remaining long idle at home, and I will now detail them. In 1794 extensive armaments were assembled in the English ports, and at Cork; their destination was the West Indies, where they were to assist in the reduction of the French islands, and their rendezvous at the other side of the Atlantic was to be at Barbadoes. The command of the land forces was consigned to Sir Ralph Abercrombie. The portion of the expedition, which embarked at English ports, was the first to sail, and with it went a regiment in which a near relative of mine,[1] not yet of age, held the commission of lieutenant. This young officer and I were bound by the ties not only of consanguinity but also of strict friendship; he was indeed my earliest friend, for we had been brought up together from our infancy;

[1] John Ross-Lewin of Fortfergus, co. Clare, first cousin to the author, and a lieutenant in the 69th Foot. His brother William, a lieutenant in the 1st W. I. Regt., also died from the effects of the climate.

he was the head of the elder branch of a family resident in a southern county in Ireland, and as such inherited a large estate, which was held in trust by guardians during his minority. Unfortunately, those persons did not show themselves worthy of the confidence which had been reposed in them, and too easily assented to the wishes of a spirited youth for a military life. He was suffered to raise men for a lieutenancy, and the West Indies became his destination. The mortality that prevailed there among the troops was so great at this period, that I naturally felt alarmed for the safety of my friend; I saw too the folly of his leaving at such a time an ample fortune, and wished to counteract, if possible, what I conceived to be the injudicious views of his guardians. I therefore formed the resolution of proceeding to the West Indies, for the purpose of persuading him to resign his commission and return home.

Some persons may be led to suppose, from what I have said, that I maintain the doctrine, that the friends of a young man do wrong in permitting him to serve his king and country in the army, because he happens to inherit a fortune. On the contrary, I think it both honourable and useful for such a person to do so, when he is to be opposed to a brave and worthy foe; when he has a chance of learning the profession of arms, and of reaping the laurels due to the successful exertion of skill and courage—

> " Send danger from the East unto the West,
> So Honour cross it from the North to South,
> And let them grapple."

If under such circumstances it be his fate to press a soldier's gory bed, why, let us say with the Frenchman, "fortune de guerre," or "better in battle," with my uncle Toby. But on this expedition a miserable and inglorious end awaited the British soldier—the dreadful fever silently but surely did the work of death, and the free-hearted and gallant sons of the British Isles sunk, worse than useless to their country, and with sad rapidity, into an unhonoured and soon-forgotten grave. Was I not then justified in exerting myself to persuade my friend, circumstanced as he was, to quit such a scene, and return to a happy home, where his presence might soon be of the greatest utility?

In accordance therefore with my resolution, I left the militia, as I have already mentioned, and, after the shortest possible stay at my father's, set off for Cove with a purse containing a few guineas, and letters of recommendation to Major-General White, who commanded the troops under orders for embarkation. As soon as I arrived I waited on the General, who received me very kindly, and advised me to join one of the corps, as a volunteer, lest my appointment should not take place before the sailing of the fleet; at the same time he gave me permission to name the corps to which I was to be attached. As I had been acquainted with the Honourable Captain De Courcy at Kinsale, while quartered there with the militia, and now found that he had joined the 99th, a part of the expedition, I consequently preferred that corps to any other, and joined it; but I had not been with it many days, when, on taking up an orderly book, I read the notification of my appointment to an ensigncy in a different regiment, my commission bearing date November 4th, 1794.

I found, among my new brother officers, a young ensign whom I had met before. When he joined at Spike Island he had rather a homespun appearance, and, on going up to his future commanding officer, an Englishman, to report his arrival, he was stopped by a repulsive wave of the hand, and the words, "My lad, we don't take Irish recruits now." —"Oh ! sir," said Newcome, "I am an ensign."—"I perceive," said the colonel with a sigh, directing his conversation to one of his officers, who stood near him, "that another *blood an' ouns* has joined us. It is too bad !" He would have been quite *au desespoir* had he then known that he was soon to have another Irish ensign in his corps, in the person of the writer of these pages.

On board the transport in which I now embarked there were three officers ; one of them was a married man, and, as I soon learned, a professed duellist. Some slight difference of opinion occurred between this person and one of the party after dinner, upon which Mrs. O'B——, his loving spouse, immediately ran into her cabin, and returned with her husband's pistols. "Look at those little fellows," said she to us ; "look at the stocks with the dates carved on them, when O'B—— killed his three men with them ! These are the things to keep puppies under !" The next morning an officer of another regiment called on O'B——, requesting him to be his friend in an affair of honour; and, while he was on shore, he received orders to go on the recruiting service, so that, to the great joy of all on board, we were relieved from the presence of this extraordinary couple.

The fleet sailed on the 9th of February, 1795. My transport had then on board only three other officers, all young men like myself; for the captain, who was to have commanded, had been taken ill and left at Cork. The consequence was that we were very improvident with respect to our sea-stock, seeing company every day during our stay at Cove, and, as we were about to lay in a fresh supply, the order to sail was given most unseasonably. The fleet had got under weigh before another captain was directed to take the command of the transport; he had to follow us in a hooker, and succeeded in getting on board at night. This gentleman, finding our sea-stock miserably reduced, with much prudence chose to live with the master of the vessel; and this slight hurt our feelings so sensibly that, in the height of our resentment, we resolved to place him in Coventry; but, unfortunately, we were the sufferers by this giddy resolution, for his first step proved tolerably well how little the loss of our society would affect him, and we were ordered to keep watch both day and night during the passage.

On the 11th we encountered such a tremendous gale that the greater part of our ships put back into Cove; but mine lay to off Cape Clear in a sea of mountains, no vessel in sight except the *Babet* sloop-of-war. On the 15th we made sail again; and, when the effects of the sea-sickness began to leave my companions and me, we entered upon a search for the remains of our stock, and found it to consist of two huge rounds of beef and several pounds of tea. We then attempted to barter with the master for sugar, offering him an equal weight of tea for whatever quantity he could spare; but, much as this proposal was to his advantage, he rejected it; neither would he sell us any of his provisions. The rations were of the very worst description; the cheese was particularly detestable, being full of long red worms; and, when we remonstrated with the master, he told us that it was cheese quite good enough for soldiers. Such insolence and such fare went both much against our stomachs, but in the conflict maintained within our breasts between resentment and a sense of military subordination, the latter fortunately prevailed, though endurance had nearly reached its utmost limits.

Our next care was to have one of the large rounds of beef boiled : nor was this without its attendant annoyance, for no cupboard in our cabin could contain it, and we had only to suspend it from a hook by means of a cord that we passed through the bone. The round, with the addition of a knife and fork stuck in it, formed an ornament of peculiar elegance; and, by its perpetual oscillation, tended to increase the nausea which young hands feel on their first trip, and which is so much promoted by the sight of any object, really or apparently, affected by the motion of the vessel; consequently, the most important part of our stock, like our commanding officer, came to be regarded as a nuisance rather than as an acquisition.

After a passage of six weeks we arrived off Barbadoes. This island, when seen from a distance, seems to be all in motion, owing to the vast number of windmills employed there in the preparation of sugar. On rounding a headland, we entered Carlisle Bay, and were quickly encompassed by bumboats, the crews of which welcomed us to Barbadoes. As my regiment had been in the West Indies a few years before, several of the old sergeants were recognised by the slaves who rowed in the boats, and amongst the rest by one named Hector; this poor fellow was pointed out to me particularly as a man who had given an extraordinary proof of fortitude. He had run away at one time, and when caught was chained by the leg to some fixture, but at night he released himself from the chain by cutting off his foot at the ankle joint. He did this probably to vex his master, since such a mutilation diminished his value as a slave. It frequently happens that the negro will resolve to starve himself to death; as he well knows that, next to taking away the planter's life, he cannot be better revenged than by taking away his own; when such sulky fits, as the Barbadians term them, come on, the poor wretch is flogged without mercy, and the combined tortures of hunger and the whip sometimes prove too powerful for his fortitude.

We disembarked on the day that we cast anchor and went into barracks, waiting the arrival of those ships which had returned to port in stress of weather.

In consequence of the bad terms on which we had been with the officer in command of our transport, three of our mess were ordered to appear before a court-martial to answer for our conduct while on

board. One was acquitted, and promoted to a lieutenancy on the same day; but another and I were kept
in arrest for some time, though afterwards directed to
do duty. The commanding officer of my regiment
took out with him a *chere amie;* and her brother and
sister were also on board the head-quarter ship, the
gentleman having been appointed to an ensigncy in
the corps. He was junior to two of us, but advantage was taken of our arrest, and he was promoted
over our heads. "Things are done differently in the
militia," thought I. Indeed, I had been led to suppose that the line possessed so many advantages that
the militia could not for a moment bear a comparison
with it in any particular; but, as I knew that conduct
such as I have had to describe would never have been
suffered in the constitutional force of the country, I
was at a loss to perceive up to this period in what the
great superiority of the regulars consisted.

We had been here but a few days, when an assistant
surgeon, who had sailed in a different vessel, joined us,
unaccompanied by any of his party. He informed us
that his transport had been captured by a French
cruiser and taken into Guadaloupe, and that Victor
Hugues, the governor, far from wishing to detain him
with the other prisoners, had dismissed him with the
flattering remark, that wherever he went he would do
much more harm than good with his medicines and
flannel shirts.

A strange coincidence resulted from the capture
of the above-mentioned ship some years after. The
young Irish ensign, whom our colonel had mistaken,
at Spike Island, for a candidate to carry a musket

instead of a stand of colours, was on board her when she became a prize to the enemy; among the captors there was a Gallo-Hibernian, who was subsequently taken himself by the *Russel* 74 and carried to England, where by some means he succeeded in getting an ensigncy. Also, on board the *Russel*, at the time of the second capture, there was another son of Erin, a midshipman, who some time after left the navy and obtained a commission in the army. Now what, in my opinion, is so remarkable is the fact, that a dozen years did not elapse before I saw these three officers all captains in the same regiment of the line.[1]

When the missing ships arrived, we found that one grenadier lieutenant of my regiment had thrown himself out of one of the port-holes of the *Hindostan* and perished. The other, a fine young man, was sick of the fever on board, and died a few days after he was brought on shore. I went to see him one morning during his illness at St. Anne's barracks'; his life was then drawing rapidly to a close; he was quite insensible, and his head was covered with flies. A person, whom I supposed to be a medical man, was standing at the bed-side: " Your poor friend is gone," said he, turning to me, as I entered the room. I did not stay long; and afterwards found that the person, who had been watching the dying moments of the young grenadier, was his own brother, a captain of the 53rd regiment. Though we did not remain many weeks at Barbadoes, the mortality among the

---

[1] What is still more remarkable, they were all three killed in action on the same day at Quatre Bras. See p. 262.

·troops was very great, and we left many fine fellows behind us to feast the land-crabs.[1]

Our force was formed into two divisions; one of them was intended to attack the French islands under the command of Sir Ralph Abercrombie, and the other to proceed with Major-General White to reinforce the British troops in St. Domingo. My regiment belonged to the latter division—a circumstance which I considered very fortunate, as I heard at Barbadoes that my friend was stationed at Cape Nicola Mole.

It may not be amiss to make brief mention here of some facts connected with the annals of St. Domingo about this period. An extensive rising of the slaves on the French plantations in that island commenced in the night of the 22nd of August 1791; and in a few days the insurgents mustered no fewer than 100,000 men, armed with whatever weapons chance threw in their way. A conflict of the most sanguinary character ensued, and the greater part of the northern district, the most beautiful by nature of that beautiful island, soon presented one wide scene of desolation and horror. A detail of the atrocities committed in the hour of retaliation for many a year of oppressive bondage, could only serve to shock the ear. Suffice it to say, that the wild justice of revenge never prompted the heart of man to the perpetration of more appalling deeds of blood. Nowhere could the offended eye find a resting place, free from the mournful traces of the firebrand and the knife. Some

[1] A species of reptile resembling the common crab in form except that it has two sharp spikes growing out of the back shell.

of the towns and forts alone were successfully defended by the French inhabitants. At length our
government resolved to send an expedition against
St. Domingo, thinking it might prove a valuable
acquisition, but it was in an evil hour that they first
thought so. The earliest landing of British forces
was effected in the month of October 1793—they
were soon in possession of Jeremie, the Mole, Cape
Tiburon, and other places on the north - western
coast; but, before our arrival at Barbadoes, the
troops in St. Domingo were so reduced by sickness,
that several of those places were abandoned by them,
and they with difficulty maintained themselves in the
remainder.

The necessary arrangements being at length completed, the whole fleet got under weigh, and sailed
out of Carlisle Bay together; then the two divisions
separated, and shaped their course for their respective
destinations : in a few days mine entered the Mona
passage, which divides St. Domingo from Porto Rico.
A slaver sailed in company, and was often close
alongside our ship, so that we could fling to the
poor wretches on board a quantity of biscuit, for
which they scrambled with great avidity. A more
shocking sight than that which this vessel afforded
cannot well be imagined ; she was crowded to excess,
and indeed it appeared to me that the slaves had
little more than standing room ; they were all naked.
I was informed that the traders in slaves found
small vessels the most convenient for their purpose
(though certainly not for the poor negroes), since,
when arrived off the Guinea coast, they could take

out their masts, and row them, so lightened, up the rivers with sweeps.

Immediately on our coming to anchor, eager to see again the companion of my happiest hours, and to enjoy his first movement of surprise at my unexpected appearance in St. Domingo, I hastened to the shore, and landed about a mile from the town. One solitary soldier stood on the beach ; he wore a uniform of my friend's regiment ; I asked him if he knew anything of Lieutenant ——.[1] His reply is indelibly engraven on my memory :—"I was his servant, sir. He has been dead these three weeks." I bowed with submission to the decree of Providence, and returned to the ship. If any man on the expedition felt discouraged and disheartened by the prospects that the nature of the service promised, I think that I should have been that man. The powerful motive, by which I had hitherto been animated, had now vanished ; and my feelings, when I set my foot a second time on the shore of St. Domingo, were those of one treading on the grave of his dearest friend : still, I trust that unswerving loyalty never ceased to lodge within my breast, and to stimulate me to do my duty, as far as in me lay, to my King and my Country.

[1] John Ross-Lewin.

CHAPTER III

THE troops were disembarked with the least possible
delay. Brigadier-General Forbes, with part of the
13th Light Dragoons, and the 32nd, 56th, 67th, and
81st regiments of the line, proceeded to take the fort
of Bomparde, distant sixteen miles. We had the
option of approaching this point by either of two
roads; the one was crossed by streams in two or
three places, while along the other there was no
water, and the latter unfortunately was chosen.
The General's reason for preferring it I have never
heard: all that I can say is, that the consequences
were very disastrous. The troops only moved off at
9 A.M., and before that time the greater number of
the men had emptied their canteens; for a considerable distance we had to pass through a deep and close
ravine, and were half suffocated by clouds of red dust;
we had not advanced above two miles when the
serjeant-major and thirteen privates of the 67th ex-

pired. Those who had improvidently drunk their
grog before moving off were soon to be seen sucking
the sleeves of their jackets for the perspiration that
oozed through them; the tongues of several were
hanging out of their mouths, amazingly swollen, and
black with flies; and in many instances, *horresco
referens*, the men had recourse to the last extremity to
allay their thirst; but the Brigadier, who commanded
us, was fortunately well supplied with sour-sops,
" which ever and anon he gave his *lips*," at the head
of the column. All the suffering and loss of life
sustained on this short march might easily have been
averted by the precaution of taking with us a few
mules, carrying barrels of water.

As we drew near to the fort, some smart skirmishing took place between us and the enemy; but the
latter were soon driven in, with the loss on our part
of a small number of killed and wounded, among
whom were Lieutenant Nesbitt and Adjutant Ross,
both of the 32nd. We then cut fascines for filling up
the ditch, and prepared to storm the place; but the
garrison beat the chamade, and were permitted to
march out with the honours of war; they were men
of all shades of complexion, from white to black.
The fort, of which we took possession, was quad-
rangular, having a gun mounted at each angle, and
surrounded by a tolerably deep ditch, the bottom of
which was planted with stakes, pointed and hardened
in the fire : there was a village near it.

We posted strong picquets on the different path-
ways leading to the fort, and at night small parties
were pushed more in advance into the woods;

since, in a war with a savage enemy, there is
nothing so much to be feared as a surprise, for a
successful attempt at which they are peculiarly fitted
by their native habits, the keenness of their senses of
hearing and seeing, their perfect knowledge of the
country, and the silence, secrecy, and celerity of their
movements.   Our next care was to select the best
houses in the village for hospitals, which were speedily
filled, as the mortality increased daily.   We were
much harassed by sudden calls to arms that were
given almost every night.   If a musquet-shot was
heard, the works were instantly manned ; and the
want of rest that we thus suffered, added to the
baneful influence of the climate, in a very short time
made it apparent that this post would not be long
tenable.

The first picquet that I commanded was posted
across a pathway leading to Jeremie, which was then
occupied by a considerable force of brigands.   A
guide conducted us through the woods by a complete
labyrinth for two miles, and then left us.   The orders,
which I had received through the Fort-adjutant, were,
" Remain until you are cut to pieces ; but if overpowered, retire on the fort."

As the men were quite exhausted, I made them
sit on the ground, holding their firelocks between
their legs ; and afterwards I directed the rear rank
to lie down and sleep for two hours, which they
did by word of command ; when their time expired,
I roused them and made them watch, while the
front rank rested in their turn.   As for myself, I was
kept on the *qui vive* all night, vainly endeavouring

to extract some meaning from the orders, which seemed to be of a very contradictory nature; but whatever they were intended to mean, there was little probability of our being able to retrace our steps should the brigands attack us. However, as it happened, the night passed over without a visit from them.

Not long after this the enemy gained an advantage over us by surprising, one morning before daybreak, the post of Palissée, distant from the fort about two miles, and on the road to the Mole. A captain was stationed there with three subalterns and fifty men of the 32nd. It seems that the brigands had crept to the edge of the wood near which the picquet was posted, and, having watched their opportunity, made a sudden rush, burst into the house, attacked our men before they could turn out, and used their knives with such effect that they cut to pieces the whole party with the exception of the captain and one private, who escaped into the woods. These two, after wandering a considerable time, and fearing that they were only saved from the knife to perish by famine—a death so particularly shocking to an Englishman—by great good fortune fell in with a detachment that had been sent out from the fort to ascertain the cause of the firing. The officers killed were Lieutenants Williams, White, and Power.

At this time I was posted, with a small party, at a coffee-mill about two miles from Palissée, and I heard the firing. I immediately collected all the farming utensils that were to be found, and began to fortify myself as strongly as my skill in engineering and the nature of the post and materials would permit; but, in the course of the day, a dragoon came out from the fort with an order to retreat, and I was thus deprived of the chance of having the honour to command at a siege.

As the enemy continued to occupy Palissée, it was deemed necessary to retake it without delay. Colonel Hamilton, of the 81st, was intrusted with the command of the force destined for this service, which consisted of the greater part of the 32nd and 81st regiments, together with a detachment of the 13th Light Dragoons, under Lieutenant Sheares. The infantry were divided into two columns, so that, marching by different routes, they might attack on two points at once.

The enemy were drawn up in the large open space that surrounds the houses, and, as soon as the heads of our columns emerged from the cover, opened upon them a well-directed fire; but, their line being suddenly charged by the dragoons, they fled into the wood with precipitation. They had never seen a body of cavalry before, and were panic-struck at their appearance, which they thought supernatural, though they must have seen horses and mules ridden by the whites resident on the island. Some of the fugitives took refuge in the cellars of the houses, and were bayonetted; seven others were caught, and set up by the men for marks to shoot at, in revenge for the massacre of the picquet, but the officers interfered and saved the lives of the poor wretches; they were kept to act as pioneers, and never attempted to make their escape while their services were required. The brigands were generally naked, with the exception of a piece of cloth wrapped round the loins; they wore waist-belts and pouches, and were armed with musquets, but had no bayonets; some of them carried knives.

A short experience having shown that Bomparde was totally unsuitable as a military position, and the brigands collecting in great numbers, it was decided to withdraw the troops to the Mole. As there was only a pathway leading from Bomparde to this point, the transport of the sick was very tedious; they were conveyed on hospital stretchers, fitted with long poles, and borne on men's shoulders; but all hopeless cases, not expected to hold out many hours, were to be left behind.

Among the sick so condemned there was a brother officer and particular friend of mine, and him I was determined not to abandon before every effort in my power had been made to accomplish his removal; but it was with regret that I saw the last fatigue party move off, after having applied in vain to the commanding officer, who declared that no men could be spared. My only resource then was to go to a few black prisoners, who were digging graves near the hospitals, and I brought two of them without orders to the sick man's room. He was lying on a stretcher, quite insensible, and swollen to an enormous size, being naturally very tall and robust, and I am confident that four of our men would have found it a very severe task to carry him to the shore. The blacks could not lift the stretcher, but made me understand that they could carry it if once placed on their heads.   I had this done, and they moved off apparently with ease.   They had no escort, not even a single person to watch them, and might have safely got rid of their burden, and escaped into the woods, nevertheless they conveyed him faithfully to the platform.   He was then taken on board one of the ships, and shortly after his honest heart, poor fellow ! had ceased to beat for ever.

The whites of the neighbourhood, who had returned to their homes after the place surrendered to us, were now destined to become refugees once more, and followed us to the coast.   Their case was most pitiable, as they had fully expected that the English would retain possession of their old district; *au comble*, the notice of the evacuation given to them was so short that they had only two or three hours to prepare—just time sufficient for collecting the few mules and asses they possessed, and providing them with baskets in which to stow old people, children, and poultry.   The strong and healthy of both sexes made the journey on foot.

It was alike impossible not to be touched by the misfortunes of the emigrants, and not to be struck by the ludicrous *tout ensemble* of their march.   In a pair of panniers, which had acquired an oscillatory motion from the unusually hurried pace of the astonished donkey, by whose flanks they hung, might be seen the grotesque figures of two antiquated French ladies—next to them another of the long-eared tribe, toiling under the weight of a scolding mother of a family, balanced by her squalling progeny, which she was vainly exerting herself to keep in order— then, seated between two panniers, one of which was

tenanted by geese, and the other by their amphibious
fellow-birds, an old man might follow, a very picture
of resignation, fixing his eyes on his beast's ears,
and apparently deaf to the cackling and quacking of
his aquatics, as well as to the often-repeated remark,
" Had you taken my advice, we should not now be
in this catastrophe," which proceeded from the shrill-
voiced beldame who, with the rest of the poultry, rode
close at his donkey's tail. After these had passed in
review, the eye might light on a mule, more vicious
and not less obstinate than the famous one of the holy
Abbess of Andouillets, and returning every blow of
its enraged guide's cudgel with a violent outflinging of
its heels, which caused the pigeons in the off pannier
to escape at each flap of the lid, seriously discom-
posed the corpulent old lady in the near pannier,
through an aperture in the bottom of which one
goodly leg had already slipped ; and likewise excited
the alarm of the living burden of the succeeding
donkey, consisting of a withered, wrinkled, sharp-
visaged female, whose general appearance, set off by
a parrot and a lapdog, plainly indicated that she had
" never told her love," and of a black-eyed niece, who
certainly would be convicted of having been more
communicative if the little *gage d'amour* in her arms
could be adduced in proof. It may be added that
the screams of the fat old lady, the lean old aunt, the
niece, the child, and the parrot were very agreeably
accompanied by the barking of Fidele, and the lusty
sacrés of the muleteer—in short, nothing was wanted
but an ambuscade of brigands to complete the charming confusion of the scene.

On the route I conversed for some time with a Frenchman, who had had several skirmishes with the brigands; in one of these encounters he took an officer of colour, and carried him behind him on his horse. "What became of him ultimately?" I inquired. "I kept him seven days," said the Frenchman, "and every morning I cut off one of his fingers; yet the rogue escaped into the woods after all with three." Owing to the number of men and horses that had been killed at different times by the blacks, in the attempt to pass along this line, and now lay in a state of putrefaction in all directions, the air became quite tainted; and habit made us such connoisseurs that we could readily distinguish the dead body of a man from that of a horse by the scent alone.

The burial-ground happened to be near one of the principal batteries, called the Polygon, and the officer of the guard had orders to attend all interments, and see that three shovelfuls of quicklime were thrown into each grave. As the hospital-carts, each carrying three bodies, arrived almost without intermission during the day, this was both a sad and a wearisome duty. The number of the hospital assistants was now reduced to the ratio of one to a hundred patients, when at least ten times as many were necessary; the consequences of this alteration to the sick were deplorable—the poor fellows, being unable to fan away the flies themselves, and having no proper attendance, died with their mouths full of them, and frequently, as their heads were shaved, they were covered with such swarms that the skin

was completely hid.   The regiments in camp were
the greatest sufferers ; as the rain at times, and
principally at night, fell in torrents, and soon pene-
trated the old moth-eaten tents.

I have passed whole nights, sitting in my tent up
to my ankles in water, and holding an umbrella
over my head.   In the morning, when the sun shone
out, the camp was enveloped in a cloud of steam.
Our living in such damp brought on various fatal
diseases, which in a few months reduced strong
regiments to skeletons.   Sudden deaths also happened occasionally ; I recollect one instance in
particular :—I was invited to dine one day by
Lieutenant R——t[1] of the 32nd, and at the hour
appointed I walked to his tent and asked the servant,
who stood at the door of it, if dinner was not
ready ; the answer was, " Master is dead, sir."   It was
too true ; for the hospital-cart was soon brought up
for the corpse of him who in the morning had asked
me to dine, little thinking then that he had eaten
his last meal !

At the advanced posts the picquets were placed
without any shelter behind *chevaux de frise ;* an officer
and only three men went on at night, and a sentinel
was posted on the pathway that led through the
woods.   I have often revisited a sentinel after an
interval of a few minutes, and found him fast asleep
without arms in his hands : the punishment for the
crime of sleeping on his post, to which a soldier is
made liable by the articles of war, is death ; but in
our present situation such severity was uncalled-for,

[1] I have not succeeded in identifying this officer.

as it was not in human nature to bear up against the exhaustion of strength and spirits experienced by our men.

The very beasts of this island seemed to have conspired to annoy us; the large monkeys frequently made so great a rustling in the woods that the sentinels, thinking the enemy were there, fired, and thus caused the whole line to turn out, which was extremely harassing. And then the asses, which were very numerous, would occasionally collect on the flank of the camp, and charge at full speed along the whole length of it, tumbling over the ropes, and breaking the poles of the tents; the men used to provide themselves with stout sticks for the better reception of these unwelcome visitors, and did not spare them. We were commonly favoured with this "long-eared rout" whenever a thunder-storm came on; and what can be more vexatious to a worn-out soldier in a tempestuous night, than to have a donkey or two tumbling over him, snapping his tent-pole, and leaving him rolled up in the wet canvas till morning!

The number of effective officers in my regiment was gradually diminished to two, another subaltern and myself, and for some time we did all the duty; but at length a few officers from black corps were sent to us. For three weeks I have been on picquet every night. Nevertheless, I continued to enjoy good health for about twelve months; but one evening, at the end of that period, I was attacked by the yellow fever at the mess-table, and rolled up in a blanket at once, and taken to the hospital. There I remained thirty-six days without amendment, though in general the disorder proved fatal in forty-eight hours. At length the medical officers abandoned me to my fate, having sapiently come to the conclusion that a few hours more would terminate my existence. I heard them express this opinion as they walked off, and it had the good effect of rousing me a little. My servant was at hand, and I had strength sufficient to desire him to dress a salt herring, which was the only thing I felt any inclination to take. I ate it with some appetite, and drank in consequence copious draughts of Madeira and water. I continued on the same diet for several days, at the end of which the fever left me, to the great surprise of the doctors.

My pay-sergeant of the grenadier company was also in the hospital at this time, and, having seen the dead bodies merely sewed up in blankets before they were thrown into the graves, and feeling great horror at the idea of being buried without a coffin, he took care to buy one, and kept it at his bedside, until he got what is called a "lightening before death"; he then fancied that he was recovering, and sold the coffin to the patient on the stretcher next to his; but, relapsing soon after, he died, and was buried without one.

At this time a little circumstance, in my opinion speaking well for our men, occurred. When I fell sick I had the payment of the grenadier company, and during my illness the money for that purpose was kept in an open trunk in the hospital, as my pay-sergeant, whom I have just mentioned, was likewise confined to his bed. The soldiers paid themselves,

C

taking what dollars they required whenever they pleased; yet, when I was afterwards called upon to make up my accounts, these men came forward, much to their honour, and scrupulously acknowledged every dollar they had taken.

The French residents on this island treated their slaves barbarously; I saw few of these unfortunate creatures that did not bear evident marks of ill-usage; the commission of the most trivial fault, when discovered by their masters, insured them an unmerciful flogging. On such occasions they were made to lie at full length on the ground, and the punishment was inflicted with a long whip, like those used by waggoners in England. I have seen an axe flung with full force at a poor wretch because he did not hold a piece of timber exactly as his master, who was chopping it, wished. The recollections of the year '91 were fresh in the memories of the planters.

When recovering from the yellow fever in the military hospital, I was disturbed one morning by the pitiable cries of some one in distress, and, looking through a window that was close to my bed, I perceived that they proceeded from a small black boy who was passing by; he was heavily chained, and carried a pitcher of water on his head, while a French lad, who walked after him, was lashing him with a whip, and tormenting him with the most wanton cruelty. My servant ran out instantly, pursued the malignant rascal, and, overtaking him near his residence, gave him a smart blow on the head in proof of a Briton's constitutional abhorrence of such dastardly conduct; but this interference on the

part of one of our nation in behalf of a slave was not
to be borne by a vindictive Frenchman, and in revenge the poor black child was burned and lacerated
with hot irons. I heard his cries for three days. On
the fourth, death came to the little sufferer's aid, and
kindly put an end to his misery. During these four
days I was kept in such a state of agitation that my
recovery was very much retarded, and often did I
regret that my servant had yielded so imprudently to
the impulse of the moment, difficult as it was to
resist it.

While I remained at the Mole, the brigands never
honoured us with a visit, and in this respect they
acted wisely; our defences were too strong to admit
of a successful attack by such a force as theirs, and
they must have been well aware that the climate
would rid them of our presence before many months
had elapsed : had our ministry evinced equal foresight, a fine army would have been preserved, and an
enormous expense avoided.

In twelve months my regiment was reduced to a
mere skeleton, with the loss of thirty-two officers;[1]
it was then completed by convalescents from other
corps, and embarked for the Bahama islands, which
enjoyed a better climate than St. Domingo.

It being the opinion of our medical officers that
there were no hopes of my recovery as long as I
remained in these latitudes, I was ordered to return
home, and accordingly obtained leave of absence. I
sailed from New Providence for England, on board
a West Indiaman, the *Fisher* of Liverpool, Captain

[1] The 66th Foot lost 26 officers and 690 men during this year.

Atkins, with other merchant vessels in company, and under convoy of *La Raisonnée* and *Squirrel* frigates, with the *Swallow* sloop-of-war ; but, a signal for a strange sail being made on the third day, the three King's ships gave chase, and we saw them no more. As it was war time, they thought cruising for prizes more entertaining than convoying merchantmen. We experienced a severe gale off the banks of Newfoundland, and shipped such a heavy sea, that another like it would have sent us to the bottom, as our ship was very deep-waisted.

During the voyage I experienced the utmost care and attention from the worthy Captain Atkins ; I had entered into no agreement with him for messing, and was charged not one-fourth of what I had expected. On making my acknowledgments to him for his kindness, before we landed, he said, " I am happy we part good friends ; but it would have been better had you gone on shore at night ; the people will think I starved you." I was certainly a miserable spectacle ; the bridge of my nose had become transparent ; and in short I could have been but one remove from the state of leanness of the remarkable Frenchman who has been exhibited lately under the name of the Living Skeleton.

After passing a day or two at Liverpool with some friends, I set off in one of the packet boats for Dublin, and, strange to say, as I approached my native country, the remains of my old attack began to leave me ; and on landing, I found that I had fairly got rid of it. When I reached home, I was received almost as one who had been raised from the dead, and I do

not doubt that my appearance was rather sepulchral.
The joy of my old nurse, in particular, was excessive,
when she was convinced of my identity, respecting
which she was quite sceptical, until she saw the mole
on my foot, that gave evidence as credible to her
as the scar on the leg of Ulysses did to the faithful
Euryclea. She had paid her priest to say masses for
me, and had hung one of my old militia coats on a
cross at the foot of her bed, before which she offered
up daily prayers for my safety.

As I was the only surviving ensign of my corps, I
was promoted to a lieutenancy[1] on stating my case
to the proper authorities, and also obtained leave of
absence until the beginning of the memorable year
1798.

[1] Commission bears date May 24, 1797.

CHAPTER IV

WHEN my leave had expired, I set out for Chatham
with a renovated constitution, which was destined to
be tried by other hardships. I sailed from Dublin
in one of the Holyhead packets. It was a rough
night, and a violent gale came on as soon as we had
crossed the bar ; the cutter began to ship a vast deal
of water, and the captain had drunk himself into a
state of stupidity ; he had left both his compasses
in the binnacle, and a heavy sea swept them off the
deck, with several other things ; two sailors were also
carried overboard, but, the end of the boom dipping
in the water, they were caught in the belly of the sail
and thrown back on the deck.

Soon after, the captain was trying to fasten a
candlestick to the table in the cabin, but, instead,
drove a carving fork through his left hand and
into the timber, with such force that it required
some exertion on the part of one of the passengers
to pull it out. We hoped that this accident would
rouse him ; but we could perceive no indication of
returning reason, except his sucking the part affected
with great eagerness. However, fortunately for us

38

there were three masters of merchantmen on board, and, as one of them had been before at the Isle of Man, they decided upon shaping their course for it when the vessel could carry sail. As we approached the land, the people on shore, who perceived our danger, continued to make signals, by which we were saved, for they led us to Derby Haven, where the vessel was run aground on a sandy beach, and left high and dry at low water.

The passengers proceeded to Castletown, where we found comfortable accommodation. As the Manx people paid no imposts at this time, their island was one of the cheapest places of abode in Europe, and an income of £50 a year would have enabled a single man to keep a jovial board.

The repairs that it was necessary to make in the cutter were completed in a week, and we then sailed for Holyhead, where we arrived without any further adventures; and I proceeded forthwith to my final destination.

The Irish rebellion now broke out; the gaols were soon filled, and Duncannon Fort was converted into a slave market; cargoes of our wretched, misguided peasants were shipped off from thence for Chatham, in every kind of craft that could be procured for the purpose. The nature of their accommodations was unthought of. As many men as the hold could contain were huddled together, without straw to lie on, or any sea-stock other than potatoes, which could not be cooked in bad weather, and of which even a sufficient quantity was not always provided; and it is a melancholy fact that several of those unfortunate people have perished of absolute want on their passage. In this manner many regiments on foreign stations kept up their establishments; and those recruits soon became soldiers, second to none in gallantry in the field. It is true that at this eventful period war raged both at home and abroad, and the hands of Government were full; but under any circumstances the nefarious proceedings of Duncannon Fort should have been instantly checked.

As soon as a batch of United Irishmen arrived in the garrison, their sticks, clothes, and bundles were heaped together and burned; they themselves were bathed in cisterns, put into the barber's hands to have their hair cut close, and provided with new undress clothing; in a short time they would become well-looking soldiers. General Fox, whose name must ever be remembered with respect by those who had the good fortune to be placed under his command, was unremitting in his attention to the messing of these men, and to their accounts, kept by the staff-sergeants, as he was determined that the Duncannon system should not spread to Chatham.

I had charge of a fine division of about one hundred and thirty men, all Irish; and they took it into their heads to salute no officer but me. One morning two of them were on sentry at the barrack gate when General Fox passed, and he observed with surprise that they took no notice of him. "Do you not know me?" he said to them; "I am General Fox." The reply was, "Faith, 'tis well for you;" but it was accompanied by no salute. The result of this act of insubordination was the appearance, in a few days, of an order that they should be drafted into regiments on foreign stations, not more than three to each. This order they refused to obey, and sent a deputation to me to say that they would fight it out, though the garrison at this time was two thousand strong, and it was with great difficulty that I persuaded them to give up their arms.

Those Irish drafts, coming over in such a wild state, caused considerable trouble at Chatham. They regarded an attempt at desertion as a very venial offence, and the knocking down of a staff-sergeant as a mere trifle ; the consequence was a great frequency of courts-martial. I recollect being a member of one, when the charges preferred against the accused were, his being out after hours, and his striking a staff-sergeant. The prisoner was a very powerful young man, and, as some Irishmen, who deal in hyperboles, would say, "so broad in the chest that one might turn a gig on it." While the said grave charges were being detailed in his presence, the expression of his countenance indicated no consciousness of the impropriety of his conduct on the preceding night, and the muscles of his face were relaxed into a constant grin, while, as he thought, the sergeant was making "much ado about nothing."

"Well, Patrick Murphy," said the President to the recruit, when the accuser had ceased, "what have you to offer in your defence?"—"I'll tell your honour dat;" replied Murphy; "as I was taking a bit of a walk wid myself last night towards Ratchister, I meets dis honest man, an' 'Where are you goin'?' says he.—'I'm goin' to take a bit of a walk,' says I.

'You'll walk wid me to de guard-house,' says he.—' I owe you no discoorse, sir,' says I : an' wid dat he lays holt of me.—'Take ov me, sir,' says I, ' if you plase ; ' an' wid dat what does he do, but draws his soord, an' makes an offer at me ?   So I jest raises up my hand, an' gives him a pat wid de backs of my nails, an' down drops de honest man.—' Get up, sir,' says I thin, ' for I'll take you to de barrack, an' complain you for tryin' to kill me wid de soord.'—He wouldn't get up for my biddin', nather would he spake a word, jist to show how much he was hurted ; so I puts himself an' his soord under my arm, an' brins him up all de way to de gate ; so I knocks, an' de man at de door says, 'Whose dere ? ' says he.—' It's I,' says I, ' one of Colonel Ogle's boys wid a sergeant.'—So he opens de door, an' calls de guard ; an' dey puts me into a place dat I didn't see de blessed light of de sun in since ; an' sure de world knows, gintlemen, dat I could kill de little man, if I liked it."

While I remained at Chatham a Russian squadron came up the Medway to be coppered.   The officers came occasionally to sup at the barrack.   It was evident they had not been accustomed to polite society ; but, though their manners were coarse, they were perfectly good-humoured.   They seemed to make no distinction between the different dishes set before them ; they helped themselves to whatever happened to be near them, and ate with excellent appetites ; cold and hot meats, preserves and pickles, cheese and confectionery, were all swallowed without the slightest regard to the order in which they came, or what should begin and what end the repast.

Their men were still less disposed to make nice distinctions between what should or should not be eaten; they apparently saw no difference between soap and cheese; and, when in the chandlers' shops, would pick up and eat any bits of the former article that remained on the counter. Besides, it was remarked some time after their arrival in the Medway, that the lamps in the streets went out earlier than usual, and, at length, some Russian sailors were observed climbing up the posts and drinking the oil. They slept on the decks of their ships, wrapped up in sheep-skin cloaks with the wool inside, which was not very conducive to cleanliness. They were much addicted to the use of spirituous liquors; and even their priests were not ashamed to be seen stretched across the steps of alehouses in the day time, and beastly drunk; still these reverend gentry were held in such veneration by the crews, that a sailor would never pass one of them, though in such a disgraceful state, without taking off his cap.

I received this year a most unpleasant command to go to Jersey with a detachment of my refractory countrymen, fresh arrivals from Duncannon, and principally intended for the 88th, the Connaught Rangers. It would have spared me a most disagreeable duty had these men been sent with them, for they became very unruly; they whipped up every article of sea-stock, laid in by the officers at any of the ports down Channel, that was left for a moment on deck; they did not even keep the cabouse sacred; and, occasionally, a fellow would leave the skin of his hands in a stewpan, while diving for its contents.

On our way we anchored in the Downs, and sent on shore for fresh meat; but it was not long on deck, when a woman burst into the cabin to make a complaint to me, as commanding officer. "Oh! my sheep's head!" she roared out; "sure I had as good a right as the best of them to get some of the meat;" and certainly her face, which was streaming with blood, testified that she had defended her right to the last extremity. Upon going between decks, I found all hands engaged in a general row, boxing, yelling, and tearing from each other the meat that the officers had provided for their own mess; and it was with difficulty that I succeeded in restoring something like order and tranquillity. However, when the lights were put out at 9 P.M. hostilities recommenced, and the battle raged with as much fury as ever; the biting of noses, ears, fingers, and toes, the scratching of faces, the pulling of hair, and the cuffing and kicking being kept up with much spirit till a late hour.

At daylight I went on board a transport bound for Guernsey, with troops of the same class, to ask the advice of the officer in command, who was my senior, respecting the proper measures to be adopted in this emergency. He told me that his people went on precisely in the same way as mine, until he made up a severe ship-cat, with which he flogged them on their bare legs when they turned out of their berths at night to fight, and he advised me to do the same, adding, that their dispositions had undergone a thorough change since they left their own country, as they were now *dis-United* Irishmen. When I returned to the ship, I followed the directions of my

superior officer ; with this difference, however, that I
employed one of the staff-sergeants on board to make
use of the cat.

In a place where there was so great a mixture of
officers of all corps in the service, and of course endless variety of character, it might reasonably be expected that unpleasantries, likely to terminate in an
appeal to arms, would occur now and then. I was
one evening in the guard-room with a Lieutenant
M——— [1] of the 37th, playing a rubber of whist, when
another subaltern, Donald G———, of a Highland regiment, came uninvited into the room, and, without
saying a word, drew a chair to the fire and sat down.
He preserved silence for about half-an-hour, and then,
suddenly turning to the officer on duty, exclaimed,
" By ———, Mr. M———, you are a scoundrel ! " He
walked out of the room immediately after this polite
sally, and left us all in no slight astonishment, with
the exception, perhaps, of M———, who merely said,
" Devilish cool, indeed ! " As soon as the guard was
relieved, a message was sent to Donald, and arrangements were made for a meeting behind the barracks.
It was apparently his first affair of honour, and,
though urged to appoint a friend, he refused to do so,
saying, " I canna see the use of a second, when a man
could tak his ain part." He went directly to a gun-
smith's at Rochester, hired a horse pistol, which he
loaded with a plentiful charge of slugs, and, putting it
under his coat, hurried to the place of meeting. He
found there Lieutenant M———, and that officer's
second ; and the latter, having paced the distance,

[1] Lieutenant Marks (?).

and placed his friend on the ground, then proceeded to act also for the other party; but Donald slipped behind him, and at about half-distance, levelled his pistol and discharged its contents at the head of his antagonist, crying out at the same time, "Tak that, you scoundrel!" Lieutenant M——'s hat was perforated in several places, and knocked off by the slugs, which also scored the skin of the top of his head, and cut ridges through his powdered and pomatumed hair; and as he passed his hand over the part affected, he quietly repeated his former comment, "Devilish cool, indeed!" The affair ended here, as the old garrison-adjutant, who had been sent to put the parties in arrest, and was directed to the spot by the report of the pistol, came trotting up, and prevented any further proceedings.

There was a Scotch lad here, an ensign in the 81st regiment, whose father, with true nationality, kept a flour manufactory in the land o' cakes, and who was so complete an original that he afforded considerable amusement to the whole garrison. Unluckily for him, he was one day invited to dine at General Fox's, and, on receiving the card, went off immediately to consult a great wag, Colonel C——[1] of the 47th regiment, respecting the proper form of the required reply, and the manner in which he should conduct himself during the entertainment. "I will write your answer," said the colonel, "and provide you with any articles of dress you may want, and also give you instructions that will serve to regulate your conduct from the time you enter the drawing-room until you leave the house."

[1] Major James Cuming (?).

"All's weel then, and mony thanks," said the ensign ; "for, as I ha' been maistly brought up in a mill, I dinna ken preceesely the manners o' grand company."

When the hour for dressing arrived, the colonel had in readiness for his pupil a pair of silk stockings, well blued, and old - fashioned knee and shoe buckles. When the ensign had finished his toilette, the military Chesterfield thus addressed him : "Well, M——, as far as the tailor makes the man, you are quite the thing ; now, therefore, attend to my instructions. The general, you must know, is a jolly good kind of man, and wishes every one to make free with him, and seem perfectly at home in his house."—"The general's aye a weel dispositioned and kind-hearted body," interrupted M——.—"So then," continued the colonel, "the moment you enter the drawing-room, go up and shake him heartily by the hand, and repeat the ceremony with Mrs. Fox, not forgetting to ask her how the children are, and talk away with them about Scotland as much as you please. When you go to the dinner-room, and all are seated, ask the general, the first thing, to take a glass of wine with you ; and, as soon as that is down, be sure to be equally attentive to Mrs. Fox ; then eat away as fast as you can. When the dishes are removed, the servants will place a large glass half-filled with water near you, and take particular care to drink every drop of it."—"I'll e'en do that," said the ensign, "but wuld I na' put a wee drop of wine amangst it ? "—"Certainly," replied the colonel, "fill it with wine."—"An that be a'," rejoined the Scot, "I'll ne'er shirk it ; for sax gude glasses o' Farintosh, as ye ken weel eneugh,

is waur nor as mony bottles o' their port and clairet."—
"Very true," said his deceitful companion ; "and now
remember that, before you go away, you shake hands
in a friendly manner with the general and Mrs. Fox,
and thank them politely for their entertainment."—
"My name is na M——," cried the *naif* ensign, "an
I forget onything of a' ye ha' been sae gude to rede
me !" And he kept his word. Everything was done,
as directed, to the inexpressible amusement of the
general and his other guests ; but, when he emptied
a decanter into the finger-glass, and drank off the
mixed contents of the latter, the company were irresistibly convulsed with laughter, while poor M——
still felt confident that he had in no way transgressed
against good manners and propriety.

The finest sight at Chatham was, in my opinion, the
portion of the Dutch fleet, nine sail of the line and
two frigates, captured by Admiral Duncan in the
victory gained by him off Camperdown on the 11th of
October in the preceding year. Some of the British
men-of-war engaged in the action were also in the
Medway during part of my stay ; two of them in
particular, the *Monarch* and the *Ardent*, were much
damaged ; and, in the first - mentioned ship, the
divisions between four contiguous ports forward were
completely beaten in.

My next change of quarters was to a dull place,
distant about fifty miles from town, and to which the
skeleton of my regiment was moving from Portsmouth, where it had arrived some days before from
New Providence. When it was about to enter the
town, all the population sallied out to see it. The first

person who appeared happened to be a remarkably corpulent captain, who had been recruiting, and had joined on the march.—" Bless us," said an old farmer, who would have wished to have a few bullocks in such good condition, "this be no skeleton, surely !" The joke went round, and no one enjoyed it more than the person who was the cause of it.

Before our arrival, a newly raised Irish corps, and I cannot exactly say whether it was the Carlow Buffs faced with black, or Colonel Matthew's Tipperary Rangers, was quartered here, when not more than half of the men had received their uniforms. The honest burghers, however, being of a peaceful way of thinking, and not all enamoured of military society, in respect to which their sentiments and those of a great proportion of the fair ones of their families were diametrically opposite, did not live on terms of becoming amity with the sons of Mars, and, accordingly, the latter resolved to be avenged on them for their want of civility. For this purpose their colonel one night sent out half the regiment in plain clothes, with directions to go a few miles on the London road, and return at daylight to the town as a desperate mob come to attack it. Never was order better obeyed. At the time appointed the wildest yells were heard at the entrance from London, and, presently, the boys rushed in, wheeling their sticks, shouting and threatening destruction to the town and its inhabitants, who, in fear and trembling, awaited the issue of this uproar and tumult, equally alarming and inexplicable. Only one or two of the boldest ventured to thrust their night-capped heads out of upper windows, to recon-

D

noitre the fearful and unknown enemy; but a few paving stones, directed so as to skim close by their stations, had the effect of causing them to withdraw themselves rapidly within their shells. The panic was still further increased when the other half of the regiment, which was drawn up to resist the supposed mob, began to fire volleys of blank cartridge, and the streets became the scene of a mock combat, to which, no doubt, the imaginations of the citizens added piles of carnage and torrents of blood: no business was attempted—not a shop was opened—and *sauve qui peut* was the cry. However, when the attack was repelled, and the din of battle died away, confidence was gradually restored—the industrious resumed their daily occupations—the idle had recourse again to their usual modes of killing time—and the good people, seeing neither blood nor dead and dying, began, I dare say, to suspect that it was all a trick.

Various minor rows also occurred before those unruly sons of Erin were removed; and, on the day that they marched out, they left one of the spinning girls in a state of intoxication, and stuck through a lamp-iron in front of the head inn—a sight at which the worthy citizens were excessively scandalised.

Our next move was to Launceston, where we experienced much civility. We now became a boy regiment, with one hundred men to do the duty.

From Launceston we were ordered to Bridgewater. In this part of England the lower classes were suffering from an alarming scarcity of provisions; a large mob entered the town, and were very riotous. They laid hands on the magistrates, who were glad to

escape with only torn cloaks, and we were called out
to support the civil power ; but, when the poor people
declared that they had been for days without food,
our officers gave them, instead of balls, all their spare
cash. Soon after, our boy recruits were drafted into
regiments serving in India, and the remainder of our
corps proceeded to Bristol, where they embarked for
Waterford.

CHAPTER V

OUR next quarter was Dundalk. On our march to
this town, we breakfasted one morning at a small inn
by the roadside, distinguished by the sign of the
Royal Oak, and where we were attended by a bare-
legged girl. An English officer, who was amused by
the to him outlandish air of the whole establishment,
asked our waiter by way of diversion if there was
any claret in the house : " Troth, then, there is and
illegant," said she, and tripped off to the binn. She
quickly returned with the wine, which, to his astonishment, fully answered her description of it, and pleased
our palates so well that we took with us a quantity of
it to the next stage.

We were sent here to be completed from the English fencible regiments, which were for the most part
stationed in the north of Ireland. They had been
employed in quelling the Irish rebellion in 1798, and,
as civil war tends in a great degree to the relaxation
of discipline, it was requisite to hand over the men
that came from these corps to a correct, steady,
and well-disciplined set of non-commissioned officers,
who would make them work well together and lay
aside their old habits. As an illustration of the high

notions of discipline entertained by our sergeants, and of their fitness for the duty that devolved on them, I may relate here an anecdote of this period.

When we received a route for Kilkenny, we were ordered to precede the baggage, and therefore direc-. tions were given to have it placed in the store, which was two stories high. I was always of opinion that the less an officer was encumbered with baggage the better ; but for such ideas I never received any credit, and my acting up to them was invariably ascribed to want of means to increase it. Be this as it may, my light portmanteau was put in the tackle, and one of the men, by a couple of quick hauls with one hand, whisked it up to the top of the store in a moment. The sergeant conceived that this was not done in a respectful manner, and called out to the fellow, "What way is that, sir, to hoist the lieutenant's baggage ? Lower that trunk immediately." And, as soon as this order was obeyed, "Now, sir," cried the exact non-commissioned officer, "clap both hands to it, and hoist away handsomely." The portmanteau was then raised as slowly, and with as much seeming exertion, as if it had possessed the respectable weight of half a ton.

Kilkenny was rather a pleasant quarter. It is re-markable for "its fire without smoke, its water without mud, and its air without fog," according to the well-known proverb, and also for its private theatricals, a species of amusement which the people of this town and its respectable neighbourhood keep up with pecu-liar taste and spirit.

We proceeded thence to the Irish capital.

"Beware of the ides of March," said a soothsayer

to Julius Cæsar;—a similar caution might have been of some use to me, as on the fifteenth of that month I lost a dinner for eight by an unlucky wager. This spread was given at an hotel; we drank pretty freely, and some experienced in consequence an exhilaration of spirits. One of my guests walked on before me towards the barracks, and on his way caught a watchman dozing on his post. The temptation was irresistible, and the guardian of the night received a smart tap on the side of his head; the assaulted instantly sprang his rattle, which soon called a bevy of his brethren to his aid, who hemmed in our hero, and in the scuffle punished him severely, as his cut and bleeding face amply testified. When I came up, my first object was to endeavour to get him away, and take him to the barracks; but so far was I from succeeding in it, that I was knocked down for my peacemaking intentions, and then dragged to the watchhouse, where I passed the rest of the night, my partner in distress being suffered to find his way home. As my recollection returned, I began to think of the consequences that might follow this adventure, since, on the seventeenth, the day of our patron saint, there was to be a ball at the Castle of more than usual splendour; and I inquired earnestly if they could let me have a looking-glass, that I might see whether my face was or was not so marked as to prevent me from appearing at the ball: but the surly charlies refused to procure one for me. However, I was told that my face was not cut, and that the blood on it only proceeded from a blow which had uncorked my smelling bottle, but was of no consequence. Notwithstanding these assurances, I feared, as I felt considerable pain below one eye, that it would turn black, and thus deprive me of all hope of enjoying the amusement that I had anticipated—an apprehension which added much to the annoyances of the night.

After daylight, I was taken in a coach to the sitting magistrate, Sir William Worthington, and I had no reason to regard him as an even-handed dispenser of justice, for, without listening to anything that I had to say, he informed me that I should be sent either to Newgate or to the barracks, and that the other officer's sword and mine should be forwarded to General Dunn, as the charges preferred against me were very serious, namely, going about the streets armed at untimely hours, and committing assault and robbery on the persons of his Majesty's subjects on his highway. It was to no purpose that I then pleaded that I was knocked down, which effectually prevented me from assaulting any person, had I any such intention ; that officers were directed to wear their swords in the streets at all hours ; and that I could not have stolen a watchman's pike and rattle, first, for the same reason that rendered it impossible for me to commit an assault, and secondly, because from the moment when I was attacked by the watch until the present time I had continued in durance vile. " No matter, sir," said Sir William, " I wait for your answer—to New-gate or to the barracks ? " I did not hesitate to choose the latter alternative, and was released. I instantly hurried to my room, and removed the mud and blood from my face ; I was delighted to find that a very small black mark below one eye was the only dis-

coloration that water would not efface : therefore to
the Castle I went, though the general did think that
it was rather cool on my part to appear there, as
he still retained my sword. A day or two after the
ball our swords were returned.

I came off duty on the morning of the twenty-third
of July, and in the evening had retired to rest at an
unusually early hour—about half-past nine—when
my servant came into my room, dressed in marching order, to my great surprise. He was not less
astonished at finding me in bed, for he told me that
the town was in open rebellion ; and that he had
heard my name called on the parade, and thought I
had gone with a detachment, as the greater part of
the regiment had marched off already. I quickly
slipped on my uniform, and hurried to the parade,
whence I was sent with a party to Thomas Street,
which the rebels had made their rendezvous.

At this time Colonel Browne of the Twenty-first
Fusileers had been killed, while returning to his
quarters, as were also Lord Kilwarden and one of
his nephews ; their bodies lay in the watch-house,
dreadfully mangled. His lordship was coming into
town from his country seat, to apprise the Government of a danger of which they had so little expectation. Miss Wolfe, who was in the carriage with him,
was permitted to proceed unharmed by the rebels.
She fled to the Castle, and made her way to the
secretary, to whom she gave the first intimation of
the breaking out of the insurrection that had been
received there. All who heard her laughed at the
statement ; one said that she was mad, another that

she was in love; but a sudden rush made through the gates by the 62nd regiment put an end to their unseasonable jesting. That corps had luckily been quartered in the old custom-house, a building not far from the Castle, and, on hearing what was doing, hastened without loss of time to the defence of this most important post, and saved it. Had they neglected to do so, the rebels would have been masters of the Castle in a few minutes, but such an unruly rabble acted too little in concert to have any chance in carrying it when defended by a regiment.

An orderly dragoon, sent from Kilmainham with a dispatch, found one of the streets through which he had to pass occupied by a host of rebels; nevertheless, this brave fellow determined to do his duty, and gallantly attempted to cut his way through the dense mass before him. In this he succeeded for a considerable distance, but was at length absolutely lifted out of the saddle on their pikes, and perished, a noble example of the spirit and devotedness of a British soldier.

When the first military parties reached Thomas Street, they had some skirmishing with the rebels; but after a trifling resistance, the latter fled in all directions. Mr. Emery, assistant-surgeon of the 32nd Regiment, was in Thomas Street before Lord Kilwarden breathed his last, and the venerable old man died in his arms. This officer took from his lordship's person his rings, some valuable papers, and a ten pound note, which was steeped in blood, and he forwarded them to Mr. Wolfe, his lordship's nephew, who immediately wrote to him to thank him

for his attention to his deceased uncle, and to request
his acceptance of the note.

We continued in the streets until daylight, breaking open houses, and searching cellars, where the
peasants usually put up. Parties of military were
then sent off in all directions to the different towns
and villages, for the purpose of disarming all suspected
persons. Lyons, Lord Cloncurry's residence, was
searched, and that nobleman's arms were taken away
and brought to Maynooth. I accompanied the troops
sent to the latter place ; the innkeeper had absconded
before we arrived there, so that we should have been
badly off for that day, had not his Grace the Duke of
Leinster generously sent a single melon to regale
twenty officers.

The disaffected in the other parts of Ireland were
too much disheartened by the unwelcome tidings, "that
rebellion had bad luck" in the capital, to venture to
take up arms ; and thus terminated a most ill-advised,
ill-concerted, and rash undertaking. The only remarkable feature in this abortive effort to effect
the separation of Ireland from Great Britain was the
secrecy observed by the rebels. So little idea had
Government of any insurrectionary movement, that
only the day before the rising, General Fox, then
commander of the forces here, issued an order to
the troops not to wear side-arms in the streets.

Emmet, the ostensible chief of the conspirators,
had been called to the bar, and was a young man of
some talent, though totally unfit to act in the capacity
of military leader to a body of men, so wild and
intractable as the insurgents whom he headed. I

believe that he was honest, and that, in adopting a line of conduct to which others were led by ambition, bigotry, desire of change, or fear of pecuniary embarrassment, he—ever ardent, enthusiastic, and high-minded—listened only to the dictates of what he thought to be the purest patriotism. He seems to have dreamed, rather than reasoned, himself into notions of the practicability of that Utopian scheme, the erection of Ireland into an independent state, maintaining herself on her own resources, and unindebted for protection to any other power. In fact, this rebel of the nineteenth century, had he lived in the days of romance, for he possessed a gallant spirit, a poetical imagination, and a susceptible heart, might have shone in the character of a devoted and fearless troubadour, who passed his days in celebrating his mistress and fighting the battles of his country.

Great numbers of the deluded insurgents, as well as Emmet, were now taken up, and executions took place daily. I was present when two young lads were hung at their own doors, at Palmerstown near Dublin, and then beheaded ; their parents stood by during the execution, and assisted in placing the bodies in the coffins ; they also took off the shoes of their dead sons, and followed the carts to the gaol for the rest of their apparel ; and all this was done without a tear, or a sigh, or any indication of emotion. Many will be ready to exclaim against what they will imagine to be a brutal want of feeling. It was no such thing. Among the faults of the rude and hard-faring Irish peasant, many as they may be, such insensibility cannot be numbered. No ; those parents

did not look upon that scene of execution with
common eyes—no ignominy was, in their minds,
attached to the fate of their sons—they saw in the
cord and the axe nothing but the instruments of their
martyrdom—and there was that in their countenances
which plainly told how the loss they suffered, of one
kind, was met by a counterbalancing gain of another.
Still, perhaps, some moment would be found, when
no Sassenagh was near, in which to pay, unobserved,
the tribute of grief at the grave of the departed ; as
well as one in which these poor misguided people
would speak proudly of the two youths, who died,
though unavailingly, in what they considered their
country's cause.

I have to regret that I had not an opportunity of
being present at the trial of Emmet, and of hearing his
eloquent and manly address, parts of which few heard
without emotion, and especially that in which he
proudly and earnestly disclaimed any past intention
of looking to any foreign power for aid in the struggle
he thought to have made for the independence of
Ireland.

On the morning of his execution I repaired to
Kilmainham, the place of his confinement. I found
there several of the staff, and a great number of
country gentlemen, who formed a lane from the cell
door to the prison gate, at which the sheriff was
waiting in a coach. At length the prisoner appeared ;
he was perfectly composed, bowed to the persons
assembled with as much ease as if he had met them
in a drawing-room, and, passing on, stepped into the
coach. When he arrived in Thomas Street, he re-

quested the sheriff's permission to address the people ; that gentleman asked him in what strain he intended to speak. " I mean to exhort them," replied Emmet, " to follow up the pursuit in which they are at present engaged." " Then," said the sheriff, " you cannot be heard." Emmet ascended the platform with a firm step, calmly unloosed his neckcloth, and looked with an upbraiding countenance on the dense multitude that surrounded the gallows ; he then desired the executioner to take another turn of the rope over the beam, and, this being done, the fatal noose was tied, the cap put on, and his station taken on the board which was to be pushed off with him. The cap being now drawn over his face, he was launched off ; at first he rubbed his hands together, as if to evince his indifference, but soon became greatly convulsed ; his wish to have the drop shortened caused a miserable prolongation of this, the last of his earthly sufferings. I have witnessed other executions, but never saw a criminal struggle so long with death. Such was the end of the erring, unfortunate Emmet.

On the following day I was called out from the castle-guard by Major Sirr to proceed with a party to the house of a person named Redmond, who resided on one of the quays ; this man was deeply implicated in the rebellion ; he had taken to flight, and his house was deserted by all his family. We broke open the doors, and, after a strict search, discovered in the yard several cases of pikes formed of the four outside planks cut from large pieces of balk, and put together with such ingenuity that, unless examined most closely, the deception could not be detected; in such cases the pikes for the arming of the peasantry were to have been sent into the country. Upon this, the Dublin yeomanry entered the house and threw all the furniture and other moveable effects out of the windows into the street, where they burned them in one large heap.

Redmond was arrested shortly after on board a vessel at Belfast, brought to Dublin, tried, and convicted. As he was drawn towards the place of execution he passed by the abode of a girl to whom he had been engaged; she appeared at the window, and they exchanged in silence a last look. There are times when one look speaks the passing thought more effectually than a thousand words, and this was one of them; it was a bitter moment, and insensible indeed must have been the heart of him among the spectators, to whom that short parting scene was not deeply affecting. When Redmond arrived in front of his own house, where the gallows was erected, he asked calmly: " Is this the spot where the fire was made ?" and then, mounting the scaffold with perfect coolness, met his fate like a brave man.

The alarm that had spread throughout the country induced several families of distinction to come to Dublin, and thus make an important addition to the society of that city. A military man's appearance at a fashionable rout was a sufficient introduction for the future to the first circles, and his attendance at a levee gave admission to all the public balls at the Castle; the other viceregal parties were of course more select, and for them cards of invitation were issued. We thus met the first people then residing in the Irish capital; their sprightliness and vivacity, wit and humour, combined with the politeness natural to their nation, gave an inexpressible charm to their society. The Irish cherish the utmost aversion to stiff formality and cold reserve; it is their ambition to place the stranger at once at his ease, and this, in my opinion, is the real test of good breediug.

After my corps left Dublin, the towns of Enniskillen, Omagh, and Kinsale became successively its quarters. Light battalions were now formed of the light companies of the regular and some of the militia regiments in Ireland. I belonged to one of them, which was at first stationed at Mountjoy House in the Phœnix Park. We had been there but a short time when Lord Cathcart, then commanding the forces in Ireland, sent one evening to say that he would see the battalion next morning, and that we were to manœuvre as light troops. General Rotenberg's treatise on light infantry tactics had been put into our hands only a few days before, and our commanding officer was totally uninformed on the subject; he therefore determined to divide the battalion into small parties, to serve out to the men a great quantity of ammunition, and to let them fire away from behind the bushes as long as it lasted. The morning came, and so did Lord Cathcart. The light battalion was soon hid among the bushes: our fire was most furious; and the park seemed all in a blaze; but it would have been difficult for his lordship to discover any plan in this military spectacle. He therefore waited patiently until our ammunition was expended, and then, riding up to the commanding officer, said : "Colonel, I am much obliged to you. Your adjutant's horse is too large. Good morning."

Our next move was to Galway. Besides our battalion, this town was garrisoned by a regiment of the line and another of militia ; therefore it was never more gay : the ladies wore their silk stockings during the whole of our stay ; dry drums, conversazioni, so termed because there were no refreshments, were held every week ; a constant round of tea and card parties also were given nightly ; the invitations to them were usually verbal, and delivered by tea-boys, who came into the mess-rooms, saying, "Mrs. —— would be glad if Mr. —— would take tay with her this evening." Some officers, who did not attend these coteries frequently, called out to the messenger, though not with much gallantry, "Your mistress only wants to win their money at cards."

One night that I was playing a round game, a Mrs. B. and I won all the silver at the table. The lady had swept her great winnings into her lap, and was rejoicing over her good fortune, when the mayor entered, and informed us that he had just received orders from the Castle to cry down the benders—Irish shillings, which were so called from their being cut out of thin silver plates and easily bent, and which passed current until replaced at this time by a new silver coinage, consisting of tenpenny pieces. Poor Mrs. B. looked thunderstruck at this unlucky announcement made by the mayor, and exclaimed, "Och ! murder, murder ! won't I get anything for my elegant benders ?" Indeed, she and I were paid for our shillings the next day at a reduction of three-fourths of their original value.

That remote corner of Ireland in which Galway is situated has so few attractions, that it has hitherto afforded a permanent residence to few strangers, with the exception of persons engaged in mercantile pursuits. The inhabitants are therefore an unmixed people, and retain their old manners, and their rich brogue in all its purity; like the Scotch also, the better classes are distinguished by the names of their country mansions; and, were it not for this custom, it would be difficult to find out particular persons, where so many have the same patronymics. Their distinguishing attributes are said to be pride, poverty, and devotion; but I found them to be eminently gifted with the social virtues, and ever ready to meet the stranger with a *cead mila faltha.*

Towards the close of the year 1805,[1] I came on the strength of the first battalion, then stationed at Kinsale. I sailed on board a Bristol packet for Cork, when ordered to join, but heavy gales drove us to Waterford. As we neared Passage, it was necessary to tack, but in the attempt the cutter missed stays, and ran through a salmon weir, carrying off the nets on her bowsprit; the crew lost all command of her, and the master, despairing of saving her, left the helm, and went about the deck, wringing his hands. In the meantime, she was nearing the rocks, and going head in with considerable velocity when I tried my hand, and put the helm hard a-starboard, which had the

---

[1] The author had been promoted to a company, August 6, 1804, and was employed in the recruiting service in Cornwall.

E

effect of throwing her up in the wind, and letting her
in sideways on a smooth ledge of rocks, where she
lay without suffering much damage : the boats of the
guardship came to our assistance ; they took us all to
Passage, and got the packet off the rocks.   I had never
been at the above mentioned village, and happened to
ask a woman I met near it to tell me its name ; she
stared at me at first, and then exclaimed, " Och ! sure
the world knows the Passage of Waterford ! "   There
is therefore no necessity that I should say another
word about a place so very well known.

At Kinsale we passed the greater part of our time
on the water, fishing and sailing in its fine bay ; this
mode of life gave rise to various picnic parties, and
one of these had rather a laughable termination.   The
stout, corpulent captain, connected with the skeleton
story, was of a hasty temper but not at all vindictive ;
he happened therefore to have a difference of opinion
with a gentleman, an inhabitant of the neighbouring
city of Cork ; and I may add that there existed another
difference between them—namely, a very great difference of stature, for the head of the militaire did not
reach even the shoulder of the citizen, a tall man.
Well, the parties were at first to decide their dispute
with the pistol, but by the interference of friends the
affair was amicably settled.   As the offence given on
either side was not so serious that it could be washed
out with blood alone—it was determined rather to
drown all unpleasant recollections in the flowing
bowl, and a grand picnic was the consequence.   On
our return in the evening, the two quondam foes, who
had sacrificed pretty freely to the jolly god, were

together in the first boat ; when it had arrived within about a yard of the pier, the tall gentleman stood up, and, extending his long arms, succeeded in laying his hands on it and tried to draw in the boat; but his heels perversely opposed this operation, and thrust the boat farther out, so that he could not even regain his standing position, and remained at full stretch with the tops of his fingers resting on the edge of the pier, his feet on the gunwale, and his whole person in imminent danger of a sudden dip in the sea. The little captain, now full of generous wine and generous feelings, seeing his tall friend practising this strange extensive motion, hastened at once to his assistance, stood alongside him on the gunwale, stretched out his arms to reach the pier, which they might have done had they been a yard longer, and, losing his balance, plunged headlong into the seà, quickly followed by the other, whose hold was completely loosed by the injudicious attempt made to save him. Neither could swim, and all in the boat were so convulsed with laughter that they could afford them no assistance before they had accomplished a series of the most extraordinary divings and plungings imaginable.

CHAPTER VI

WE remained at Kinsale, Charlesfort, and Bandon until the July of 1807, when we embarked at Cork for Portsmouth, as a great armament was assembling in the English ports. The land force, consisting of thirty thousand men, was commanded by Lord Cathcart, and the naval by Admiral Gambier; the destination of the expedition was kept a profound secret. My corps was at this time a beautiful one, mustering one thousand strong, and did not leave a man behind, a very unusual circumstance with regiments. On the 16th of July we reached Portsmouth, after a passage of eight days; and on the 17th, all the transports with troops on board having arrived, the whole fleet weighed and sailed for the Downs. It was then currently reported that we were to attack the Boulogne flotilla. The transports that had my regiment on board went to Ramsgate harbour and landed us; and we were immediately marched to Deal, where we stayed three or four days, and were then suddenly sent to Ramsgate again to be in readiness to re-embark. It was rumoured here that the fleet was to sail for the Baltic, and to keep open the navigation of the Sound.

On the 27th of July we embarked and sailed with the rest of the fleet, which had rendezvoused in the Downs. We now learned for the first time that the real object of the expedition was to seize the Danish fleet at Copenhagen, though this act of hostility was not preceded by a formal declaration of war with Denmark. The British government had received information of an intended union of the Danish and French fleets, and was determined to be beforehand with at least one of the parties. This departure from the rules generally observed by civilised nations, may not be considered strictly honourable, but it was politic as far as good faith and policy can be separated. Had the Baltic fleets, with the Dutch from the Texel, succeed in effecting a junction with that of France, we might have found it a matter of no small difficulty to cope with them, and the conduct of the Danish government was in every respect marked by a decided hostility to British interests.

We entered the Cattegat without accident. The castle of Cronberg, which commands the entrance to the Baltic, and is built on the island of Zealand, fired at the ships within range; the fleet therefore kept close to the Swedish shore. As we passed, the Danish cavalry patrolled along the beach from Elsinore to Copenhagen; they wore yellow jackets, helmets ornamented with flowing black horse-hair, and broad buff belts, and rode long-tailed black horses. The old master of the transport on board of which I sailed was continually boasting, during the voyage, that with

my company he would drive all the Danes before
him ; but, when he saw the enemy's dragoons on the
shore, at that distance making a very warlike and
imposing appearance, he changed countenance, and,
giving his trousers a couple of tugs, exclaimed,
"These be rummish chaps, I tell ye—you'd better not
meddle with them." It is needless to say that we
heard no more of his heading my company, or of his
feeling even the slightest inclination to land. The
country looked beautiful, and seemed to be highly
cultivated. We anchored on the 8th of August out of
range of the defences of Copenhagen.

I crossed the Sound to Helsingborg, in Sweden, to
pass a day there ; it is a small town, but had at least
one very good hotel. I found a German waggon
drawn up at the door of this establishment ; the
vehicle, which had two strong long-tailed horses
harnessed to it, was without springs, but the seats,
which were three in number, hung from leathern
straps. A tall, slim fellow, wearing a high-crowned
hat with a tin plate to the front, and mounted on a
stout nag, was cracking his whip and passaging his
steed before the waggon, and seemed perfectly pleased
with his figure and equestrian skill. Presently nine
British surgeons, dressed in their uniforms, were in
possession of the three seats, and the carriage set off
for a neighbouring spa at a round pace, with the tall
horseman riding on in front as avant-courier. I
might have visited the spa too, but that I found mine
host of the head inn abundantly provided with capital
claret—a beverage that has always been more grateful
to my palate than any water, however good. The

troops in this town were a remarkably fine body of men ; they wore blue jackets, single-breasted, round hats, turned up at one side, and feathers, long gaiters, and the broad buff belts of the time of Charles the Twelfth.

Five days after we landed, and proceeded to invest the town. The paymaster of the 50th regiment hired a cart, to convey himself, his clerk, and his books, to the encampment; but the Danish driver, not under-standing the directions given to him, drove them into Copenhagen. The drawbridge was not raised for some time after, so that, had our troops advanced at once, they might have entered the city without diffi-culty. Mr. Montgomery, the gentleman above men-tioned, was treated with much civility by the Danes, and was suffered to depart with clerk and books as he had arrived.

Our first work was the erection of batteries. The troops bivouacked in the fields, building wigwams of branches of trees, and thatching them with sheaf corn. The Danish gunboats and praams threw heavy shot amongst us occasionally, but they did little damage. The royal family retired into Holstein; and the greater part of the country people in the vicinity fled into Copenhagen at our approach; but we were well supplied with provisions.

About the 25th we began to work day and night, erecting mortar batteries within a quarter of a mile of the city. The weather was sultry, and the dews at night were very heavy. The Danes did not seem to be inclined to venture out; and the few that showed themselves were picked off by our riflemen. At length they made two sorties; the first along the lower road, near the beach, on the extreme left of our line, where a heavy battery had been lately erected, and two field-pieces placed behind a traverse on the road by the British. Sir George Smith, a zealous and indefatigable officer, though in very bad health, had been stationed since the investment at this post, and soon repelled the attack; it was a point of much importance, as the battery covered the landing of our stores.

The second sortie was made not quite so much to the left as the former one : the Danish force consisted of detachments of the Danish guards, Norwegian life regiment, and volunteer rifle corps. The advanced picquets of the left wing of our army alone were engaged with them ; and succeeded in repulsing them. The front of the picquets was protected by a sunk fence, which was calculated to afford them tolerable cover, and all, except that of the 50th regiment, took advantage of it ; but this picquet, crossing the fence, became of course more exposed than the others, and lost one officer and fifteen men, killed and wounded. There was a shrubbery on part of the ground to which the enemy advanced in this affair ; but it gave little security to the troops that occupied it : they left several fine tall men of the Danish guard dead in it. One of the officers of this corps was taken prisoner : he came up to me, after having first surrendered to a sergeant, I think, and not looking sufficiently before him, did me incalculable mischief by thrusting one of his long legs through a melon frame, under which I had intended to bivouack. These sorties of the Danes cost them some men, and neither were nor could

have been of any advantage to them : their troops did
not want for bravery, but were quite inexperienced, and
required a campaign or two to make them soldiers.

It was found necessary to destroy a large armed
hulk that was moored across the channel, and an-
noyed our left : a heavy battery was therefore erected,
and a mound of earth thrown up to cover the furnace
for heating the shot. One morning that I was employed with a fatigue party at this work, a young
officer of the quarter-master-general's department
rode up to me. He had been inquiring his way to
the advanced posts. He accosted me, saying, " I
perceive, sir, that you are raising an epaulement ; let
it be a special observance of yours to make your base
equal to your perpendicular." Another morning, that
the regiment was in line, a shot rolled slowly along
the front ; and one of the men, thinking it quite spent,
advanced one foot to stop it ; but its force was greater
than he had imagined, for it broke his leg above the
ankle. The limb was amputated, but the man died.
Now, if the above-mentioned officer had been present
when this accident occurred, in all probability he
would have observed to the wounded man, that he
was evidently wrong in acting as he did, since the
momentum equals the quantity of matter multiplied
by the velocity, whereas he seemed to have thought
that it depended solely on the latter. As soon as our
battery was completed, we began to fire red-hot shot
at the hulk, and set it on fire in half-an-hour, when it
burned to the water's edge.

Sir Arthur Wellesley proceeded with the light
brigade into the interior of the island, to prevent the

militia from assembling. On the 29th he defeated the Danes near Kioge, and took about eleven hundred prisoners. This duty was performed effectually, but the men were guilty of many excesses. The Danes pay the greatest respect to the remains of their deceased relations, keeping the churchyards uncommonly neat, and adorning them with well-executed monuments, chiefly of white marble. Some of these were wantonly injured by the soldiers, and several of the tombs were broken open by them in the expectation of finding money, rings, and other trinkets. Not content with these insults to the dead, they stripped many living females of their necklaces and ear-rings, sometimes tearing the latter through the flesh ; but immediate steps were taken to put a stop to such outrages.

All persons of consideration living in Copenhagen have also neat villas in its environs, standing in the midst of gardens and pleasure-grounds, which are kept in excellent order ; a great proportion of them have observatories, as the Danes are a studious people, and particularly fond of astronomy. Those who resided in the country, and had fled when our fleet anchored, abandoned in their precipitate flight all their effects, except their plate, jewellery, and some other easily portable articles.

Though every individual of the army, who was possessed of proper feelings, must have regretted the destruction of property that ensued, and exerted himself accordingly to prevent all wanton injury, still the nature of the service required that all ornamental improvements of the Danes, happening to impede in the least our progress in the siege, should be levelled or removed. If a fine garden afforded the best site for a battery, one was raised there, and the fruit-trees were cut down to be made use of in its erection ; and the crops, which were standing on our arrival, were more effectually destroyed by our bivouacking in the fields than if an immense flight of locusts had descended on them ; so that the country within two miles of the walls of Copenhagen was speedily converted by us into a melancholy waste. Among the men there were certainly many addicted to plunder, and I regret to say that the example set by some few officers showed that they too were not free from a propensity so disgraceful to the character of a soldier. I knew one who packed in a cask a handsome service of china, with the view of carrying it off on our return ; but he did not take the precaution to fasten down the head at once, and another person, either through dislike to the act of plunder or to the plunderer, placed, unobserved, a nine-pound shot in a tureen that was uppermost. When the cask was opened afterwards in England all the china was found smashed to atoms by the working of the shot.

On the first of September the city was summoned in vain. The batteries were finished on the following day, and at night we began to throw shells ; I once counted thirteen in the air at the same moment. On the 4th the town was on fire in several places ; the cathedral was all in a blaze ; the flames ran up the interior of the tall steeple, which looked like a huge pillar of fire, and presented a beautiful though awful sight.

I crept down to the wet ditch to hear what was

going on in the city; and such a state of horror and
confusion as, judging by the sounds that proceeded
from it, the inhabitants seemed to be in, is indescrib-
able. Amidst the general din, the shouts, exhortations,
and cries of the people in the streets, and the crash of
falling roofs and walls, I could distinguish the rattling
of the engines, and the noise of the firemen exerting
themselves to check the conflagration, but their labour
was endless and unavailing; no sooner was one fire
extinguished than another broke out; at length the
steeple came down with a tremendous crash, and
scattered the blazing material to such a degree that
everything in its vicinity was consumed.

When one third of the town had been laid in ashes,
and eleven hundred of the inhabitants killed, a flag
of truce came out, and on the 6th it was stipulated
that all vessels and naval stores belonging to the King
of Denmark should be yielded, and immediate possession of the citadel and arsenal given to the British,
on condition that the island of Zealand be evacuated
by them within the space of six weeks. It was also
agreed that a mutual restitution of prisoners should
take place, and that all public and private property,
with the exception of the royal shipping and naval
stores, should be respected. The drawbridge was
then lowered, and the inhabitants rushed out, anxious
to ascertain the state in which their houses and
grounds were after an occupation of so many days
by the troops of an enemy. A sad sight was to meet
their eyes, and realise their most gloomy apprehensions—all their property plundered and destroyed,
excepting the bare shells of the buildings.

One elderly gentleman came up to two or three of our officers, who were standing with me where his villa stood when last he saw that spot, but it had since been razed to the ground. We were not very conversant with his language, but he pointed to the ruins, and then, turning to the burial-ground of an adjoining church, gave us to understand, that the only home we had left for him was there. Though he was grieved and dejected, his manners were still composed and gentlemanly—he neither in word nor look seemed to upbraid the authors of his loss, which he was too old then to think of repairing; and, when he had done speaking, he politely handed to us his snuff-box. We were glad to profit by the opportunity of shutting up in it, unperceived by him, one or two gold pieces; they might have been of use to him, and I do not think that he could have been offended with the liberty that we had taken.

On board our fleet there were little more than fifty men killed and wounded; and, during the whole siege, the loss of our army amounted to only two hundred and eight men.

Our brigade, having borne the brunt of the siege, took possession of the dock-yard as the post of honour; we were also appointed to go on board the prizes as marines.[1]

Our officers were permitted to go into the town by obtaining tickets; the Danes were very civil to them. The shells and rockets had fallen in every quarter. Several heavy shells went through the roof of the royal palace, which stands in the centre, and

[1] The 32nd had been originally raised as marines.

that division, which had contained the public places
of amusement, was reduced to a heap of ruins. The
garrison consisted of the Danish guards, the Norwegian life regiment, the volunteer rifle corps, and
some artillery. The guards were the largest men I
have seen in any army, and wore long scarlet coats,
powdered hair, and long queues. The Norwegians
were very able-bodied men also ; they wore scarlet
jackets, breeches, and gaiters. The volunteers consisted of students and citizens. They were a very
strong corps, and dressed in green uniforms. A small
pamphlet, containing an account of the siege, was
printed in Copenhagen ; it stated that the first shell
which fell in the town killed two of the finest girls in
it, and that the first rocket destroyed an infant in the
arms of its nurse, who was standing at a window ; the
writer, after the mention of these accidents, exclaims,
"Oh ! England, Queen of nations ! mother of such
noble and valiant sons ! is this thy work ? "

An alarming circumstance occurred while we kept
possession of the dockyard : a positive order had been
issued, forbidding our men to smoke, under any pre-
tence whatever, as long as they should continue on
duty there; but a sentinel, who was posted near the
window of a large store that contained live shells and
the loaded muskets deposited there by the Danes on
their surrendering the place, suffered two of his comrades to go in through this window for the purpose of
smoking unseen ; these men proposed to light their
pipes by igniting some powder which they put into the
pan of a firelock, not thinking that it was loaded ; it
went off, and the sparks falling among some loose pow-

der, the shells near it began to explode, and fly up through the roof. The whole building was quickly in flames. We that were in the dockyard were soon at work, while the troops outside fancied that there was a row with the Danes. The boats from the fleet hurried to the shore, and the captains of the navy were seen everywhere that their presence could be of service; the musketry continued to go off among the men's legs, and a heavy shell would occasionally explode; yet few accidents occurred. The store was completely destroyed, but by the greatest exertions the fire was confined to it. A captain of the navy, half-suffocated by the smoke, ran to my quarters for a drink, but our stock of liquor had long disappeared in the confusion : as a last resource he took down some phials of physic, which he perceived on a shelf, and emptying their contents into a cup, drank off the mixture : my apartments had been previously occupied by the Danish apothecary. When the fire broke out two young officers took a boat, crossed over to the citadel, and told Lord Cathcart that the dockyard was on fire. His lordship said with great coolness, "Go back, gentlemen, and put it out."

On the 21st the fleet got under weigh, and presented to the inhabitants of the opposite coasts of Sweden and Denmark the most imposing spectacle that had ever appeared on the waters of the Sound and Cattegat. The King of Sweden, Gustavus IV., came to Helsingborg, where the Sound is about four miles and a half across, to witness it. All the line-of-battle ships saluted the King of the Goths and Vandals, as they passed in succession. The Swedes were as pleased

spectators of this grand scene as the Danes were sor-
rowful ones; for the two nations hate each other most
cordially. In evidence of this animosity, it may be
mentioned, that every device on the public buildings
and works of all kinds in Copenhagen is emblematic
of some disaster that had befallen the Swedes in past
wars.

At the dockyard I got into one of the Danish gun-
boats, with a party of soldiers and a few sailors, to go
on board the *Princess Sophia Frederica*, 74, one of the
prizes, in which part of my regiment was embarked.
Just before I left, Admiral Essington came up to me,
and taking hold of me by the button, said, "Don't go
to leeward, whatever you do;"—but to leeward I went
of the whole fleet. It began to blow very hard, and
we came to an anchor, firing musketry as a signal
of distress; the nearest ship to us threw out a line
fastened to a buoy, which came down before the wind,
but it was too short to reach us; however, a boat-
swain's mate of one of the men-of-war, whom we had
in the gun-boat, jumped overboard, holding the end of
a rope between his teeth, and, swimming to the buoy,
succeeded in splicing the two lines.

We were then hauled up to the ship, which, I was
glad to find, was the *Princess Sophia*. This vessel
made a great deal of water on the passage, which
was rather a rough one, and the pumps were continually at work. The pilot became alarmed, and
wanted to desert the ship when off the English coast,
but he was not permitted to land until we disembarked
at Deal.

The ships and stores brought off from Copenhagen

were valued in England at four millions and a half sterling, and it was supposed cost the Danes about ten millions ; but as no formal declaration of war had been made, it was decided that the captors were not entitled to prize-money, and a sum of only eight hundred thousand pounds was granted by way of compensation to that portion of the army and navy which had been engaged in the siege of Copenhagen. A captain in the army received about ninety pounds.

I landed very ill, having had an attack of the measles on board the seventy-four, but, recovering a little, obtained leave of absence, and went up to town with the intention of proceeding thence to Ireland.

F

CHAPTER VII

I WAS surprised to learn in town that the regiment
was ordered to hold itself in readiness for immediate
service. I therefore abandoned all idea of returning
home, and repaired to Portsmouth, the place of
embarkation. There I found considerable bustle;
the 26th, 29th, 32nd, 50th, and 82nd regiments, with
some battalions of the German legion, were already
embarking. General Spencer commanded the troops.

We sailed in the middle of December, uncertain
whether for Portugal or the Mediterranean, and
passed our Christmas most drearily in the Bay of
Biscay, lying to in most dreadful weather, the whole
fleet being dispersed. On the 31st of the month it
blew a perfect hurricane, the most vivid lightning
flashing round us, the sea running mast high breaking
over the ship in every direction, and at length pooping us, and bursting in the cabin windows. One
would absolutely have thought that we should have
been blown out of the water. We saw at different
times ships, with signals of distress flying, driving
under bare poles.

There is no situation in which a young officer is ever placed so truly uncomfortable—I may even say, wretched—as the being on board of a crowded transport suddenly ordered to proceed to sea before he has had time to stow away his sea stock, or to make other necessary arrangements, and where he has to encounter heavy gales and mountain-waves, with the nausea, their common concomitant. It is on such an occasion that every little comfort enjoyed at "sweet home" is recalled to his recollection, with its true value set upon it ; and though I will not go so far as to affirm that the presence of these accumulated unpleasantries tends in any degree to damp his military ardour, occasionally an involuntary sigh for terra firma escapes him, and reflections the least agreeable disturb his mind.

Even I, who at this time considered myself an old hand, found myself not prepared to meet with perfect equanimity some circumstances that attended our voyage—the sudden sailing of our vessel—the want of proper convenience for stowing away our sea stock— the pooping of the ship, when the sea burst through the cabin windows with such force as to wash one of our officers from his seat and carry him under the companion-ladder (where he remained for some time paddling in the water, with a fur cap that he wore pulled over his eyes, and fancying that he and the ship were going to the bottom)—the consequent destruction of our store, which was collected in the cabin—our hamper of glass and crockery pitched from the locker, and all its brittle contents smashed to pieces—while casks of pickled salmon and smoked herrings, a round of beef, reindeer tongues, cheese, pickles, eggs, cognac brandy, bottled ale, lemons, oranges, almonds (with pestle and mortar used in bruising them for milk), boots, shoes, slippers, dressing-cases, hat-boxes, bedclothes, mustard, vinegar, and biscuits, *cum multis aliis*, were rolling or floating from one side to the other in a flood of salt water, not forgetting an unlucky half-dressed wight or two slipping and floundering through this heterogeneous mixture—this vast olio.   I say that much philosophy, much stoic firmness, must have entered into the composition of that man, who, similarly circumstanced with me, could look unmoved upon the sudden and calamitous fate of all these creature comforts, upon a scene of such utter ruin, waste, and desolation.

However, we weathered the storm, and bore up for the Channel. To the westward of the Scilly Isles a large lugger, armed with sixteen guns, and full of men who were mustered fore and aft and ready for boarding, came down upon us ; but we had seen her in the morning, and prepared for her reception by loading the six eighteen-pound carronades which our transport carried, and keeping the soldiers stretched on the deck in their greatcoats in order to deceive the privateer. When she ran alongside she soon saw what we were, and, at our desire, hauled her wind on the other tack. We would have fired into her had we not thought she might by chance be a Jersey privateer, though we had little doubt of her being French.

We arrived in Plymouth Sound on the 5th of January 1808, having experienced a succession of violent gales for seventeen days, till the rigging had absolutely become white. We found one of our fleet here dismasted : the pilot who came out to us said that several of the ships had foundered, but his account luckily proved to be incorrect. We remained at Plymouth a few days, and then proceeded to Falmouth, to wait there for some ships from Portsmouth, in which we were to put to sea again, our destination being the Mediterranean it was rumoured.

Adverse winds detained us at Falmouth until the 1st of March, when we weighed, had a fine run of five days to Cape St. Vincent, and anchored at Gibraltar on the 9th. We learned here, to our surprise, that three of the transports, with the greater part of our regiment on board, had arrived safe, and sailed for Sicily. We were also informed that, on our departure from England, it was settled that General Spencer should attack Ceuta, but that Sir Hew Dalrymple, Lieutenant-Governor of Gibraltar, having received intelligence of the growing disaffection in Spain, which threatened to manifest itself in a general rising, had sent the troops to Sicily as fast as they arrived, with the view of protecting that island from an invasion by the French, who had assembled a strong force in Calabria, and that a portion of these troops had since received counter orders and were to return to Gibraltar, being replaced by the Germans under General M'Farlane.

Ceuta is on the Barbary coast, and distant from Gibraltar about seven leagues ; it is a fortress of vast strength, and has but one landing place, from which not more than two or three persons can approach the town abreast. It was the general opinion in the army that any attempt to take it would be a failure. Under any circumstances, success being so very problematical, an attack on Ceuta could never be justly considered a prudent step, but would be the excess of folly at a time when the Spaniards were so well inclined not only to desert our enemies, but even to join with us against them.

Among the numerous duels fought here, I recollect one particularly, in which two midshipmen were the principals, and the master of the ship their mutual and only friend; the parties exchanged shots, and one fell mortally wounded. Intelligence of this sad termination of their dispute quickly reached the ears of the Governor, who, much incensed, commanded the immediate presence of the master, and, on the arrival of the latter, asked him how he could stand by while two boys were trying to murder each other? —"I assure you, sir," replied the old seaman, "that I acted like a father to both of them." The Governor was doubly enraged by this reply, rendered with the air of a man who is firmly persuaded of the propriety of his conduct, and ordered the nautical second to leave his sight instantly, exclaiming, as he retired, that he ought to be hanged.

While we stayed here I paid a visit to a merchant vessel which had an immense quantity of fowls and eggs on board, and had been taken by the Moors from the Spaniards. Her captain told the Commissioner that if he would make an English frigate of her he would fight the Prince of Darkness himself; but he was informed that, however he might be able to

perform the part which he had assigned to himself, the
Commissioner found the other totally impracticable.
At the same time permission was given him to go
into the dockyard, where he might pitch upon anything he pleased that he thought requisite for the
fitting up of his prize as a man-of-war, for it was
necessary to keep these people in good humour. The
Moor gladly availed himself of this permission, and
attended punctually at the arsenal at the appointed
hour; but seeing such a variety of stores, he became
perfectly bewildered : one moment he would ask for
a twenty-four pound carronade, and the next, for a
long nine ; then an eighteen-pounder would look well
in his bow, and a couple of sixes fit in his stern ; in
short, he armed his ship with guns of various lengths
and bores, and took a quantity of shot and shells, with
the utmost disregard to the probability of their match-
ing his artillery, or otherwise. Such a frigate as he
made of her, and such a crew as he commanded, alike
set description at defiance. He himself indeed wore
a turban, but the seat of knowledge of his first lieutenant was inelegantly covered with a blanket, made
tight under his chin by means of a large skewer.

During our stay at Gibraltar, all accounts from
Spain went to confirm the opinion that its inhabitants would not submit much longer to the foreign
yoke, without making some effort to throw it off.
Patriotism, loyalty, and religion still maintained their
influence throughout the Peninsula, and conspired
to unite its people in one unalterable and undying
sentiment of detestation toward the invaders of their
land. That land, by perfidy and stratagem, had fallen

an easy prey to a nation which they always disliked and now detested; their princes, who, notwithstanding their weakness, were the beloved scions of a beloved stock, were, with a solitary exception, either captives or exiles far from the royal palaces of Spain; and their revered religion was in danger of insult and detriment, their churches of profanation and sacrilege, and their clergy of persecution and degradation, from the insolent and triumphant infidels of France. When once the proud, national, and determined Spaniard had taken breath, and recovered from the first shock of surprise and grief, he could not tamely crouch at the feet of the usurper, though surrounded by the victorious and formidable legions of the mightiest monarch of Europe.[1] Each Spaniard, too, felt himself singly to be a match, and more than a match, for a Frenchman; and his uncalculating valour and extreme ignorance led him hastily to overlook the weighty advantages of military talent, experience, and discipline.

At length, rumours reached us of the outbreaks that preceded the general rising, of the movement at Toledo on the 23rd of April, and of the violent commotions at Madrid on the 2nd of May. On the 15th, some of the troops stationed at Gibraltar, and among them that part of my regiment which had not proceeded

[1] The whole Spanish force consisted of 90,000 of what were called the regulars, and 30,000 untrained militia; of the former, 20,000 were with Junot in Portugal, and 15,000 with the Marquis de Romana, in the north of Europe; while Napoleon had 120,000 men in the Peninsula, and his troops of all arms in all countries were nearly 550,000 strong, not including national guards. The French had possession of Madrid, Barcelona, Monteiro, Figueras, St. Sebastian, and Pampeluna. They were also masters of Portugal.—H. R-L.

to Sicily, embarked with Major-General Spencer, and steered for Cadiz. We arrived off that port the next day, and found Lord Collingwood's fleet there before us; they had been watching the French Admiral Rossilly's squadron of five sail of the line and one frigate, which lay in the inner harbour. Three days prior to our arrival, the cries of "Viva Fernando Septimo!" and "Guerra con la Francia!" made the welkin ring throughout the isle of Leon. The exasperation of the insurgent populace against the lukewarm and the timid was excessive, and they barbarously murdered their Governor, Don Francisco Solano, and his secretary, who were suspected of being in the French interest. A similar fate awaited Governor Filanghieri at Corunna, the Conde d'Aguilar at Seville, and hundreds of others against whom the cry of "*traidor*" was directed.

The British Admiral endeavoured to persuade the new Governor of Cadiz, Don Thomas de Morta, to accept his assistance in taking the French ships, with the view of making them his prizes, but the Spaniard refused, on the plea that those vessels, in case of a reverse of fortune, would serve for the conveyance of his party to South America. We were joined, while yet at anchor, about five miles off this port, by the Sixth regiment, from Gibraltar, and the parts of the different corps that had returned from Sicily; these last had been on board ship seven months, with the exception of ten days, during which they had been stationed on shore at Palermo.

By this time the insurrection had become very general, under the direction of the Supreme Junta,

which consisted of twenty-three patriotic men. On
the 10th of June, the inhabitants of Cadiz, the Caraccas,
and the neighbouring villages, erected batteries commanding the inner harbour, and commenced a heavy
though not well-directed fire on the enemy's squadron.
The French Admiral, finding that there was no chance
of escape, and that he must surrender either to the
Spaniards or to the British, struck to the former, as
he could not clear out of the inner harbour without
suffering much greater damage than had been already
inflicted on him, and as there was a better prospect of
the final recovery of the ships by his nation, if they
remained at Cadiz.   The crews of the French men-of-
war were packed on board Spanish gun-boats, from
the ends of whose booms little effigies of Napoleon
were hung, to increase the annoyances of the prisoners.
But we can hardly censure the Spaniards for their
desire to display, in every way, their hatred of the
invaders of their country, when we recollect the per-
fidious and cruel treatment that they had uniformly
experienced at their hands, and especially the fusillades
of Madrid.   In consequence of the crowded state of
these small vessels, a bad fever broke out among the
French prisoners, and carried off numbers of them.
Junot sent off some troops to overawe the people of
Cadiz, but General Avril, who commanded the detachment, saw fit not to continue his march, after intelligence of General Spencer's movements reached him.

On the 12th the fleet of transports got under weigh,
and we sailed for the mouth of the river Guadiana,
which divides Spain from Portugal. The troops on
board amounted to about 5000 men. On coming to

anchor again, we sent an officer up the river, and he ran considerable risk of being taken by the French.

While we remained at the anchorage, a practical joke was near being attended by very unpleasant circumstances. One of our old captains entertained an unaccountable antipathy to cats; so strong was this feeling, that he turned pale whenever one of those animals came into a room where he happened to be, and consequently it was often a source of great torment to him. One unlucky though very fine day, when the cabin skylight was taken off, while he sat under the aperture, playing a rubber at whist, and in no wise suspecting a young ensign who was looking down on him from the deck with no peaceful intentions, the arch subaltern, at the instigation of the demon of mischief, suddenly caught a large Barbary cat, and let it drop on the veteran's bald pate. The frightened animal maintained its hold for a few moments, fixing its sharp claws in the unprotected skin of the said part, which nodded under the weight, like the head of a mandarin; but when the horrified captain recovered from the first effects of the shock, he drew his sword, rushed upon deck like a madman, and would certainly have run the ensign through, had he not, with prudent foresight, perched himself out of harm's way on the mizzen top. Fortunately, the injured person's choler was not of a very lasting character: a short time sufficed to cool it; a pardon was granted to the offender, and he ventured to descend from his place of vantage.

The Algarves were now in a state of insurrection. Our presence contributed to inspire the patriots with

confidence, and induced the French colonel Maransin
to retreat with his force of 1600 men to Mertola. The
insurrection in Portugal commenced at Oporto, in
consequence of the prompt conduct of General Bel-
lesta, who commanded the Spanish troops in garrison
there, and immediately marched for Spain, carrying
off the French staff as prisoners. The proud Spaniard,
however, made no effort to rouse the Portuguese ; but
they quickly followed his example, by declaring against
the French. The Bishop of Oporto was the principal
leader there, and he opened a correspondence with
the British Government, but all his statements
were gross exaggerations. The armed peasantry had
various encounters with the French troops, and were,
of course, invariably defeated, and often with great
loss.

Since the breaking out of the insurrection in Spain,
the Central Junta had sent deputies to England,
where they had been received in the best manner ;
the enthusiasm that prevailed there in favour of the
Spaniards, now engaged in a noble struggle for liberty,
was unexampled, and the Government made promises
of money and material for their army, and directed
Sir Hew Dalrymple, the governor of Gibraltar, to
give them every assistance in his power. On the 4th
of July, his Majesty issued a proclamation, declaring
that Great Britain was at peace with the Spanish
nation. ·

Our present movement was to cover, in some
degree, Castanos' rear, as he was at the head of a
body of troops in Andalusia, and was daily increasing
his numbers, and making preparations to attack the

French corps that had marched into the province for its subjugation, and was commanded by General Dupont. The subsequent surrender of the latter, with 16,000 men, to Castanos and Reding at Baylen, on the 19th of July, is well known as the most decisive achievement of the patriots during the campaign. However, Major-General Spencer prudently declined to give them any more active support, or to unite himself with their still tumultuary force. We remained at this anchorage only a short time, and again set sail, as we thought for Lisbon, to assist in capturing the Russian squadron in the Tagus; but, meeting adverse gales off Cape St. Vincent, we came to anchor near it, and continued there for a few days.

When we weighed from Cape St. Vincent, we steered eastward again, and returned to our old anchorage off Cadiz. During our former visit we could perceive from the transports the firing that preceded the surrender of the French ships; and, now that Cadiz was open to us, we were desirous to see what damage they had suffered. We therefore got into the boats, and proceeded to the inner harbour. Its entrance was defended by strong forts, called the Puntals and Matagorda;[1] the basin is magnificent, of vast extent, completely land-locked, and secure from

[1] The fort of Matagorda was dismantled and abandoned by the Spaniards when Victor blockaded Cadiz in February 1810; but as it was an important work to the defenders of that city, it was re-occupied by 150 British immediately after the landing of General Stewart, and maintained against the French in a very gallant manner for eight weeks. Captain M'Lean of the 94th commanded the detachment, and did not evacuate the fort until the parapet was destroyed, half of his men *hors de combat*, and the Spanish ship of war and gun-boats that had assisted him compelled to withdraw.

all winds. We pulled round the French squadron ; they were six splendid ships, and, to our astonishment, showed no traces of injuries received from the Spanish shot, heavy as the fire had been. The French officers were permitted to remain in them ; they saluted us frankly, and we would have gone on board had not an order been issued forbidding us to do so.

We could now visit the superb city of Cadiz, and did not fail to profit by the opportunity. The inhabitants received us with much politeness ; but our light infantry officers, who wore bugles on their caps and breastplates, were not a little chagrined at their being mistaken for musicians. The red cockade, with the words "Fernando Septimo" in centre, was generally exhibited ; we afterwards wore it, adorned with spangles.

When we had been on shore for the space of ten days, we received orders to re-embark, and two other regiments landed to occupy our quarters. On the 22nd of July they returned to their ships, and in the course of the day all the transports weighed and proceeded to sea.

CHAPTER VIII

EARLY in the summer a force of 9000 men was assembled at Cork, under the command of Sir Arthur Wellesley, an officer who had gained much reputation by his services in India and Europe. The public were not then informed of the plans which the Government had *in petto* for the employment of those troops; but it now appears that they were to have been sent out to South America, and to have joined General Miranda. This project was at once abandoned, when intelligence was received of the breaking out of the Spanish insurrection, and Sir Arthur Wellesley was directed to proceed with the expedition to Corunna, for the purpose of co-operating with the insurgents. On the 12th of July the fleet sailed from Cork. Sir Arthur, who outsailed it, reached Corunna on the 20th, and heard there of the total defeat of the Spanish generals, Cuesta and Blake, on the 14th, at the battle of Medina del Rio Seco. He found the Junta of Gallicia, too, more anxious for money and arms than for men from England; he was therefore induced to alter his plan, and he determined upon a campaign in Portugal. He then repaired to Oporto, and, after some communication with the Portuguese leaders and British agents, decided upon landing near the mouth of the Mondego. He had previously sent orders to Major-General Spencer to join him with his division, but that officer anticipated them.

We were off the rock of Lisbon on the 5th of August; and an officer from Sir Charles Cotton's fleet, then cruising near the mouth of the Tagus, brought us directions to go on to the Mondego, eighty miles to the northward, where we should meet the troops under Sir Arthur Wellesley. On the 8th we anchored in Figueras Bay, into which the river Mondego empties itself. The surf on the bar was then so great that the disembarkation seemed to be impracticable. Some boats that made the attempt were swamped, and about twenty men and a few horses were drowned. Captain Malcolm, who commanded a seventy-four, had the direction of the debarkation; having some particular business to transact with Sir Arthur Wellesley, who was at the camp, he pulled off from the ship in his gig to go on shore, and, running in on the top of a sea, was upset, and driven, boat, crew and all, a considerable distance up the beach without sustaining any serious injury : the instant that he got on his legs again, he made for a horse that was near him, mounted, and galloped off, as if nothing had happened, to the camp. At length it was observed that a certain rock broke off the surf in some measure, and it was thought that the troops might be landed inside it from the flat-bottomed boats.

As many as the boats could safely carry were then ordered into them, and they pulled off in succession to the rock. The Portuguese on this part of the coast were very zealous, and, being expert swimmers, rendered great service during the whole operation. They swam about the boats, diving under the heavier waves, and reappearing in the hollow of the sea, ready to pick up any soldiers whose boats might be swamped. According as the flat boats reached the rock, the Portuguese placed our men across their shoulders, and carried them, their arms, ammunition, and three days' provisions, in perfect safety to the shore. No people could have behaved better, and very few would have behaved so well; they were full of enthusiasm; they regarded us their future deliverers from the insolence and oppression of the French, and they certainly adopted a handsome method of giving us a welcome to their land.

The debarkation was completed during the day, and we proceeded to the camp by a deep and sandy road, about two miles in length. The British troops that passed that night together on Portuguese ground mustered 12,500 strong. About 20,000 French were stationed within the confines of the country, and masters of the most important points. The Portuguese general, Freire, had only 6000 men under his command at Coimbra, and they were wretchedly organised and not to be depended on in case of a general action; still they were not in want of arms, as Sir Arthur Wellesley himself supplied them with 5000 stand and a quantity of ammunition, and the whole population wished us success. We had now

G

to contend with a gallant, well-tried, and long victorious enemy, and the most prescient could not foretell the duration of the approaching struggle ; but we were now engaged in a noble cause, far more grateful to our feelings than our northern expedition of the preceding year had been, and we enjoyed a fair opportunity of showing to the world, that, notwithstanding our insular situation, the sons of our sea-girt lands could fight as well on terra firma as on the briny wave—nor will many who are capable of judging venture to assert that the proposition has not been proved to a demonstration.

On the 9th the advanced guard took the road to Leira, where the Portuguese had collected a magazine of provisions ; they entered that place on the following day, but General Freire's people appropriated the provisions to their own use, although intended, it was stated, for the British. On the 10th the main body moved off in the same direction, marching from ten to twelve miles a day, and at night making wigwams of the branches of the fir-trees that crowned the hill-tops. The valleys produced olives and grapes in abundance, besides other fruits, corn, and a variety of common vegetables. We entered Leira on the 11th. The Portuguese general behaved very unhandsomely, not only in seizing the magazine, but in declining to join us with the force under his command. It was with great difficulty that Sir Arthur finally prevailed on him to give him about 1600 men, horse and foot, and of course it was important that Portuguese troops should take part in the first action fought by us for the deliverance of their country. Our fourth day's

march brought us to the splendid monastery of
Battalha, erected in memorial of a victory gained by
the Portuguese over the Spaniards near its site. Sir
Arthur Wellesley and his staff were entertained there
by the ecclesiastics. I had some conversation with
one of the priests, a native of Tipperary; he was
liberal in his praises of the country, of the wine, and,
probably forgetting himself, of the women also; his
brogue, untravelled as Goldsmith's heart, was truly
rich and genuine. But, although there may have been
more *bon vivants* among the religieux of Battalha than
an equal number of the monks of La Trappe could
exhibit, it is only just to say that we found them both
friendly and hospitable. I think it was here that
the intelligence of King Joseph's flight from Madrid
reached us.

Our first affair with the enemy was a trifling
skirmish at Obidos on the 15th, between five companies of British riflemen and the French outposts,
in which some lives were lost on both sides without
results. The force at this time opposed to us was a
body of about 6000 men, who had advanced from
Lisbon under the command of General Laborde.
This officer had intended to effect a junction at
Leira with General Loison, who was marching from
Abrantes, but his plans were defeated by our movements on the 9th and 10th. The 16th was passed in
making inquiries and arrangements, and reconnoitring
the position taken up by the enemy; the choice of
such a position, and the manner in which it was
subsequently defended, do equal credit to the military
genius of the French general.

The villages of Celdos and Roleia are built opposite
to each other at the extremities of a large valley, and
nearly equidistant from the small town of Obidos,
which is remarkable for its fine aqueduct and ancient
castle. The French were posted on an elevated but
level space in front of Roleia; the rear was covered
with low trees and close underwood, and several
passes led from it to the neighbouring mountains, of
which a remarkably strong ridge offered an excellent
second position at an easy distance. The advantages
presented by the nature of the ground in a great
measure compensated for the disparity of numbers;
and, circumstanced as Junot and Loison were, it
was of considerable importance to the French that
Laborde should resist our progress here.

On the morning of the 17th, at daybreak, we broke
up from our bivouac. Flank movements were made
to threaten the enemy's rear with a portion of the
British and Portuguese; but it appeared to some
officers that sufficient time was not allowed to give
those movements the desired effect, a circumstance
tending to occasion a great and unnecessary loss of
lives; since, by acting on his flanks with strong
bodies, he could not have maintained his position
without incurring the risk of being assailed both in
front and rear. We continued to advance in three
columns. As we approached the enemy, the utmost
order was preserved, and the columns were increased
and diminished with as much regularity as if we
were at a review. When within musket-shot of the
enemy, the line was formed, and we advanced over
the uneven ground, doubling when an obstacle pre-

sented itself, and moving up when we had passed it,
with great exactness. The enemy appeared at the foot
of the position outside the wood, but retired under
cover as we advanced; this we had reason to expect
from old soldiers, who knew how to take advantage of
their ground. The columns pushed on, surmounting
every obstacle, and drove the enemy before them to
the second position. Here the mountain-passes were
defended with great pertinacity. The 29th British,
with the Hon. Lieut.-Colonel Lake at their head,
were obliged, by the nature of the ground, to climb
a height in single files by a goat-path. On the
summit, the 70th French were drawn up to receive
them, and when Colonel Lake[1] gained it, the sum-
mons to him to dismount and surrender, his refusal,
and his death were the work of a minute, and thus
a void was made in that regiment which it was not
easy to fill again.

The grenadier company, and a splendid one it
was, had followed their commanding officer closely;
they were very much blown from the exertion
of climbing the steep and from the heat of the
weather, and all of them, with the exception of
fifteen, were killed, wounded, or taken; but the rest
of the regiment continued to ascend with the utmost
gallantry, and finally succeeded in dislodging their

[1] Major Fletcher, "Recollections," vol. ii. p. 137, describes Lake as
being mounted on "quite a charger nearly seventeen hands high" and
dressed in an entirely new uniform. "Even his hat, feather-epaulettes,
sash, &c., all new. His hair was powdered and queued, his cocked hat placed
on his head square to the front." Major Fletcher said, "Well, Colonel,
you are dressed as if you were going to be received by the King." Lake
smiled and replied, "Egad, sir, if I am killed to-day, I mean to die like a
gentleman."

opponents. This regiment, supported by the 9th,
performed wonders. The enemy, being now forced
from the passes, commenced his retreat, formed in
column, and moved off in perfect order with his
cavalry in the rear. We were unfortunately weak in
that arm, having, thanks to the wisdom of Government, only 200 men of the 20th light dragoons, and
250 Portuguese horse; accordingly Laborde retired
unharassed by us. He himself was wounded in the
action, and about 600 of his men were killed and
wounded; he also lost three pieces of cannon. The
British loss in killed, wounded, and prisoners was
500, and of this number 15 officers and 205 rank and
file belonged to the 29th regiment. The prisoners
from this corps were sent off without delay to Lisbon.
On their march thither, those men never ceased to
lament the loss of their gallant commanding officer,
and to extol his many virtues. When one of their
escort understood this, he immediately stepped forward and declared that he deeply regretted his having
been the person who had shot such a man, that it
was the colonel's obstinacy which had caused so
unfortunate an event, and that he never would have
fired at him had he known his worth in time. The
fighting was over before four P.M. Sir Arthur
Wellesley followed as far as Villa Verde, but, hearing
that General Anstruther was off the coast with reinforcements, he altered his route. The heat during
this day was excessive; and one or two of our soldiers
died from the effects of drinking cold water; and
as our men found some precipitate in the French
knapsacks, it spread directly that the wells were

poisoned. The use of the precipitate was to destroy vermin.

The army rested for the night some distance beyond the field of battle. The next day we marched to Lourinha. On the morning of the 19th Sir Arthur Wellesley took up his position at Vimiera, a pleasant village in a fine valley, which is watered by a small river called the Maceira. The land surrounding the valley is very high, especially on the left bank of the river. Within two or three miles of the village the sea runs up in a sandy bay, into which the Maceira falls, and there General Anstruther was directed to land the troops and stores. The surf was high, and during the debarkation some boats were upset, and a few men drowned. On the 28th, the whole were landed; and with this addition our army amounted to 16,000 men.

As a great alteration was effected here in the personal appearance of our troops, I cannot leave it unnoticed. The short queues that were worn by both officers and men, were cropped on the field this day, in obedience to orders that had arrived from England. When I joined the militia in 1793, all military men wore their hair clubbed, that is, each had a huge false tail attached by means of a string that passed round the upper part of his head, and over it the hair was combed and well thickened with powder or flour; a plastering of pomatum or grease was then laid on; a square bag of sand was next placed at the extremity of the tail, rolled up with the assistance of a small oblong iron until it touched the head, and tied with a leathern thong and rosette so as to confine it in a proper position. After the arrangement of the tail, the officers' fore-tops were rubbed up with a stick of hard pomatum —a most painful operation, especially on cold mornings, and often calling the "salt rheum" to the eyes; when this was over, the friseur retired a pace or two for the purpose of frosting, which was effected by means of an elastic cylinder, filled with powder, and so constructed as to expel, and let fall upon the hair, a light shower of it; and lastly the powder-knife prepared the head for parade, by arching the temples and shaping the whiskers to a point. In this agreeable manner half an hour of every morning was consumed. The men powdered only on "dress-days," as Sundays, Thursdays, and days of duty were called. Each dressed his comrade's hair, so that an hour was lost in dressing and being dressed.

The year 1796 was most auspicious for the army, as false tails and sand-bags were condemned, and the pay was doubled. But so wedded do many persons become to old customs, that some corps were to be seen dressed in this manner in '97. The Clare regiment were quartered that year at Waterford, and still continued to wear their hair clubbed. At length the general commanding there sent for one of the grenadiers to come to his room, and, as soon as the man made his appearance, the following colloquy commenced: "My lad, how long does it take to dress your hair in this manner?"—"An hour, plase your honour, to tie an' be tied."—"And does it incommode you in doing your duty?"—"Very much, sir; I can't turn my head without moving my body along with it, an' I'm afraid to eat after my hair is dressed, for fear of its getting creased on me."— "Go," said the general to his aide-de-camp, "and get my dressing-case." The scissors were immediately in requisition, and the general cut off the grenadier's false tail, as well as the wings that projected over his ears. Major O'Brien, who commanded the corps, was then sent for, and ordered to have all his men trimmed in the same style without delay. In the course of the day, some washing-tubs filled with false tails and sand-bags were conveyed to the banks of the Suir, and their contents consigned to the stream. Hair-powder was used by the army as late as 1806. The flank companies wore the hair turned up behind, and made to rest on pieces of glazed leather, which were called flashes. The 29th, which, on the day of our landing at the mouth of the Mondego, was the finest regiment of the line that I ever saw, continued to wear the skirts of their coats hooked up in the old way, and their hats square, instead of fore and aft.

It was announced on the 20th that Sir Harry Burrard was in the offing, and before night he came into Maceira roads. It was Sir Arthur Wellesley's wish to have moved on to Mafra, and to turn the enemy, who, it was supposed, had taken up the position of Torres Vedras, about ten miles off ; but Sir Harry positively objected to this, because he should be thus placed at a distance from his supplies. He was in want of cavalry, and in daily expectation of the arrival of Sir John Moore with a force of 10,000 men, which had been employed up the Baltic, and would now be an important reinforcement to the British army. In the meantime, Marshal Junot called in all his garrisons and detached corps, and, having made the necessary arrangements, advanced towards Vimiera.

The greater part of our infantry were posted on the high land on the left of the river. The village of Vimiera was occupied by cavalry, artillery, and commissariat. Major-General Bowes's brigade, consisting of the 6th and 32nd, was posted in the rear of the village, on a sugar-loaf hill. The riflemen and the 50th, under General Fane, occupied the right of a table-land before Vimiera, and General Anstruther's brigade the left, at the extremity of which there was a church. Those officers had six guns, six and nine pounders. The western range of heights, that rather commanded the centre, were at first occupied by picquets, but immediately before the action three brigades crossed over to them.

On the morning of the 21st, about eight o'clock, Junot's army was first observed advancing along the road from Torres Vedras to Lourinha. The action commenced an hour after. The French force was divided as follows: One division of infantry, consisting of 6000 men, commanded by Laborde; another, of rather inferior strength, led by Loison; a third, weaker still, under Kellerman; and 1300 cavalry with Margaron at their head. The whole were more than 14,000 strong, and the artillery amounted to twenty-three pieces. The British were superior in numbers, but inferior in point of guns and cavalry. As the enemy approached the British position they subdivided their columns, so as to make simultaneous attacks on several points. The table-land occupied by the brigades of Generals Fane and Anstruther was attacked in greatest force. Laborde led his division against it with great resolution, driving our skirmishers before him, but suffering from the well–directed fire of our artillery. The head of his column appeared within twenty or thirty yards of the 50th regiment, who, being drawn up in line, poured in a most destructive volley, and charged with the bayonet. The enemy stood for a moment, and then broke and fled, but many of them fell. The cool and intrepid conduct of the 50th in this battle was beyond all praise. It was necessary that they should bring their right shoulders forward, in order to give their fire with full effect, and this was done by a simultaneous movement of the men with the greatest precision, though the enemy were within so few yards of them. Had this corps given way our commissariat and military chest would have been in danger.

The second battalion of the 43rd was hard pressed in the churchyard and vineyards it occupied by Kellerman's grenadiers, but after a bloody struggle it repulsed the attack. General Fane's brigade was equally successful, and, as the troops that had been opposed to it retired, the squadron of the 20th light dragoons increased their confusion by a dashing charge ; but, continuing the pursuit with inconsiderate eagerness, they were encountered and driven back with loss by Margaron's more numerous cavalry, and their colonel, Taylor, lost his life in the vain combat. General Kellerman repeated his attack on the centre, but with no better success. Generals Brennier and Solignac also failed in all their efforts to dislodge General Fergusson on our extreme left.   At one time six guns were taken from Solignac, and the 71st and 82nd were left in possession of them, while General Fergusson followed up his advantage over the broken troops ; at this moment Brennier made a sudden attempt to retake them, and with temporary success, but those two regiments quickly rallied and drove back the French. Junot, though completely beaten, drew off his infantry in fair order under cover of his cavalry, as we were so weak in the latter arm.   His troops fought bravely in this action, and suffered a loss of more than 3000 killed, wounded, and taken ; General Breunier was among the prisoners ; thirteen guns and twenty-three waggons laden with ammunition also fell into our hands.   The British had 783 killed and wounded, and only one man missing.   Sir Harry Burrard was in the field, but honourably refused to take the command.   Upon the final defeat of the French, Sir Arthur Wellesley urged the necessity of following up our advantage, and moving with the utmost celerity on Torres Vedras, but in vain.   Had his advice been taken the French should have either made a most disastrous retreat or seen themselves cut off from Lisbon.

When the firing had ceased, I walked over a part of the ground where the action had been most severe—

> " The field, so late the hero's pride,
>   Was now with various carnage spread,
> And floated with a crimson tide,
>   That drench'd the dying and the dead."

Upon entering the churchyard of the village of Vimiera, my attention was arrested by very unpleasant objects—one, a large wooden dish filled with hands that had just been amputated [1]—another, a heap of legs placed opposite. On one side of the entrance to the church lay a French surgeon, who had received a six-pound shot in the body. The men, who had undergone amputation, were ranged round the interior of the building. In the morning they had rushed to the combat, full of ardour and enthusiasm, and now they were stretched pale, bloody, and mangled on the cold flags, some writhing in agony, others fainting with loss of blood, and the spirits of many poor fellows among them making a last struggle to depart from their mutilated tenements.

There is no time more fit for reflection than an hour of calm succeeding the stormy moments of a great battle—no place more fit than such a spot as that on which I then stood. Amid the excitement of the fight, the din of arms, the absorbing desire of victory, the soldier sees with an unshrinking eye the blood of friend and foe poured out around him—his own may soon mingle with it—and his sharing cheerfully the same dangers, and his readiness to revenge the fall of his comrades, must supply the place of less stern feelings. But when the thunder of the cannon has ceased, the roll of the musquetry has died away, the smoke has cleared off, and the trampling and shouts

---

[1] Fletcher mentions that on passing a hut he heard "God save the King" being sung in a lusty shout. He entered and found an Irishman undergoing the amputation of a leg. He apologised and was about to retire when the patient stopped singing and said, with the most perfect coolness : "Come in, sorr—no inthrusion—you're heartily welcome."

of combatants in the mortal strife are heard no more, while the only sounds that reach the ear are the cries and groans of wounded men, and while the eye wanders over one scene of carnage, then does the mind become painfully alive to the horrors of a field of battle.

A great number of the 43rd lay dead in the vineyards, which a part of that regiment had occupied ; they had landed only the day before, and they looked so clean, and had their appointments in such bright and shining order, that, at the first view, they seemed to be men resting after a recent parade, rather than corpses of the fallen in a fiercely-contested engagement. This corps, which suffered so severely, had passed us in the morning in beautiful order, with their band playing merrily before them. How many gallant fellows that we then saw marching to the sound of national quicksteps, all life and spirits, were before evening stretched cold and stiff on the bloody turf !

Immediately after the action, an officer [1] of my regiment happened to pass near an old French soldier, who was seated by the road side, covered with dust, and desperately wounded ; a cannon-shot had taken off both his feet just above the ankles, but his legs were so swollen that his wounds bled but little. On seeing the officer, the poor fellow addressed him, saying, " Monsieur, je vous conjure donnez moi mes pieds," and at the same time pointed to his feet, which lay on the road beyond his reach. His request met with a ready compliance. The pale, toilworn

[1] The author himself.

features of the veteran brightened up for an instant on receiving these mutilated members, which had borne him through many a weary day, and which it grieved him to see trampled on by the victorious troops that passed ; and then, as if prepared to meet his fast-approaching fate becomingly, by the attainment of this one poor wish, he laid them tranquilly beside him, and, with a look of resignation and the words, "Je suis content," seemed to settle himself for death.

During the attack on our left, the 71st were ordered to oppose the enemy with the point of the bayonet. The pipers of the regiment, in the advance to the charge, struck up a national Scottish air, as is generally their custom, and in the middle of it, one of them, a Highlander named George Clerk, received a severe wound in the groin, which brought him to the ground ; but he supported himself in a sitting posture, exclaiming, with apparent indifference, "The deil tak ye, if ye hae disabled me frae following, ye winna keep me frae blawing for 'em," and he continued to play and encourage his comrades until the enemy fled. This gallant soldier recovered from his wound, and was promoted to the rank of serjeant and piper-major by Colonel Pack; the Highland Society in Edinburgh also presented him with a pair of very valuable pipes.

It was here, too, if I mistake not, that the 71st were opposed to the French 70th, and that after the action a soldier of the first-mentioned corps, looking at the buttons of some men of the other that lay dead near him, uttered the bon-mot, "I well knew we were one too many for them."

The three Lieutenant-Colonels that fell at Roleia and Vimiera, namely, Lake of the 29th, Stuart of the 9th, and Taylor of the 20th light dragoons, were highly esteemed and deeply regretted by their respective corps.

Sir Harry Burrard being immoveable, the French retraced their steps without molestation, and we waited at Vimiera. On the 22nd Sir Hew Dalrymple arrived from Gibraltar, and took the command of the army. These bungling changes of officers, and the unaccountable detention at home of our cavalry regiments, with the exception of a part of the 20th light dragoons, were equally discreditable to the judgment of the ministry, injurious to the interests of the country, and provoking to the feelings of the army in Portugal. On the evening of this day, a body of the enemy's horse was observed, and the troops in advance stood to their arms ; but a flag of truce, with the trumpeters, was soon distinguished. General Kellerman had come out to make terms. He was conducted to Sir Hew Dalrymple, and, having declared Junot's disposition to evacuate the kingdom of Portugal on honourable conditions, and demanded time for the arrangement of a suitable convention, he and the British general agreed to an armistice for forty-eight hours ; and now, to use the expression of Sir Arthur Wellesley, it seemed that all we had to do was to prepare to shoot red-legged partridges.

It has been said that it was a common observation of the same officer's, that twenty words of Portuguese were sufficient to enable one to pass comfortably

through the country; but few of our officers, at this
time, knew half that number. The inconvenience,
consequent upon such ignorance of the language,
was particularly felt in the commissariat department,
the members of which were necessarily placed at
once in close communication with the natives. One
day I saw a commissary sadly perplexed, through
inability to make some muleteers comprehend that
he wanted them to be ready at the same place on the
following morning; at length, he turned to a group
of officers that were standing near him, and requested
their assistance as interpreters, if at all acquainted
with the vernacular tongue of the equally puzzled
peasants. One of the persons to whom this request
was directed, instantly stepped forward and offered
his services, saying in a confident tone, " I think,
Sir, that I can explain to them anything you may
require."—"Then, Sir," rejoined the pleased commissary, " be so kind as to tell them that they must
be here early in the morning with their mules."
Upon which the interpreter, addressing himself to
the muleteers, proceeded thus, " Portuguesios, the
commissario—wants the mulos — to-morrowo——
presto—la, la ; " pointing to the village of Vimiera.
—" O, Sir !" cried the commissary, in a tone of
disappointment, " I feel much obliged to you ; but
I can go as far as that myself." The said officer
bore the sobriquet of " Jack the Interpreter " for a
long time after this unlucky attempt to display his
acquirements as a linguist.

It was about this period, if my memory does not
fail me, that Colonel Pack, who commanded the 71st,

H

directed his quartermaster to take out a party to get some vegetables, as otherwise the men would ramble about in quest of them. In obedience to this command a serjeant was called, and the quartermaster said to him, " It is the Colonel's orders to parade three men a company immediately, to *steal* vegetables." The Colonel, who was more precise than Irishmen generally are, happened to be still within hearing, and the word "steal" grated so harshly on his ear, that he exclaimed, very much vexed, " Pooh ! pooh ! Mr. Fr———r, I did not say, sir, to steal vegetables, but to procure pompions." However, as there was no intention of paying for the articles required, this was very much like a distinction without a difference.

The disgraceful Convention of Cintra was concluded and signed on the 30th of August, in the palace of the Marquis Marialva. Sir John Moore's force had then disembarked at the mouth of the Maceira, and our part of the army occupied Torres Vedras, and a position in the rear of that town.

It was stipulated, in this treaty, that the French army should not be considered prisoners of war ; that transports to convey them, their horses, artillery, and baggage of every kind to France, should be provided at the expense of Great Britain ; that, on their arrival in their own country, they should be at liberty to serve in any portion of the globe ; and that all Portuguese who had espoused in any way the French cause were to be protected from all persecution on account of their traitorous conduct. The intelligence that such a Convention had been acceded to by our three chiefs was received by the army with one feeling of indignation.   The Portuguese were equally incensed, and with still greater reason ; they had seen the French army march into their country without baggage ; they had since seen them laden with the plunder of their towns, villages, and churches ; and they were now to see their despoilers, though beaten in the field and in most difficult circumstances, suffered to depart with their ill-gotten store, freely, and on board British ships ; their allies were to provide means of transport for their enemies, with all their arms, horses, and booty, to wish them *bon voyage*, to send them to amuse themselves at home as long as it should please them, and then to return and fight with renewed vigour on the same theatre of war. I myself have seen the large cases containing the plunder of the churches and dwellings of the Portuguese, as they were conveyed to the transports provided for the French, and some of them were so well filled as to require the united strength of eight men for their removal.   It is a matter of regret that a general so distinguished as the present Duke of Wellington, should have attached his signature to the Convention of Cintra ; but it must be borne in mind that he was only third in command, that he objected to different parts of it, especially to the fifth article, by which the plunder of Portugal was secured to the French, and that he had had sufficient proof already of the obstinacy of at least one of his seniors.

There was some little delay before the French garrisons evacuated the frontier fortresses, owing to the interference of Portuguese politicians and Spanish

officers, but they were finally shipped off.   The garrison of Almeida was marched under a British escort
to Oporto, and embarked there.   While their effects
were being removed, a case filled with church-plate
burst asunder.   The rage of the populace at this
sight knew no bounds ; they flew to arms, and would
not suffer the French to embark, unless as prisoners
of war ; they also plundered the baggage of those
troops, seized their arms, and would ultimately have
taken away their lives, but for the great exertions
made by the authorities and the British officers to
prevent this last act of violence.

The French at Lisbon embarked in three divisions,
the embarkation of the first being covered by the
second, and that of the latter by the third, which was
in turn protected by the British.   The first division
embarked on the 15th of September ; Sir John Hope,
who commanded at Lisbon, took possession of the
citadel three days before, and adopted other precautionary measures, lest any serious tumult should be
excited by the inflammatory appeals made to the
public on the subject of the Convention.

At this period, thinking that our army would
remain for some time in a state of inaction, I
obtained a letter from one of Sir Arthur Wellesley's
staff to Colonel Clinton, the adjutant-general, and,
proceeding to Belem, near which Sir Hew Dalrymple
had established headquarters, I procured leave of
absence to return to England.   The day was far
advanced before I could effect this, and my way lay
through the principal part of Lisbon.   We had embarked at Portsmouth in such haste that there was

no time to provide ourselves with saddles, and I
was mounted on a raw-boned horse, across whose
back some bread bags were thrown, and over them a
rope, in which, as a substitute for stirrups, my feet
rested ; and, to make the matter worse, the streets
were crowded to excess, it being a Sunday evening. To
avoid the public gaze I turned off into the country,
and trusted to chance for finding the camp, which
was about six miles off. It was dusk when I
reached a comfortable-looking country house, built
close to the road on which I was moving, and,
as I perceived the owner of it looking out of a
window, a mutual salutation took place, the Portuguese addressing me in good English ; we then
entered upon other topics, and it appeared that he
had passed some time in those parts of the West
Indies which I had visited. As it was nearly dark, I
made certain that an invitation to pass the night
would follow from this conversation, and therefore I
prolonged it as much as possible; but my expecta-
tions were wofully disappointed, for he at length
wished me a good night, and, saying that I should
have considerable difficulty in finding out the camp,
drew in his head and closed the window. I am no
advocate for corporal punishments, but I must confess that at the moment I should have had no objection to his receiving one hundred lashes, well laid in,
for his inhospitality. I continued to ride on for
some time, and in a narrow lane two ill-looking
fellows, armed with long guns, came up to me ; they
said something that I did not understand, and I was
not sorry to hear them afterwards direct me to go

forward. I had not left them long when I reached the great aqueduct that supplies Lisbon with water, and, it being then very dark, I seated myself under an arch, and, tying the horse to one of my legs, invoked the drowsy deity, Somnus. At the first glimmering of the morning's light I proceeded in search of the camp, and, on coming to a peasant's house, was shown the proper direction to take. Some of the officers thought it would have been an enviable thing to procure leave of absence had there been a vessel going to England, but as they did not know of any means of transport to be found at Lisbon, they pronounced my application for leave of absence to be unwise.

In the course of the day I repaired again to the city. I experienced the greatest difficulty in getting a place to pass the night in; all the hotels were crowded with French officers and soldiers, who were to embark the next morning, for they were well aware that it would be unsafe for them just then to separate into small parties. The last house that I went to was the *Lion d'Or*, and there I was informed that it was quite impossible to find accommodation for me; but, as I had heard that the proprietor was a Canadian, I asked him if he knew a relative of mine [1] who resided in his country; his reply was in the affirmative, and he then got me something for dinner, and expressed his regret that he had only a garret in which he could put me. He concealed my cocked hat, and, observing that I wore a great coat, said he thought I might pass over the French

---

[1] Ralph Ross-Lewin, Captain 5th Foot, and Town-Major of Quebec.

dragoons, who lay stretched on the stairs, without being recognised as a British officer. He also told me that the French officers owed him such heavy bills that he must proceed with them to France, as his only chance of obtaining payment. When the house was perfectly quiet, he took a lantern and led the way upstairs to my apartment, stepping cautiously over the sleeping troopers ; at length we came to a small room with a wretched bed at one end of it, and my conductor, having shown me into it, retired. My first care was to place every article of furniture there against the door ; and then I stretched myself on my humble couch, but had no sooner done so than I was assailed by such myriads of bugs that I did not for a moment venture to dispute the post with them. In a few minutes more I heard some persons attempting to force the door, and as I had a considerable sum of money about me, and as the attempts to effect an entrance were renewed repeatedly, though without success, I passed the remainder of the night standing opposite to the door with my sword drawn. At daybreak I was relieved from this unpleasant situation by the sound of the sabres clattering from step to step as the dragoons descended the stairs. The next night I was more comfortably lodged.

The French were embarking at Belem, and I saw there about eight thousand of them in column ; they were highly appointed. General Kellerman happened to pass near the spot where I was standing, and saluted me ; so did all his staff. On my return to the Great Square, a landing place, I perceived an unusual commotion among the people, and found that it was occasioned by the sight of the large packing cases, and the officers' baggage, that the French soldiers were conveying to the boats : the mob carried stilettos in their sleeves, and proceeded to stab every straggler they met. The British officers took all the single Frenchmen that they saw under their protection, and thus saved the lives of several. The baggage of many of the officers of the embarking army was seized, and trunks, valises, cases, and hampers of sea-stock were broken open and their contents speedily demolished. Among other matters the populace laid their hands on some bags of Brazil sugar, for which they scrambled with uncommon eagerness ; in the melée the hair of some of them was so well powdered with sugar, that their heads began to turn from black to white, and the eyes of others received of it so abundantly that they left their owners in total darkness. Some boats, carrying French cavalry appointments and a few dragoons, and rowed by English sailors, happened to pass near the quay, and soon became objects of attack. Showers of stones were flung at the soldiers ; but the Portuguese not unfrequently took such unlucky aim that they hit friends as well as foes, and our sailors, feeling this very sensibly, began without delay to give our allies a wider birth.

At this time a great crowd was collected not far from the citadel, and I was informed that it was preparatory to an attack on a few French soldiers, who still remained in that quarter : another British officer immediately hastened with me to their rescue.

On reaching the spot we found a serjeant and twelve dismounted cavalry seated on a wall, with their arms piled in front of them, and gazing with contempt on the mob. We told them that we had come to their aid. They thanked us, but said that they only despised the Portuguese, and that they were guarding some of their appointments, which they would not leave until carts arrived to remove them.

The army of Junot originally consisted of above 27,000 men, but, owing to losses in battle, by sickness, by desertion, and by shipwreck, only 21,000 returned to France; soon after their landing, they joined the troops then marching for Spain, and re-crossed the Pyrenees.

Though I had obtained leave of absence, it was still not very clear to me that I should soon be enabled to get away from Portugal; for, as yet, no regular communication with England had been established. My only resource was to wait on Sir Charles Cotton, with the request that he would give me a passage in the next man-of-war sailing for any British port. I found the admiral on the quarter-deck of the *Hibernia*, bowing to their boats a deputation of the first people in Lisbon, who had been waiting on him. When this ceremony had ended, the lieutenant on duty made my request known to Sir Charles, who immediately, and with the utmost affability, desired me to come to the gangway, and pointing to the *Plover* sloop-of-war, said, " She is the first vessel for England, and if you go on board and tell Captain Brown that you have been here, I dare say that he will not refuse you a passage." The officers of the *Plover* received me with much politeness; they told me that they were making preparations to receive Sir Arthur Wellesley, General Fergusson, and a numerous staff, who were also about to return home. Of course my request was granted, and a time appointed for me to repair on board.

On the 21st of September Sir Arthur Wellesley, General Fergusson, &c., came off to the ship. She was very much crowded; it was even found necessary to dismount six guns in order to make more room. We sailed late in the evening. Outside the bar of Lisbon a large Algerine frigate ran alongside, with lanterns over her guns, and her crew at their quarters, showing their ebony visages at the ports; she looked more like a ship in the service of his infernal majesty than anything of this world: she was watching for vessels belonging to Portugal, which was then at war with Algiers. She sailed past us quietly, and we were not displeased to get rid of her so easily.

We had rough weather and a good deal of sea, the landsmen suffering very generally from nausea. Captain —— had some of his sails on deck every day; he was continually making alterations in them, and apparently they had the desired effect, for the *Plover* sailed remarkably fast. We came up with the Russian squadron off Scilly, though they had sailed ten days before us, and on the 4th of October we let go our anchors at Plymouth.

Mr. W——m, one of the staff, amused himself during the passage by firing at his cocked hat, which was suspended from the point of a yard, and of course he succeeded in piercing it in many places with balls. When we landed at Plymouth the people imagined that the various perforations they beheld in the covering of this officer's head had been the work of the enemy's bullets, and were filled with amazement at the hair-breadth escapes which, they concluded, he must have experienced.

The inhabitants of Devonshire were so incensed by the Convention of Cintra that they seemed to have forgotten Roleia and Vimiera, and consequently received Sir Arthur Wellesley with every mark of disapprobation ; indeed, hissings and hootings greeted him at every town and village of that county through which he had to pass on his way to the metropolis. But the people of England should have considered that, had he been left to follow up his victories, there would have existed no necessity, in the opinion of any person, for such a Convention, nor for anything more, very probably, than the fixing of the hour on which the troops of Junot should lay down their arms.

Before leave of absence had expired, my regiment returned to England from Corunna.[1] Our corpulent brevet-major, already mentioned as captain, carried his pinguid bulk miraculously through Sir John Moore's disastrous retreat from Sahagun to the coast ; but during the battle of the 16th of January he was so overcome by weariness that it was no longer possible for him to keep pace with his corps if ordered

---

[1] The author's brother, Thomas Ross-Lewin, took part in this retreat and in the subsequent action, in which the 32nd lost 250 rank and file killed and wounded.

to execute a movement; under such circumstances he was advised to go to the rear, an advice which he disdained to follow, for he was perfectly brave, and scrupulously nice of his honour. The men then procured a large elbow-chair for him, and he remained seated on it while the firing lasted. His covering sergeant, when standing behind the chair, had the staff of his pike broken by a musquet-ball, which passed close to the major's head.

The regiment on its return home was quartered at Horsham, and there I rejoined it.

CHAPTER IX

IN July 1809, a most extensive armament was collected in the Downs ; the army consisted of upwards
of 40,000 men, and the fleet of thirty-nine sail of the
line and thirty-six frigates, besides numerous gun-
boats, bomb-vessels, and other small craft ; the
latter was commanded by Lord Gardner, and the
former by the Earl of Chatham, the son of the great
statesman of that name, but "no more like *his* father
than I to Hercules." My regiment formed a portion
of the land force. The destination of the expedition
was at first kept a profound secret, and an embargo
was laid on the shipping in all the parts of Great
Britain and Ireland, to continue until we should sail.
The troops were embarked on board the ships of
war as well as the transports ; and Government
made a handsome allowance to the officers of the
navy, in consideration of the increase of the numbers
at their mess. Each seventy-four took a regiment.
The object of this expedition was two-fold; it was
only at the moment of sailing that it was said that a
diversion in favour of our allies and an attack on the

French fleet near Antwerp were meditated. We sailed from the Downs on the 28th of July, and were off the Dutch coast in the morning, nearing the island of Walcheren. The fleet soon came to anchor, and immediate preparations were made for our landing, which was effected without opposition at a point about ten miles distant from Flushing. That place was strongly fortified, and garrisoned by French troops.

The 71st regiment was the first to land, and pushed on towards Ter Veere, detaching Captain Ness to the left with his company, to attack a battery which was situated on the shore, and had begun to fire on the shipping ; this work was carried in a very handsome manner, and some prisoners were taken from the enemy. Captain Ness having secured the guns, &c., joined the left wing of his regiment under Colonel Pack, who were warmly engaged with detachments from the garrison of Ter Veere ; the latter retired into the town at night, closely followed by their opponents nearly to the gates. In this affair there were several killed and wounded on both sides, and the French lost not a few prisoners ; but by some fatality the right wing of the 71st did not come up. Colonel Pack learned from the deserters, who were numerous, that the garrison was much weakened, a part having been withdrawn to strengthen that of Flushing ; pursuant to this information, he determined to make an attempt to surprise Ter Veere that night, and with this view he again detached Captain Ness, with a sergeant and a few men, to reconnoitre the approaches. This officer and his party passed a French picquet unobserved, and had nearly reached the drawbridge, when a dog, which had followed them, began to bark, and alarmed the sentries on the ramparts, who challenged. A brisk fire was quickly opened on the reconnoitring party and the support, which was then moving up to them, and had already surprised and taken prisoners a picquet of the enemy's. As the alarm now became general in the place, the fire increased, and the British detachments retired along the dyke, suffering severely. In the morning Ter Veere was regularly invested, and it surrendered in the course of the day. It is a small town in the north-eastern part of the island.

All the enemy's posts outside Flushing were also driven in ; and we entered Middelburg, the capital of Walcheren and an open town, without opposition, having first promised to respect property. As we were approaching Flushing, the general commanding our brigade met one of our assistant-surgeons in his proper place at the rear of the column, and at once cried out to him, " Sir, why are you not with your company ? "—" I am an assistant-surgeon, sir," was the reply.—" Go directly, sir, to the colonel," said the general, " and desire him to place you in arrest." The next morning the general was seated in the garden belonging to his quarters, when a spent ball happened to hit him in the jaw. The nearest medical officer was quickly sent for ; and the first that the messenger came to was the above-mentioned assistant-surgeon, who was then in the act of dressing a soldier's wounds. The doctor hastened to the general, determined to take advantage of the opportunity now afforded him of being avenged on that officer for his unreasonable conduct on the preceding day ; his hands were covered with the soldier's blood, and, before there was time to desire him to wash them, he popped his fingers *sans ceremonie* into the general's mouth. The doctor always related this circumstance with great seeming satisfaction.

A strong division of sailors was landed, when we appeared before Flushing, to assist in the erection of batteries. Their station was on the extreme right ; they threw up a considerable work, armed with twenty-four pounders, and their fire from it soon became so incessant as to excite general astonishment. One morning that I happened to be at the advanced posts, I perceived some smoke issuing from a house on the line of picquets, and directed my steps towards it, with the view of causing the fire from which it proceeded to be extinguished, as it was drawing the attention of the enemy on the ramparts to this point, and heavy shot were continually passing through the building, and close to the spot where we were posted. When I reached the house, I found inside it one of our sailors boiling some potatoes in the midst of the rubbish, part of which had fallen into the pot. " You must put out your fire directly," said I to him, " you are drawing upon us the fire of the garrison." " Well," he replied, with a ludicrous assumption of an air of wisdom, " that is foolishness ! However can them fellows in that there town know that I be a boiling on my taties here ? " And, though stones and mortar were tumbling about his ears every moment, he would not give up his point, until I threatened to have him confined.

The picquets continued to skirmish with little intermission. The 32nd regiment was much engaged, and behaved with distinguished spirit ; Sir Eyre Coote expressed his high approbation of the conduct of this corps, and said that when the 32nd was at the advanced posts he could sleep sound. At this time the French understood irregular firing much better than our men ; the file did not separate ; one fired at random, knowing that a British soldier would pop up his head to see from what point the shot proceeded, and the other, being at the present, was ready to fire at the first person that should show himself. We lost several men by this stratagem. On one occasion I dined with Major Johnson [1] of the 32nd, and one or two other officers, behind some hurdles at the advanced posts. His old cook had prepared the dinner and laid it on a table which he had procured, when he said that he would take a peep at the French, who were within a few yards, and "have a crack at them ; " he went accordingly and stationed himself some paces off, out of sight of us ; but he must have exposed himself incautiously through the desire to observe the effects of his fire, for he was shot through the heart. We quickly discovered his fate. An attempt was made to bury him under an apple-tree, but so many balls came whistling through the branches and knocking the leaves about, that it was found necessary to bring him to

---

[1] Afterwards Major-General Johnson, M. P.

I

our dining place, which was sheltered by the hurdles, and there we made his narrow home, at the spot on which he had set our table. When this task was performed, we replaced the table, and dined over the old cook who had dressed our meal.

One morning, before a part of the line of advanced posts had been relieved, the old picquets belonging to it, by some mistake, moved off, and our vigilant and active enemy had nearly profited by this occurrence to our annoyance. The 32nd regiment was to take the outpost duty there on that day, under the command of Major Johnson ; this officer was proceeding to the place of his destination by the usual, but circuitous, route, when he observed that the picquets had quitted their ground, and that the enemy might make a sudden attempt to occupy it. Accordingly, seeing that there was no time to be lost, he procured some planks in an adjoining house, passed his men by means of them over a deep ditch, and thus was enabled to take a shorter way and reach the important point before the French. They were, however, in motion and creeping on, when they were checked by a sharp fire, which they returned, though finally compelled to fall back to their original station.

On the 7th of August the garrison made a sortie, the greater part of them were drunk, and they were easily driven back. A laughable occurrence took place, in which our fat brevet-major was concerned. He happened to be posted in an advanced position, and, having a quiet moment, took advantage of it to perform the operation of shaving behind a haystack. His wig was off, and only half of his task accomplished, when a party of French sallied out and attacked his post. The alarm was given, and he rushed instantaneously from his toilet, just as he was, and razor in hand, to head his men. He soon repulsed his assailants ; but had the fortune of the fight gone against him, and he been taken prisoner, his extraordinary figure, without coat, hat, or wig, his face half covered with soap, and his hand armed with a razor instead of a sword, would, no doubt, have excited much merriment at his expense among his lively and sarcastic captors.

On the 13th the bombardment commenced, and the town was set on fire in several places. Lord Gardner in the *Blake*, sailed up to the town, followed by the other line-of-battle ships ; each as they passed in succession fired a broadside, and, the facing of the parapet being of cut stone, the splinters flew about to such a degree that the French artillerymen deserted their guns. On the 14th the capitulation was arranged. The hour appointed for the garrison to march out was six the next morning ; but Lord Chatham wished to see them defile before him, and, as his lordship was not an early riser, it was 1 P.M. before he made his appearance. This argued very reprehensible selfishness in that nobleman, for, by his laziness, the unfortunate French troops were thus kept under arms seven extra hours on a re- markably warm day. They were five thousand strong, and there was a considerable number of Irishmen among them.

After the fall of Flushing, a part of the army pro- ceeded to South Beveland, and some regiments em-

barked and sailed up the Scheldt towards Antwerp.
We arrived within ten miles of it, and came to an
anchor in sight of the French fleet. But while we
were occupied with the siege of Flushing, the French,
who were at first in some consternation, quickly recovered from it, and made preparations for defence,
and Fouché hastily mustered 40,000 of the National
Guard in Paris, and sent them into the Netherlands
under Bernadotte. The latter, not imitating the
dilatoriness of the Englishmen, but resolving to
profit by it, was soon at Antwerp, which, as well as
Fort Lillo, he provided with strong garrisons, having
in and about those places a force of 30,000 men.
Heavy chains were thrown across the river ; the broad-
sides of the French ships were brought to bear so as
to sweep the entire channel ; strong batteries were
erected on the banks of the river ; and the surrounding country was laid under water. Under such circumstances the Lords Chatham and Gardner thought
that any attempt to destroy the French ships and
naval stores must prove unsuccessful, and therefore
wisely resolved to make none. The fleet soon
dropped down the Scheldt, and we were relieved
from the tantalising spectacle of the noble prize that
we lost through supineness and incapacity. Some
gun-boats came out from Cadsand and threw heavy
shot at the transports, but did no damage. This
roused the indignation of the master of letter V.
transport ; he paced his quarter-deck with as pom-
pous an air as if he were an admiral, and at last,
pulling up his trousers and turning to his mate, gave
the following fearful order—" Mr. Fountain, give

them our gun." This was a four-pounder that would not go off.

We disembarked at Flushing, and thus terminated the main part of an enterprise which was grandly conceived but wretchedly attempted. Upon his arrival off Walcheren the admiral should have sailed up the Scheldt without delay, and Lord Chatham, leaving a few thousand men to mask Flushing, should have pushed on with the remainder of his force to Fort Lillo, of which he could have made himself master. Antwerp, which was defended only by a burgher guard and the French fleet, would have fallen an easy prey to our army and navy. Still, it had been well for us had our ill-fortune left us after this signal failure ; but by some fatality our Government determined to hold the island of Walcheren. For this purpose twenty-one regiments were stationed there: the rest of the troops returned to England.

Flushing presented a sad picture of the effects of a bombardment. All the streets at the land side were reduced to a heap of ruins, and there was not a house in the town that had not sustained some damage.

There were a great number of old gentlemen at Middelburg,[1] and we were rather surprised to see so many persons living to an advanced age in this unhealthy climate. They were, it is true, quite emaciated, and scarcely able to support their immense wigs and cocked hats. They seemed to walk out more for the pleasure of giving and receiving salutations than for anything else. Their tenaciousness

[1] Three miles distant from Flushing.

of etiquette, and adherence to the strictest rules of the old school, were remarkably scrupulous. They still wore the large frills and ruffles, and the gold-headed cane was never missing. If the hat was taken off to a stranger, it was never replaced before he appeared covered ; the contrary practice would have been regarded as a gross infraction of the rules of good breeding. On passing the house of an acquaintance, the polite man uncovered, although none of the inmates should be visible at the windows. An arch wag of the 6th regiment, whose notice this punctilious observance of forms did not escape, used to take his stand about the centre of the principal street, awaiting the approach of some respectable old gentleman. As soon as a proper subject would make his appearance, the officer would take off his hat with a grave air of politeness, and of course instantly receive a return of his salute. He would then walk in the opposite direction, remaining uncovered, and looking over his shoulder ; the Dutchman's rigid notions of etiquette would not permit him to do otherwise, and in this manner the well-bred pair would march until they gained their respective ends of the street, and lost sight of each other. No sooner had one martyr to etiquette and decorum been disposed of in this manner, than the tormentor would re-occupy his old position, and play the same game with another. If the wind happened to be high, the sport was better, for in that case clouds of powder flew from the unprotected wig, and the tormented found himself under the necessity of re-turning home to have it re-dressed.

The good old lady, at whose house I was billeted,
would not allow me to provide anything, saying that
she hoped I would be satisfied with their mode of
living. The first thing that was given to me on my
leaving my room in the morning was a glass of gin
or cordial ; this was followed by a cup of coffee and
a pipe : dinner was served at one o'clock, and consisted of an abundance of vegetables, with little
meat, and less wine : at six a pipe, a cup of coffee,
and a glass of liquor were taken : at nine we sat
down to supper, the principal meal, and had wine,
grog, and smoking. Such hours did not suit me,
and besides, like most British officers similarly circumstanced, I felt a disinclination to subject those
friendly people to any additional expense, as they
had been placed under heavy contributions by the
French, who insisted upon being provided with
everything they required, without payment ; I therefore joined eleven other officers of my regiment in
forming a mess. We discovered a store that contained, among other matters, some casks of good
English beef, excellent bottled porter, and prime
claret, and hiring the room above it, we made ourselves very comfortable. The great market also was
very conveniently situated, and on Mondays well
supplied with the requisite *munitions de bouche*. We
provided ourselves with enormous wigs, which by
the first rule of our mess we were enjoined to wear
during dinner ; the president and vice - president
sported three-deckers, as those which had three tiers
of curls were called. The novelty of our club
attracted hundreds of people every evening to the

space in front of our windows, and, when we appeared at them, they greeted us with immense cheering and loud bursts of laughter.   We had a tolerably strong proof, that nothing is so conducive to the health of persons residing in this climate as good living, in the fact that not one member of our club was for a moment unwell during our stay in Walcheren, although our sick list had amounted on the 4th of September to 9000.

The mortality was truly dreadful.   The 23rd, 81st, and 91st regiments were struck off duty on the 1st of October, as on that day they had no men out of hospital.   An order to bury the dead at night was issued, with a view of concealing the frightful extent of the daily ravages of the fever in our ranks.   All the carpenters in Middelburg were fully employed in making coffins for the British.   In one day the 81st buried twenty of their men, and on the 24th of September, the 6th, who had come out one thousand strong, had lost one hundred men, and had seven hundred in hospital, while of the twenty-one regiments, there were only 5500 men fit for duty ; in the course of the following week, this number was again reduced to 3000.   By the 14th of November we had sent to England 8000 sick.   The Dutch physicians were quite adverse to our system of treating the sick, and very fairly proposed to take charge of one hundred of the soldiers in hospital, and to allow any of our medical men to select an equal number, in order to see which could effect a majority of cures out of their respective lists of cases.   This offer was rejected ; but why remains to be answered.

It now became evident that we should be shut up in Flushing, unless a reinforcement of 10,000 men was speedily sent to us from England, as the French commander was pouring troops into the Bevelands. General Don had arrived in the room of Lord Chatham, who had returned home, and at length it was made known that his duty was the superintending of the evacuation of Walcheren. A short time previous to the general evacuation of the island,[1] I was sent home with sick. We had on board our transport detachments from different regiments, with several officers, and our medical man was an hospital mate, who had never lived out of London, before he left it in all the might of a Hippocratian champion to combat the formidable fever. He was a fat, smiling, good-humoured little fellow, and spoke very sensibly on all matters connected with his profession, but in other respects betrayed almost incredible simplicity and ignorance of the world. Here was a man educated in the first capital in Europe, possessing fair abilities, well acquainted with his profession, and yet more incapable of thinking for himself and acting with judgment, when placed in circumstances at all new to him, than the most illiterate peasant of the rudest district in his country. He drew the most extravagant inferences from many even of the ordinary occurrences of his new life, gave implicit credence to everything he heard, however jestingly told and however improbable, constantly expressed

[1] The 32nd mustered little more than two hundred men on embarking. The returns for 7th September 1809 show that the regiment numbered 558. The loss was but slight in comparison to that of other battalions.

his serious alarm lest we should fall in with a privateer and be captured, and in every possible manner
exposed his peculiar fitness to become the butt of
every lover of mischief. There are few situations in
which such a character can fail of attracting the
immediate and particular attention of many a
tormentor, and our circumstances were then very
unfavourable to the permanence of the worthy
doctor's quiet; we had just escaped the pestilential
air of Walcheren, we felt the invigorating influence
of the fresh sea-breeze, the weather was remarkably
fine, the water smooth, and all we seemed to want
was a little fun. It was morally impossible, therefore, that one so well qualified to afford this desideratum as our medical friend indisputably was, could
long be suffered to remain undisturbed.

The first thing done was to increase, or at least to
confirm, his dread of privateers; a sail never came
in sight that he was not persuaded that it looked
very suspicious; the danger of our situation was a
favourite topic whenever he was present; and often
was the desire expressed that we might reach the
shores of England in safety, though the desponding
tone of the speaker evinced how faint were his hopes
of "a consummation" so "devoutly to be wished:"
it was not surprising then that, bewildered by his
apprehensions, this singularly unsuspecting and un-
discerning person readily consented to keep watch
day and night, during the passage. Of course his
activity and devotedness secured to him an equipment befitting the arduous office he had assumed;
he was provided with a waist-belt, a brace of pistols,

and a cutlass, which were never for an instant laid
aside, and also a spy-glass and a speaking-trumpet,
one or the other of which was generally in requisition ; and, to render the use of the latter instrument,
when in his possession, as great as possible, he was
taught a useful selection of sea-phrases. The master
of the transport, too, to carry on the joke, put a
blank cartridge into one of the guns, and declared
that he depended on the gallant doctor alone for the
preservation of the ship. It must be confessed that
our protector performed his duty in the most exemplary manner, and was constantly on the *qui vive,*
while free from the improper interference of others ;
when tired of standing or walking, he would rest
himself by sitting on deck, but he never visited the
cabin until late at night, when the officers, by sending
up to him a series of tumblers of punch, had led him
to drink so freely that he was carried down in a
state of unconsciousness : still, the rising sun saw him
at his post again, and he always apologised to the
commanding officer for his having been found below.

After a day or two had passed, a small Welsh brig
edged down to us to hear the news from Walcheren,
and, as she came within hail, the Welshman saluted
the master of our vessel in the usual seafaring
manner—" How are you, sir ? How are you ? "
Upon this the doctor, who had been watching the
stranger with much jealousy, at once put his trumpet
to his mouth, and cried, " If you don't sheer off
directly, I will fire into you." The old Cambrian
gave his trousers a tug, not knowing what to make
of such incivility ; but, as he did not instantly comply

with the doctor's orders, the poker was ordered out
hot from the cabouse fire, and the before-mentioned
gun discharged at the brig.   This was too much for
our new acquaintance, who, undoubtedly concluding
that we were all mad, was heard to call out to his
helmsman, " Port ! " and shortly after, " Hard-a-port
there ! " being evidently in a violent hurry to part
company.

The following morning it was intimated to the
warlike son of Esculapius, that he was to board
the next privateer that should approach us by night,
and to have a sufficient party to accompany him.
This service he agreed to undertake to a certain
extent, declaring his readiness to exert himself to the
utmost of his power, but adding that he should never
be able to climb up a ship's side, and could only
remain in the boat, to take care of the wounded ; he
then proceeded with the drummers to the cabin, to
instruct them in the art of applying tourniquets and
bandages.   He selected the worst of his shirts to
break up for lint, others for bandages, and a few of
the strongest for muffling the oars ; but, as his own
vessel might happen to be boarded, he knew not how
soon, he guarded against the rapacity of the enemy,
by packing his dollars in his neckcloth, and cutting
the chain of his watch with his scissors, lest its ticking
should discover that he had one.

That evening the commanding officer sent up
a message to him, with permission to come off
watch for a short time to join in a rubber at whist.
The proposal was accepted ; but our trusty protector did not leave the deck before he had

appointed a person to act in his stead, with strict orders to keep a good look-out. According to a preconcerted arrangement, and before he had done playing, a cry on deck announced that a privateer was alongside. The effect was electric. The doctor dashed down the cards, sprang from his seat, snatched up his arms, and rushed toward the cabin-door ; but, before he could reach it, a body of sailors, disguised, and armed with cutlasses, burst in. They seized and pinioned him in an instant, forced him up through the skylight, and from thence expeditiously transported him into the boat on the booms, where he lay lamenting his hard fate, that, after all his past vigilance and toil, he should at last be surprised and taken prisoner. For a short time he was suffered to remain in that disagreeable situation, but, as he might lose his dollars were he to be too long in the hands of his captors, it was thought fit to relieve him, by driving the privateer's men overboard. On being released, he thanked us all for our bravery, and declared that no consideration should ever induce him to quit the deck again ; but he was soon so well primed with punch, that he passed the night in the cabin as usual. On such occasions his mattress was spread on the floor, and he lay stretched on it till daybreak. But these frolics had nearly ended fatally to the innocent and confiding object of them, for on that night the weight of the dollars so oppressed the organs of respiration, that he was almost suffocated, and would inevitably have perished, had not some one, by great good fortune, observed that his face was turning quite black.

As we approached Portsmouth, he discovered that he had lost his certificate from the senior medical officer at Middelburg, and his advisers at once warned him of the hazard of venturing on shore under such circumstances, unless in disguise. They suggested two modes of effecting his escape from the transport; the one was packing him in a hogshead, the other, dressing him up as a soldier, with knapsack and firelock. The latter was speedily rejected, because no person of his figure would have been taken as a soldier, and his appearance in the garb of one might very probably excite suspicion; but the former was approved of, the principal only stipulating that, during the process of his removal, the officer on whose carefulness he placed greatest reliance should attend and see that the bunghole was kept open, in order to prevent any risk of suffocation. But while these matters were in agitation, the anchor was let go in Portsmouth Harbour, and so anxious were the officers to get on shore there that the doctor was forgotten, or left unnoticed. I returned to the transport the morning after we landed, and found the poor fellow sitting disconsolately on a chair in the middle of the cabin; he told me that this had been his position all night, but that he had enjoyed no rest, as an unlucky mouse had encaged itself in a round wire-trap, and the cat had been rolling this engine along the floor during the whole night; he also mentioned his fixed determination not to leave the ship until he should receive an answer to a letter which he had dispatched to London.

My first day's march was from Portsmouth to Havant, and I found the convalescents already so sensibly benefited by their native air, that there was no necessity for procuring waggons to convey them. The landlady at the head inn requested me to inspect the dinner she had provided for them, as soldiers were too apt to grumble at their fare ; I did so, and told her that I did not think it possible that they could consume all the eatables on the tables, especially as they were only recovering from the effects of the Walcheren fever. " Bless you, sir !" said she, " I have been on this here road these five and thirty year, and never yet seed a sick sodger at dinner-time."

Horsham was named as the future quarters of my regiment. On my way thither, I turned off to Brighton, the head-quarters of the district, and procured leave of absence from Lord Charles Somerset. The island of Walcheren was evacuated by the last division of our troops on the 23rd of December, after having blown up the fortifications of Flushing. The disastrous consequences of this ill-conducted expedition created considerable discontent at home, and certainly with perfect justice, for, in addition to our failure before Antwerp, the mortality that thinned our ranks could not have been equalled in the most sanguinary campaign, and the services of nearly half the men of whom the army of Walcheren consisted were lost for ever to the country. Lord Castlereagh and Mr. Canning themselves quarrelled on this unpleasant subject, and finally fought that duel in which the latter was wounded.

CHAPTER X

In the spring of 1810, I joined the regiment at
Hailsham, from leave of absence. The immediate
vicinity of this town is remarkable to Hibernian
travellers, as being the part of Sussex where potatoes
were first planted. The person who introduced
these vegetables there was a clergyman; he began
to cultivate them in his garden, about eighty years
prior to my visit to Hailsham, and from this circumstance he was subsequently designated " the potatoe
parson."

We were afterwards stationed at Bexhill. We
found here the 1st and 2nd light regiments of the
German Legion. Our infantry are much indebted
to them for practical information relative to outpost
duties, which, notwithstanding their great importance,
British troops at one time discharged in the most
negligent manner. Our allies in Flanders complained
very much of the deficiency of the Duke of York's
army in this particular; and in the earlier Peninsular
campaigns, our people, both cavalry and infantry,

betrayed an unpardonable absence of vigilance and professional knowledge.

After some time we proceeded to Guernsey, which we found to be a very pleasant quarter. Sir John Doyle was then the lieutenant-governor, and his presence greatly contributed to make Guernsey so agreeable. He was an officer whose conduct, whether regarded as that of a commander, a soldier, or a gentleman, has always elicited the warmest praise from all who knew how to appreciate real merit. Talented, brave, and courteous, he conciliated the esteem of all classes; his popularity with the people of the island was unbounded; and the kindness and benevolence of his disposition deservedly obtained for him the distinguishing title of "the soldier's friend."[1] Few men were possessed of superior social qualities, and most delightful parties were frequently given at the Government House. The society in Guernsey is incomparably better than that which is usually found within so limited a space. The young people are educated at the best English schools and at the universities; and, from the common intercourse of the islanders with France, they have the double advantage of an acquaintance with both French and English society; consequently, they are remarkably well-informed and well-bred. A mixture of the different grades in society can never take place here easily, as they are regularly classed: the "a thin class of sixties," as it is called, consists of the inhabitants of the highest degree, and

[1] In a journal kept by Major Wardell, 66th Regiment, he is referred to as "that kindly old Irish veteran."

K

they refuse to associate with persons of an inferior one ; but, should an officer of the army or navy marry a fair thirty or forty, she gains a step or two of rank by this union, and is admitted into the highest circle. In Guernsey, differently from all other places in the world, it is on a dark night that one can best distinguish the rank of persons passing through the streets—the cause of a fact apparently so strange is simply this, the first-rates have the exclusive privilege of burning three lights in their lanterns; the second-rates are allowed only two, and the third, &c., must contrive to find their way with the aid of only one. The Norman laws are still observed here, and some families enjoy particular privileges ; for instance, the Le Marchants are the only persons who have a right to keep a dovecote.

The Royal African corps was stationed for some time on this island, as an insular situation renders desertion more difficult of accomplishment, and this regiment is composed of deserters and bad characters removed from other corps. They are intended, as their name denotes, to be employed on the coast of Africa, and were at this time in daily expectation of an order to proceed to Sierra Leone. They were inspected, preparatory to embarkation, by a general officer (not Sir John Doyle), and he, feeling confidence in his oratorical powers, did not express his appro-bation of what he had seen to the commanding officer, as is usual, in a whisper, but ordered the battalion to form square, and then spoke nearly as follows : " Royal African corps ! Your appearance this day—your military appearance I mean—de-

mands my warmest praise. You are a credit to the
corps to which you belong." This part of the speech
excited the risibility of the unconcerned spectators.
"You are going to a place where there is an abundance of vegetables, and I am very sure that you will
do justice to them." Here the oration ended ; and
the general and staff moved off the ground, leaving
the soldiers in doubt whether he had addressed them
jestingly or seriously.

Towards the close of the spring of 1811, it began
to be suspected that my regiment, which was now
effective, was to go out again to the Peninsula, as
well as other troops, to reinforce Sir Arthur Wellesley
on his third campaign since the retreat to Corunna.

At length we received orders to embark, and sailed
from Guernsey on the 24th of June 1811. During
the passage two or three of our subalterns, being yet
unacquainted with the truth of the Italian proverb,
"Giuoco di mano, giuoco di villano," amused themselves by performing practical jokes to the annoyance
of some of their brother-officers. One morning their
pastime consisted in throwing every article within their
reach from their berths into that of our major, the
worthy representative of the Tunbelly family, and the
person most frequently marked out for their butt ;
nor did the shower of missiles cease before the supply
was quite expended. Still, to their great surprise,
the object of the attack gave no indication of his
usual irritability, and, on the contrary, appeared to
bear the unprovoked aggression with perfect good
humour. The cause of this unexpected calm was
soon disagreeably elucidated ; the major had a port-

hole at his berth, and, as fast as the missiles came, he, by means of this aperture, slily made offerings of each and all of them to old father Neptune. The disconcerted air of the playful subalterns was very laughable when they began to be aware that the tables were fairly turned on them, and that books, boots, slippers, dressing-cases, eye-glasses, with various other articles too numerous to mention, had all disappeared " at one fell swoop."

After a fine passage, we anchored in the Tagus on the 4th of July, disembarked without delay, and on the 19th proceeded up the Tagus in boats as far as Villa Franca.   Thence we marched to Abrantes, and, crossing the Tagus by a bridge of boats, advanced to Nize, where we found Lord Wellington.

The army was in motion, directing its march to the north of Portugal ; and it was rumoured that his lordship had ascertained the separation of the forces of Soult and Marmont, and the retrograde movement of the latter, leaving the garrison of Ciudad Rodrigo to defend themselves as they best could; that it was now thought a favourable opportunity to make an attempt on that fortress ; and that on this account the British cantonments between Elvas and Campo Mayor were now broken up, after being occupied only six days.   We recrossed the Tagus at Villa Velha, and marched to Castello Branco, where I remarked particularly the fine episcopal palace and the beautiful gardens attached to it.   Thence we continued our march northwards, hutting almost every night, and relieved by few halting days.   When the army bivouacked the space occupied by each regiment was limited to the ground immediately in the rear of the spot where we halted ; and all trees came to be regarded as billets, being taken possession of according to rank.   They were of use to us, not only for the shelter they afforded, but because we could tie our mules and horses to them, and establish at them places for unloading our baggage.   It not unfrequently happened that some one of us, after his cattle were released from their burdens, and other preparations made for the night, would be obliged to shift his quarters, on account either of the arrival of a senior officer, or of an encroachment on the ground by another regiment.

At Nave d'Aver we joined the sixth division, commanded by Sir Henry Clinton.   There was a great scarcity of fuel here, and the inhabitants preferred constant complaints against our men for burning the little timber that was to be found.   Colonel B——— [1] of the 36th, who had the command of the brigade *pro tempore,* issued positive orders that neither officer nor soldier should attempt to use for firewood any part of the materials of the dwellings in the village. On the day after this injunction had appeared, the colonel observed some of our men busily employed in unroofing a house, and, irritated by this proof of disobedience, he directed an officer who was with him to go and make prisoners of the whole party. The officer went ; but he soon returned, with the intelligence that the roof of the building on which they were at work was about to be removed for fuel to the colonel's own quarters.

[1] Colonel Robert Burne (?)

Lord Wellington's headquarters were at Fuente Guinaldo on the 10th of August. We had reached, on the 17th, the miserable village of Barquilla in Spain, distant about four leagues from Ciudad Rodrigo, and thence we moved to Villa de Porco.

The British and Portuguese army, with the exception of Sir Rowland Hill's corps of 14,000 men, then in the Alentejo, went into cantonments on the line of the Agueda. Our infantry were about 38,000 strong, and our cavalry under 4000, Lord Wellington being, as usual, weak in that arm.

We now began to feel the want of money severely ; the commanding officer [1] and I lived together, and a wretched mess we had. We were miserably unprovided, having nothing to eat besides rations of the worst kind. One of our officers, a very tall and handsome young Englishman, could not satisfy his appetite with the quantity of rations allowed him, and, having no money to purchase any additional food, wasted away gradually. He died at length, absolutely through want of nourishment.

It was with great difficulty that the commissariat cattle could be brought up, as they were procured at a considerable distance from our present quarters ; and, when they did arrive, the mind was irresistibly struck by the strong similitude they bore to what we fancy the lean kine of Pharaoh to have been, for they were so hungry, and so nearly in a state of starvation themselves, that they seemed much more likely to create a famine than to prevent one. The tough,

[1] Afterwards Sir Samuel Venables Hinde, K.C.B. Commanded 2nd Brigade of the 6th Division at Salamanca and elsewhere.

stringy, and carrion-like flesh that the commissariat bullock afforded was rendered doubly unwholesome by overdriving, which caused the poor animal to enter the camp in a burning fever. I have often seen the Portuguese drivers hold a little corn in their hands near the mouths of the wearied and famished beasts to coax them a few paces further. As soon as the skin was whipped off the meat was served out, and constituted, with the addition of ship biscuit, our regular fare. The colonel was at one time half-starved, for he suffered from so sharp an attack of rheumatism in the face that his jaws could ill contend against the tough nature of our food. One day, in particular, he quite despaired of being able to eat his dinner, preferring the pangs of hunger to the torture of masticating a piece of gristle that the commissary had sent us, when behold! our cook entered, bearing in triumph a dish on which a fine roast pig appeared dressed in the best style, and, placing it before us on the table without uttering a syllable, touched his forage cap and withdrew. We had stared at him in amazement, and now exchanged a couple of inquiring looks, which asked very intelligibly, "What is to be done?" But our eyes did not long remain fixed on the doubtful visages opposite, for, as if the pig were a basilisk, they were irresistibly attracted towards it. The smoke that curled up from the inviting dish was most grateful to our nostrils, and the visual and olfactory organs communicated so effectually agreeable sensations to the palate and mouth that our teeth began to water, those of the colonel seeming even to forget the rheumatism. The internal contest between some qualms of conscience and the inclination to gratify a useful sense was of short duration. The pig was killed, and we could not restore it to life ; if we could perhaps we would ; if we did not eat part of it, Robert, who was so much in fault, being guilty of the plunder and the murder of the little pig, would be rewarded, and not punished, by having it all to himself ; and to cause him to suffer the severe punishment awarded by military laws would strongly resemble ingratitude on our part. We therefore concluded that it was as well not to send back the roast pig ; though, at the same time, we could not suppress the feeling that our denying ourselves such a gratification as the enjoyment of the feast before us would be an act of the most exalted philosophy, and well worthy to be recorded in the annals of Villa de Porco, independently of all allusion to any appropriateness of the incidents to the name. But we trusted to no further reasoning, lest the pig, *pedente lite*, should grow cold ; and accordingly we discussed the delicious little animal, perfectly agreeing, however, in the opinion that Robert was one of the greatest scoundrels in the army. I have a faint recollection of such an event as payment made subsequently for the stolen pig, and think that it might have been occasioned by our conscientious qualms resuming the offensive with fresh activity, when hunger had become quiescent.

No two nations in the world, not even the Danes and Swedes, hate each other so cordially as the Spaniards and Portuguese. The one holds in contempt what he calls the servility of the other ; and

the latter, in turn, detests what he thinks the arro-
gance and vain pride of the former.   Portugal, too,
was once under the domination of Spain, and effected
her emancipation only after a fierce and bloody
struggle ; and such circumstances cannot but tend
very powerfully to confirm the jealousy which so
frequently exists between the people of two neighbouring states.   The difference of manner and
costume is very perceptible, even between the
higher classes of both nations.   The Portuguese
gentry are much more supple and complaisant in
their manners, and more gaudy in their taste, than
the Spanish : but we had now more opportunities of
observing the peculiarities of the bordering peasantry.
We were barely within the confines of Spain, and,
nevertheless, the cultivators of the soil we had left
were as unlike those among whom we had come as
they well could be ; and even the dwellings of the
villagers of Leon are superior in construction, cleanliness, comfort, and general appearance, to those of
the province of Beira.   At one side of the stream are
heavy wooden shoes ; at the other, nothing but light
sandals.   The Portuguese peasant appeared clad in
coarse brown cloth, his uncombed hair hanging
loosely about his shoulders, his gait listless and
lounging, and his whole air indicative of helplessness
and indolence ; and although he met us with *vivas*,
and in his general demeanour was civil and obliging,
yet it was impossible to respect him.   On the contrary, the Spaniard's costume was tasteful, and calculated to display to advantage the symmetry of his
figure ; his hair neatly combed and plaited ; his step

firm and measured ; his attitudes manly and graceful ;
his manner bespeaking gravity and self-possession ;
and his whole deportment lofty and commanding,
suiting well with his naturally proud and haughty
spirit : in fact, the peasantry of Spain have in
appearance a decided superiority over the same
class of the natives of any other country with which
I am acquainted. They have often told me that a
Spaniard was either one of the best or one of the
worst men in the world. They received us without
enthusiasm, yet they were not uncivil ; they gave
us for our money what they had to dispose of, but
evinced no zeal, no strong desire, to promote our
views ; it grieved them to the heart that the aid of
strangers should seem necessary for their deliverance
from the tyranny and usurpation of a detested race.
Nor did this reflection lose any of its bitterness
because the troops of Portugal stood in the ranks of
their allies ; indeed, they could never be brought to
confess that they needed any assistance from us
beyond supplies of money and arms ; but the
Portuguese candidly admitted that men were also
wanted.

The next move of the sixth division was to
Gallegos and its vicinity ; but it was subsequently
stationed more to the right.

On our entering Spain, my friend the colonel,
who was an indifferent linguist, felt himself so
much at a loss, when addressing or addressed by
the natives, that an interpreter was deemed to be
an indispensable addition to his establishment. The
fellow whom he appointed to this office had been

taken by the French on the retreat to Corunna, and detained by them in the country for several months before his release was effected ; and during that time he had learned to speak Spanish with fluency: he was therefore kept in constant attend- ance. While we remained within the Spanish border, the colonel frequently suspected, from the gestures and manner of several of the inhabitants, that they had complaints to prefer, and he was always most anxious to remove every just cause of dissatisfaction ; but he was never able to elicit from them, through the medium of his interpreter, any statement of grievances.   The looks of the landlords of houses in which he happened to be billetted were par- ticularly discontented, and it excited his surprise beyond measure to see them depart, after each con- ference, apparently with increased dissatisfaction at his manner, which he had intended to be perfectly conciliatory.

A considerable time elapsed before the solution of this mystery. The interpreter was a young man with a most amiable and prepossessing countenance ; innocence and simplicity seemed to be so strongly depicted there that a stranger would never imagine it possible for any guile to lurk beneath. But never were appearances more deceitful. There was not a worse character in the whole army. He pilfered everything that came within his reach, and took the lead in all acts of plunder and outrage that were supposed to have been committed by the regiment ; yet he had the address to conceal his guilt for a very long period. When a complaint was made, the colonel would call this man, and ask him what the complainant said. Perhaps the Spaniard might declare that the interpreter, with others of the servants, had broken open his store-room and robbed him of his wine, his onions, his garlic, and his money, and request that a search might be instituted for the recovery of the stolen property. "What does he say?" would be the colonel's question. "He only wishes you, sir, to make free with everything in the house, and begs that your servants will call for whatever you or they may want," would be the arch-rogue's reply. "He is a remarkably civil man," the colonel would observe; "tell him that I feel much obliged to him, but that it was always my wish to pay for anything I am provided with." "Yes, sir," the interpreter would say, adding, in Spanish, as he turned to the plundered host, "The colonel desires you will quit his presence directly, and he does not believe one word that you say." This deception was finally detected through the interpreter incautiously attempting it in the hearing of an officer who understood the language.

While we were thinking of laying siege to Ciudad Rodrigo, the French force in Spain was considerably augmented by the arrival of reinforcements from France, a great part of which consisted of troops long inured to war. Several thousand men joined Marmont; and Count Dorsenne commanded a separate corps that kept the Asturians and Galicians in check. The French at first evidently hoped, though in vain, to induce Lord Wellington to advance to Salamanca. They then determined to advance

against him, and we soon heard that Marmont had
collected an army of 60,000 men, between Placencia
and Salamanca. At this time our effective force was
little more than 40,000 men, British and Portuguese.
The next intelligence that came in was that the
French marshal was actually on his march; the
ground occupied by our army began to be narrowed; and we were prepared to see the enemy
soon make his appearance, and to give him a warm
reception whenever he did. It must be confessed,
however, that some of our regiments were in rather
bad fighting order; but others were very well, and
the four regiments of infantry and one of light
cavalry that had arrived in July, were remarkably
strong and effective.

Up to this period a trifling affair would now and
then occur, with various success, between our people
and the enemy; but the garrison were in as great
danger from want of provisions as from our attempting to besiege them. On the 24th of September, a
part of the French army made its appearance in considerable force, and convoying a long train of waggons
and mules, laden with supplies, which entered the
fortress in the evening. The next morning two
large bodies of the enemy were observed to approach, the weaker marching on Espeja, and the
stronger on Guinaldo, where a defensive position
had been selected by Lord Wellington for the whole
army, if necessary. In front of Guinaldo, on some
bare and extensive heights, General Colville was
posted with the 5th, 77th, and 83rd British, and the
9th and 21st Portuguese infantry, a few pieces of

Portuguese artillery, two squadrons of the 11th light dragoons, and an equal number of German hussars. The other brigade of the third division was at some distance from them, on their right.

The artillery, which were on the summit of the same height with the 5th and 77th, and in front of them, opened a smart fire upon the cavalry of the stronger division of the enemy, who rode across their ravine and up the ascent, while their infantry were still far behind. The grape and canister of the Portuguese did considerable execution upon the assailants as they advanced ; but at length the battery was taken and the gunners sabred. Still the bold dragoons were not to have it all their own way ; for the 5th, the regiment nearest to the guns, charged them in line with the most daring courage, first punishing them severely with a well-directed fire, and then rushing forward with the bayonet, and throwing them into such confusion by this unheard-of mode of attacking cavalry with infantry, that they gave way and fled. After chasing them down the slope, the 5th returned to their ground with the guns in their possession.

The enemy's squadrons made various charges at other points, but, notwithstanding the disparity of numbers, they were uniformly repulsed by ours. However, to avoid being cut off, it became necessary for the third division to retreat. This was done in the best order by both brigadiers ; though followed by the French cavalry and horse artillery, and having to traverse an open plain. The infantry, protecting the cavalry, formed squares, and so destructive was their fire to the enemy, who at first charged furiously, and so steady their conduct, that they soon kept them at a respectful distance, though constantly threatening to renew their attacks, and causing us some loss with their horse artillery. At the same time, after sharp fighting, particularly between the cavalry, some of our outposts on the left flank were driven in.

General Picton's division halted on the lofty ridge of the position of Guinaldo, where General Cole's was also posted. From the Agueda, on the right, to the steep termination of the ridge on the left, was a distance of about three miles; and the ground in front was a wide plain, where the French appeared in great force. In the night there was a general movement of the different divisions of the British army. It was Lord Wellington's intention to retire at once to a strong position on the Coa; but he was prevented from carrying it into effect by a mistake made by General Crawford, that officer having attempted to join the main body with his division by a wrong route, and being in consequence compelled to retrace his steps, by which means much precious time was wasted. My division was marched from Gallegos and Espeja, and took post more to the right; and it was generally expected that Marmont, with his superior numbers, would endeavour to force us into an engagement.

During the whole of the day of the 26th, the marshal contented himself with making a grand display of his force, and threatening the position of Guinaldo; but while he was thus employed, the light division crossed the Agueda and joined the army. In the morning he had 35,000 infantry and a splendid body of cavalry within gun-shot of Picton's and Cole's divisions, and early in the evening he could muster 60,000 bayonets and 120 pieces of cannon ; yet he left us in undisputed possession of our ground. After dark, the British commander thought it prudent to fall back ; and he effected his purpose without the slightest confusion, or the most trifling loss, either of prisoners or baggage.

On the morning of the 27th, the enemy appeared on both the roads by which the right wing was retiring. On one of these, the road to Aldea de Ponte, they followed very briskly, and attacked the fourth division and General Pack's Portuguese on the heights between that village and Nave d'Aver ; but they were repulsed after a smart contest, and driven back with our light troops at their heels : our men, indeed, continued the pursuit too long, and were compelled to retire in their turn before a fresh column of the enemy's infantry. It appeared to be Marmont's intention to drive us either into the Coa or across it without delay, as if we were a frightened flock of sheep ; but, to borrow a phrase from the fancy, " he had all his work to do yet " : at least Lord Wellington thought he had, and, to convince him of it, halted this night at Rendoa, where our division was posted, and took up a strong position, with the Coa in our rear and on both our flanks. Here he offered battle to the marshal, but the challenge was not accepted. Perhaps it was a fortunate circumstance for the British arms that no engagement ensued; for although our position was formidable, and in all probability would have been defended triumphantly, there still remained some chance that Marmont might succeed in forcing it, through his great numerical superiority; and, if such an untoward event did occur, the allied army, placed as it was with such a river in the rear, and not a single bridge within its reach, would be in imminent danger of total annihilation.

The campaign was now over. The French retired in three separate divisions; and on the 29th we crossed the Coa and went into cantonments, having left two divisions to watch Ciudad Rodrigo. Lord Wellington's headquarters were at Frenada. My regiment occupied Chiras.

The wet season now set in; and we had woeful experience that the roofs of such houses as we tenanted were far from being proof against the heavy rain which fell incessantly.

We had neither money, books, good provisions, nor any kind of amusement, and passed a most dreary time; and, what made matters still more disagreeable, the army was so very unhealthy that considerably more than one-fourth of our number was on the sick list. As the Portuguese have no fireplaces in their rooms, except the kitchens, our officers were compelled by the dampness of the weather to build some. We found the recesses of such windows as happened to be glazed the most convenient for this purpose, for we easily supplied the place of a chimney by taking out a pane, and running a tin tube through the aperture; but where the windows

L

were only provided with shutters, which was generally the case, we had to make the fire-place in some
other part of the room, and run the tube through
the main wall.

Of all bad winter residences a Portuguese house
is the worst. The natives themselves looked very
pictures of misery at this season, as they sat, wrapped
up in their large cloaks, in wretched, gloomy, unfur-
nished rooms, through the doors and windows of
which the cold wind whistled, while the rain dropped,
dropped eternally, from various parts of the old
boarded ceilings ; they seem not to know what
comfort means, and the filthiness of their abodes is
insufferable. What inestimable service a visit from
a colony of Hollanders, well provided with their
brooms and water-engines, would render to Portugal !
The people are also very disgusting in their persons ;
none of them in this part of the country could be
free from vermin, and numbers were absolutely
covered with them ; of course, their beds were
stocked with myriads. I usually slept on the large
chest, an article of furniture always to be found in a
Portuguese house ; and by doing so, I avoided rats
as well as the other annoyances. The Barrosa bed
was of the greatest utility ; it consists of a case, made
of tarred canvas, and lined with ticken, which, when
filled with straw, may be laid on the wet grass without any danger that the damp will penetrate, and
when empty it may be rolled up into a very small
compass.

Before we left Chiras, an officer's wife, who was
coming up from Lisbon to join her husband, met

with a provoking adventure. She was a person of rather masculine appearance, which was increased by her wearing a habit and a black hat ; she rode single on a mule, and was approaching Celerico, when the Ordenança, or armed peasantry, apprehended her upon suspicion of being a spy. She was taken to a place of confinement, and neither her entreaties first, nor her threats afterwards, availed aught to effect her liberation. They declared their conviction, judging from her costume, and, as they said, suspicious appearance, that she or he, for they entertained strong doubts of her sex, was certainly a spy ; and accordingly she was marched back to Lisbon as a prisoner, and there given up to the proper authorities. Fortunately for the captive lady, the assistant-surgeon to the regiment happened to be in the Portuguese capital at the time ; he was sent for at her request, and his appearance and testimony in her favour sufficed to relieve her from her very distressing situation.

Early in October 1811, Lord Wellington saw fit to repair the works of Almeida sufficiently to make it a place of arms, though not to restore it to its former strength, and four hundred men of our division were constantly employed there. The fatigue parties were relieved every fourth day. On the 14th I was sent to the fortress on this duty, with a detachment from my regiment. I found half the town a mere heap of rubbish, for General Brennier, previously to his escape from it with the greater part of his garrison, having blown up three of the bastions, and we the others ; the explosions had also destroyed the neighbouring houses, and the firing of the great magazine in the centre of the town in the year 1810 had been attended by still greater destruction. The inhabitants were consequently reduced to the extreme of wretchedness, and several squalid, shivering, and apparently half-famished beings, were to be seen wandering about the ruins of their former habitations. Accounts of victories and conquests, of battles won, and cities taken, read well in the newspapers at breakfast, while the politician sits in his easy chair, and sips his chocolate by a comfortable fire at home ; but one who has witnessed the horrors that a field of battle or a stormed city presents, must ever receive such tidings with mingled sensations, joy for the success and pity for the sufferers.

During the period which elapsed between October 1811 and June 1812, the sixth division, under General Graham,[1] performed many trying and difficult marches, but did not take part in any affair of interest,[2] being usually employed as a covering force

[1] Sir Thomas Graham, afterwards Lord Lynedoch.

[2] I have consequently omitted many pages of the original. The following notes may, however, be taken from the Major's account of these operations. In the middle of February 1812, the 32nd spent a week at Estremos, and Major Ross-Lewin formed an acquaintance with one of the local priests. " While taking me through the church, which was, of course, one of the lions, he explained to me the manner of interring such bodies as are honoured with a narrow house within its walls, a distinction granted only when the deceased persons have belonged to the higher classes. They are committed to old mother-earth in their clothes, without coffins, and should they be larger than usual, the dimensions of the grave are never altered for them, but they are made to fit it, being pounded down with heavy mallets; nor does the disrespectful treatment of the remains of the dead end here, for they are suffered to lie inside the church only as long as all others, for which surviving friends are inclined to purchase places, can be accommodated without disturbing them ; and

during the great sieges of Ciudad Rodrigo and Badajoz. After the fall of the latter fortress, the 32nd regiment joined in the general advance upon Salamanca.

The want of money was much felt at this time.

the moment that this ceases to be the case, the old occupants of the graves are unceremoniously ejected in favour of the newcomers, and cast into vaults outside the edifice. My cicerone conducted me to this unfashionable end of the Necropolis, but I had reason to wish that his civility had not carried him so far. I never beheld a more loathsome spectacle; the eye, wherever it turned, was offended by the sight of numerous halfconsumed bodies, and the stench they emitted was intolerable." The following reference to the conduct of the 88th at Badajoz may prove of interest to Irishmen. For a detailed account of their gallantry the reader should see Lieut. Grattan's "Adventures with the Connaught Rangers," a new edition of which has been brought out by Professor Oman. In this it is stated that the Rangers lost 25 officers and 556 men in eighty-eight days.

"The 88th regiment lost a great number of men in the attack of the castle, and after that had succeeded, in the attempt to force open the iron gate that obstructed their passage into the town. They made a rush at this impediment, *and vainly exerted themselves to drive it in with their shoulders, while the French at the other side kept up a galling fire on them through the grating;* but at last an officer, aided by a few men, turned round a gun that happened to be near, and blew the gate open. The Rangers then dashed in, and all resistance quickly ceased. A part of them also engaged in a bloody struggle with a portion of the garrison for the possession of a round tower; the spiral stairs, from the very foot to the summit, were sternly contested; blue and red coats were stretched together on every step; and when the assailants had at length fought their way up, the slaughter of the ill-fated defenders was completed by flinging all of them who had escaped the bayonet over the battlements. It is proper to add, however, that of the French soldiers found in the town none are known to have sued for quarter in vain.

"It were well, indeed, that our men had been as temperate in other respects, as they generally were where only revengeful feelings were to be gratified; for the pillage and excess, usually consequent upon the capture of a town by storm, were here carried to a deplorable extent. Such a scene of drunkenness has rarely been witnessed. The garrison had kept their spirits in a deep cistern, cut out of the solid rock, as a precaution against fire; and, when it was afterwards emptied, two soldiers and a drummer were found drowned at the bottom of it. An officer of my acquaintance had been one of the first to enter the town, and, as he

My purse was not lighter than that of most other officers of the army, and yet all it contained was a half-doubloon, a gold coin worth eight dollars. The division moved one morning before daybreak, and as I was in the act of mounting my horse to proceed with it, my treasure slipped out of my pocket, which was also my purse, and fell in the muddy lane ; but its escape was not unobserved. I dismounted instantly, and stood motionless, until the whole division had passed, and a glimmering twilight appeared ; I then began to squeeze the mud in my immediate vicinity with my hands, but to no purpose ; and having passed nearly three hours in this spot, I at length relinquished the search in despair, and told two drummers who happened to come up at the moment, that I had lost a half-doubloon, which they

passed under the windows of a respectable-looking house, an aged couple, who appeared at them, loudly and earnestly implored his protection. He instantly flew upstairs, and entered an apartment just in time to save their daughter, a girl of exquisite beauty, from the violence of some soldiers. He succeeded for the moment in clearing the house of the intruders—a task of no little danger at such a period, all discipline being then suspended —and he placed a sentinel at the door of the apartment, engaging to reward him handsomely if he would only protect the family from further insult. The fellow promised readily, and the officer hastened away to attend to some requisite duty ; but, on his return, which he delayed as little as possible, to this family, who had excited within him so lively a feeling of interest, he was greatly shocked to find those respectable persons in extreme tribulation : for the soldier, whom he had intended to be their protector, had proved the very reverse, and, joined by some of his comrades, had faithlessly plundered them of money, plate, and other valuables ; but, even so, they would have cheerfully borne this loss, had it purchased for them exemption from a cruel pang to which their parental feelings were subjected.

"It was with great difficulty, and after the lapse of many hours, that anything like order was restored in the streets of Badajos. It is painful to contemplate so rapid an alternation of light and shade in the soldier's character; to behold him one hour a hero and the next a brute."

might think it worth their while to look for. When
I was once more in the saddle, I cast a lingering look
on the spot which bore the impression of my feet,
and, to my inexpressible consolation, but to the disappointment of the drummers, I beheld the picture
of his most Catholic Majesty shining brightly in a
frame of mud, which had been well defined by my
right heel; in the next moment it was securely
deposited in my pocket; and in the third I was
cantering along merrily to overtake my regiment.

CHAPTER XI

WHEN Marshal Marmont retired, on the approach of our army, from Salamanca, he left there about 800 men to garrison some fortified convents and other works, which he had done all in his power to strengthen ; and he had succeeded in making them so formidable as to defy any sudden attack, and even render a regular one very troublesome. The reduction of these works was now to give employment to the sixth division, and, Lord Wellington having placed himself at the head of it with his staff, we entered the famed city of Salamanca.

Our reception was the best possible ; every demonstration of joy and welcome was shown by the inhabitants ; even the nuns forgot the strict rules of the convent, and appeared at the windows waving their handkerchiefs, while the whole male population made the welkin ring with their stentorian *vivas.* It was a proud moment, one on which memory dwells with pleasure ; for dead indeed to all generous feelings must have been that British heart which did not beat quicker and glow with increased enthusiasm, when a British army was thus hailed as protectors and deliverers from a powerful tyrant's yoke, by the assembled thousands of one of the fairest cities of Spain.

The great square, in which we formed in column, is very handsome. The length of each side is nearly three hundred feet ; the houses are built uniformly, have piazzas at the lower story, iron balconies at the second, and a stone balustrade round the roofs. Some of the arches are ornamented with medallions, representing in bas-relief the busts of various celebrated Spaniards, such as Cortez, Pizarro, Cid Ruy, &c. In such a place, and with such memorials before us, we received the enthusiastic greetings of the people of Salamanca. The university was accounted the first in Spain, and to it the sons of the grandees generally came to finish their education ; but the French, as usual, had plundered the colleges and expelled the students. The Irish College is a very large pile. At one time eight hundred young men pursued their studies within its walls, but, like the rest, they were forced to disperse upon the unprincipled seizure of their revenues by Napoleon. During our stay I was fortunate enough to become acquainted with Doctor Curtis, then the head of that society, and subsequently the Irish Roman Catholic Primate ; he was a very intelligent man, and all spoke highly of his scholastic attainments. The Irish students were very great favourites with the Spaniards, who were particularly pleased with their stature and general personal appearance. The cathedral is a magnificent structure ; it is 420 feet in length, and, though richly decorated, it has not lost that solemnity which is so often wanting in Roman Catholic churches, in consequence of the profusion of gilding and tawdry ornaments with which they are bedizened.   Marmont made this city his principal depot, and on that account had taken such pains to convert its ancient monasteries into strong defences.

At eight in the evening we began to make our approaches, breaking ground before the Convent of San Vicente ; and I had the first working party of my corps.   We covered ourselves in the course of the night without much loss, although the French had destroyed several fine buildings to give a more extensive range to their fire ; at one time they even had it in contemplation to blow up the superb cathedral.

Our first batteries were soon found to be ill-placed ; the ground was too low, and the men were not sufficiently covered.   We lost, in consequence, some valuable artillerymen and soldiers of different corps.   On the 23rd another battery, erected on higher ground, was completed and armed, but the fire from it was not very well directed.   This battery bore on one of the flank defences a palisadoed work, and Lord Wellington seemed to feel much anxiety with respect to the probability of its answering his purpose.   Before it opened, I observed, during the day, that a four-pound shot frequently came in at one of the angles ; and some time after I perceived Lord Wellington viewing the enemy's works from it, and resting his glass on the above-mentioned angle; but I immediately warned him of the shot, and he changed his position. Colonel Dickson, who joined him in the course of two or three minutes, also walked up to the angle, when his lordship hastily called him away, repeating the caution that I had given. I saw another shot pass over the same spot not long after, and it might have deprived our army of its able commander had he not been apprised of his danger.

In the evening of the 23rd, a flag of truce came out, but the proposals made by the besieged were rejected, and at eight o'clock the firing recommenced. That night it was determined to storm the enemy's works. The storming parties consisted of the light companies of the Queen's, the 32nd,[1] and the 36th, commanded by Lieutenant-Colonel Hinde of the 32nd, and those of the other brigade by Lieutenant-Colonel Bingham of the 53rd. Twenty men carrying ladders preceded them, and all advanced at the same time, led on by Major-General Bowes, who had the chief command. The instant that our troops showed themselves, a dreadful fire was opened on them, and the result was precisely such as most officers anticipated—a failure attended with severe loss of life. In a very few minutes the assault was repelled, but little more than half of the assailants returned. Major-General Bowes was killed. We sent a flag of truce for leave to bury the dead and remove the wounded, but it was not received. Previous

---

[1] Thomas Ross-Lewin was a lieutenant of the light company. Between the 18th and the 24th of June the 32nd lost 10 killed and 28 wounded.

to this attempt, the only effect from the fire of the batteries had been the partial damaging some of the defences, but no breach had been made.

The next day, the 24th of June, being the anniversary of St. John the Baptist, the Spaniards were to have devoted to gaiety, but our ill-luck the preceding night cast a gloom over the city.

If I do not mistake, it was on the following evening that a captain in the same regiment with me sallied out, when it was growing dusk, to buy some brandy. As he walked under the piazza in the Plaça Mayor, he met a little man, dressed in round hat and blue great coat, and accosting him said, " Can you tell me, sir, where the best brandy is sold in this town ? " " Indeed, I cannot say," replied the unknown. " D——n me," cried the captain, " but you can, for I know it from the colour of your nose ; " and immediately laying his hand on the little man's collar, and at the same time pushing him forward, he added, " I will never let you go, my old cock, till you show me where good brandy is sold." " Well, well ! " said the stranger, stopping at a shop, " I think you will find it here." The stranger was right, and thus got rid of his troublesome companion. But judge, reader, what must have been the captain's dismay when he discovered next morning that the person whom he had treated so unceremoniously was no other than General Sontag, who commanded one of our brigades.

Our vesper entertainments here were not all of the same character. One evening, as I was coming out of the trenches with two other officers and a party of men after our tour of duty, General Clinton [1] rode up to us, and said that he wished one of his officers and a part of the picquet, volunteers, to amuse the enemy by firing at the windows of one of the fortified convents, while a working party should endeavour to cover itself near the gable end of the building. Accordingly I proceeded with thirty men to a point near the convent, where we were sheltered by a wall, and there awaited the arrival of an engineer, who, the General informed me, was to come to show us the way. The working party had preceded us; but just as I had drawn up my men behind the wall, we heard a sudden discharge of musketry, and almost at the same instant they tumbled in on us, spades, shovels, pickaxes and all, in the most ludicrous confusion. They had discovered a deep ditch running parallel to the gable which they were to have undermined, and this unexpected obstacle, together with the rapid and deadly fire from the loopholes, caused them to scamper off in such a violent hurry, though not before several of them were hit. They did not renew their attempt—no engineer came near me— and the party was at length withdrawn, as otherwise they would have been speedily annihilated without having done the least service. In such a case as this, according to the military dictionary, "to amuse an enemy," means to make oneself a target for him to practise at; in other cases it not infrequently occurs that the phrases "to amuse an enemy" and "to annoy" one are nearly related.

[1] Afterwards Sir Henry Clinton, G.C.B.

Some days after the commencement of our siege, I rode out to see the position that Lord Wellington had taken up three miles in front of the city, his right resting on the Tormes. I met a number of the inhabitants, who evinced the best disposition, and were bringing firewood to our men, who were in great want of it, there being few trees in the neighbourhood of Salamanca. The French army had retired a few leagues farther, but a portion of it returned and occupied the villages in front of ours ; still all Marmont's efforts to secure a communication with the garrison failed completely, and without doubt he repented his imprudence in leaving so many good soldiers behind him in such a post. On the 20th there had been some slight skirmishing between the cavalry of the two armies, and on the following day the enemy had been in possession of some rising ground on our right flank, from which it was thought necessary to drive them ; this duty the seventh division performed, and no attempt was made to recover the position. The French then retired two leagues, followed by our light cavalry. On the morning of the 25th it was ascertained that Marmont had crossed the Tormes in force during the night, and various movements of the covering army took place, two divisions of infantry and a part of the cavalry passing to the same side by the fords of Santa Martha ; but the French marshal retraced his steps in the course of the day, finding himself wholly unable to deceive or baffle his vigilant and skilful adversary.

The experiment of setting fire to one of the fortified convents was now to be tried, and on the 26th the shot was heated for that purpose at the first batteries erected. It was projected with a force barely sufficient to let it drop on the roof of the building, which, together with a heap of timber that lay near, was soon in flames ; but the progress of the conflagration was for some hours arrested by the exertions of the garrison. At the same time the fire from the battery on the right, which was the last erected, broke down the palisades. Ensign Fitzgerald of the 32nd, who had sent in his resignation, and was on the eve of retiring from the service, was killed that day by a fragment of a shell.

On the morning of the 27th, the fire from the batteries proving very destructive, the French commandant requested a delay of three hours in order to make terms, but his request was refused, and directions were given for storming. Ensign Newton [1] of the 32nd led the forlorn hope ; the assault was completely successful ; the fort, in which a breach had been made, was quickly carried ; and the whole garrison surrendered at discretion, after having kept an entire division at bay for the space of ten days. Immediately after the surrender I walked over the different forts. Human ingenuity could not have been exercised more effectually than it had been by the French engineer who planned these defences. Several of the French soldiers had got access to the wine and spirits, and were crawling about in a state

---

[1] He was mentioned in despatches for his gallantry on the 23rd and 27th June, but was subsequently killed at Salamanca. He was a native of Canada, his father, an Irish gentleman, having settled in that country.

of brutal intoxication. The hospital was kept with the greatest regularity, and an officer of the Queen's, who had been made prisoner at the first attempt to storm, and had undergone amputation of one leg, had experienced the utmost care and attention. Many of the enemy were severely burnt when the great convent was set on fire ; but few fell at the assault.

The capture of the forts diffused extreme joy among the people of Salamanca. They had a grand service and the Te Deum in the Cathedral, at which Lord Wellington and his staff were present, a merry ball in the evening, and illuminations which continued for three days.

St. Anthony being the tutelar saint of Spain, his day was ushered in by the ringing of bells and other demonstrations of respect and rejoicing ; the richest stuffs were hung out at the windows ; and an extensive framework, covered with black cloth, was raised in the great square ; broad flights of steps led to the top of this temporary stand, and on them were placed the pictures of the greater part, if not all, the saints in the calendar, collected from the different churches, together with numerous family portraits from the most ancient houses ; so that old admirals and generals, statesmen and lawyers, courtiers and grandees, came in for their share of adoration, as well as the canonised virgins and martyrs, hermits and friars, bishops and presbyters.

The forts were now blown up ; the guns, a considerable supply of clothing, and other stores that fell into our hands, were given to the Spanish

authorities ; and the sixth division, which had lost
nearly five hundred in killed and wounded, marched
to rejoin the army.

On the morning of the 29th, Lord Wellington
moved towards the Douro, from which Salamanca is
about eleven leagues distant. The enemy fell back
as we advanced. This part of Spain is quite open,
level, and very bare of timber. The agriculturists
here entertain an inveterate dislike to trees, whose
shade and appearance they seem to think far less
desirable than their harbouring birds that commit
depredations on their corn is injurious. A march
through such a country is remarkably dull and
wearisome, and, as the weather was excessively
warm, we had every reason to regret the antipathy
of the natives to arboriculture. When we were not
actually in motion, we occupied the villages in the
daytime, and passed the nights in our bivouac.

Lord Wellington seemed to threaten Madrid, and
Marmont at length crossed the Douro, destroying
some bridges, and fixing his headquarters at Tordesillas.   His rearguard was attacked on the 22nd of
July at Rueda, and routed by the British cavalry
under Sir Stapleton Cotton. Lord Wellington's
headquarters were then established at the last-mentioned place ; on the 11th we were at Alego on the
Douro, the French in a strong position on the opposite side. We were disadvantageously posted, owing
to an unfavourable bend of the river. The next
rumour was that Lord Wellington wanted to draw
the enemy after him ; but in the interim his opponent
had been joined by a fresh body of horse, and by a

M

strong reinforcement under General Bonnet, which gave him a numerical superiority, and enabled him to execute some skilful manœuvres. On the 15th the allied army moved to the left. The main body retired to Villa Pena, six leagues from Salamanca. On the 17th the whole French army crossed the Douro ; and by a forced march they had nearly succeeded in cutting off the fourth and the light division. There was a good deal of skirmishing in front of Villa Pena, which was much to our advantage. On the 19th the French and British commanders displayed their tactics. On the 20th Marshal Marmont moved to his left, and our army in a parallel line to our right. Our march this day was long and rapid ; the two armies were separated by a valley, and moved on opposite heights in sight of each other, the French drummers beating at the heads of their brigades, and some Spanish cavalry in the intermediate space occasionally firing on the enemy. On the 21st both reached the Tormes at the same time. Lord Wellington came up to the spot where I was standing, threw himself on the ground, and was observing the enemy through his glass, when he asked an officer who was near him if they were crossing ; the answer being in the affirmative, he instantly mounted, ordered the leading regiment of our column to ford the river, and galloped off.

His order was quickly obeyed. The sixth division, after crossing the Tormes, remained on its banks that night ; and such another night I have never witnessed. With the darkness the rain descended in torrents, and a terrific thunderstorm burst over our heads ; peal succeeded peal with increasing vehemence; the electric fluid absolutely hissed through the air; and such was the vividness of the flashes, that at one time I was deprived of sight for a few moments. The horses of the 5th dragoon guards became dreadfully frightened, broke from their pickets, and ran over the men, who were stretched on the ground, inflicting severe injuries on several of them. It was, indeed, as wild and fearful a night as ever preceded a memorable day of strife and slaughter; no sound was heard but the heavy splash of the incessant rain, the trampling of the terrified horses, the shouts or groans of the men, save when they were all confounded in the stunning reverberations of the aerial artillery, which at brief intervals pealed forth an awful note of preparation for the bloody work of the morrow. I caught one of the horses that had broken loose, and, the lightning being my lamp, never saw terror more forcibly pictured in the appearance of any animal—his nostrils expanded, his eyeballs almost starting from their sockets, his mouth white with foam, and his whole form paralysed and trembling. Several of the horses could not be stopped, and galloped into the enemy's lines. They were ridden by the French officers the next day.

Before dawn the enemy, as usual, was under arms, and the troops began to take up their positions. At the same time the third division and General d'Urban's Portuguese cavalry, who had passed the night on the right bank, in consequence of Marmont's leaving a part of his force at Babila Fuente, crossed the river. Our left rested on the Tormes, and our right was posted on the less of two rocky heights, called the Arapiles, which rose abruptly from the plain. The marshal occupied a mountain ridge, close to which a deep wood was very favourably situated, and at a very early hour a strong body of his troops were in possession of the greater Arapiles, which made it necessary for us to extend our right behind the little village of that name. Skirmishing was commenced almost as soon as the hostile troops could distinguish each other. The whole strength of the allied army was under 42,000 men ; that of the enemy was full 47,000. Still it was not Marmont's game to bring on a general action, as the usurper, Joseph, was on the march to join him from one point, and he expected the immediate arrival of a considerable reinforcement from another ; besides, his communications with the north and centre were perfectly open. Lord Wellington's communication with Ciudad Rodrigo was likewise free, so that he was under no necessity to strike a blow to maintain it ; but he still knew that, should his opponent's force be increased in the manner he anticipated, he would only have to retreat at once into Portugal, and therefore it was his object to seize the first favourable opportunity of engaging the enemy.

The chief part of the day was spent in manœuvring. Marmont, whose object seemed to be to turn our position and cut off our retreat, endeavouring to deceive the British commander ; but he did not know his man. In this manœuvre the French marshal incautiously weakened his own line, and his antagonist was too much on the alert not to profit by this

blunder. The enemy began what was destined to
be the serious business of the day by a heavy
cannonade. At this time the sixth division was
halted in columns of companies. A battalion of the
Light German Legion marched by us, and, as the
last section of this corps was passing an opening in
the heights on their flank, the first shot that I saw
take effect came through, and killed five of them.
The enemy next threw out a thick swarm of
tirailleurs along his front and flank, and simul-
taneously extended his left, apparently with the
view of cutting off our communication with Rodrigo.
Our first and light divisions were then on the
extreme left ; the fourth and fifth divisions in rear
of the Arapiles ; and the sixth and seventh divisions
in reserve. The third division and cavalry occupied
the right. The enemy began an attack upon the
village of Arapiles ; but they could not dislodge the
Guards, who held it. It was now that Lord Wellington saw that the favourable moment had arrived,
and he rapidly made dispositions for the onset.

General Pakenham was directed to turn the
enemy's left with the third division, supported by
artillery and Portuguese horse. Upon their ascend-
ing the heights, a large body of cavalry came on to
charge them, but the 5th regiment, being thrown
into a good position, poured in such a well-directed
volley, that the dragoons went to the right about,
and retired in confusion. The division then pressed
on, and, everywhere outflanking the enemy, drove
them from point to point and made a great number
of prisoners. Sir Stapleton Cotton advanced with

our heavy cavalry, and in a brilliant charge cut to pieces a brigade of infantry ; but the arm to which he belonged suffered a severe loss here, by the death of General Le Marchant, who was killed by a musket ball.

The fourth and fifth divisions, supported by the sixth and seventh, moved against the enemy in front nearly at the same time ; and General Pack, with a Portuguese brigade, against the greater Arapiles. The latter officer failed in all his attempts to dislodge his opponents from this steep and rugged hill, and his men suffered severely. On the retreat of this brigade, the enemy pushed forward a large body of infantry, attacked the fourth division, who till then were gaining ground, with great spirit, and caused some confusion. General Cole was wounded in the conflict. But the fifth division came up, and, by a judicious movement, under the direction of Marshal Beresford, retrieved the fortune of the fight at this point ; and the enemy, taken in flank, were compelled to retreat. Our success on the left and centre of the French was completed by the sixth division, who succeeded in carrying the greater Arapiles. As we advanced we marched over a brigade that was lying on the ground.[1]

By this time the loss sustained by the enemy was

[1] "The advance was so rapid that very many of a body of riflemen, more numerous than the British, covering the retreat of the main body of the defeated army, threw themselves on the ground as if dead, and were run over. It is not generally known that many of them fired at the backs of the advancing line."—Extract from letter of Lieut. Smith, of 11th Regiment, 6th Division, quoted by Cannon in his *Records of the 11th North Devon Regiment.*

considerable. One of their colonels lay immediately
in front of the colours of my regiment; he was
badly wounded, and begged hard to be removed from
the field; and our commanding officer humanely
directed the drummers to take care of him. I saw
him afterwards perfectly recovered at Salamanca.

Close to the wounded colonel one of his own men
was seated with his leg broken; he had a large calabash full of wine slung by his side, and as soon as
some of our men caught a glimpse of it they determined to make free with its contents; but he
understood what they said, and instantly raising the
calabash to his head, endeavoured to empty it with
all possible expedition. Two soldiers ran forward to
stop him, but he sturdily resisted their efforts; and
when they at length succeeded in wresting the calabash from him, they found to their disappointment
that he had transferred all that had made it valuable to his own interior.

But our work was not yet finished. Notwithstanding his discomfiture at all other points, the enemy's
right was still unbroken, and was quickly reinforced
by the beaten battalions. Marmont was wounded, and
obliged to quit the field; but the command devolved
on General Clausel, who, with equal firmness and
ability, rallied the fugitives, and, with the approach of
evening in his favour, exerted himself to prevent our
further success. His new position was well selected;
both his flanks were protected by a numerous cavalry,
and the face of the heights offered an unobstructed
range for the formidable artillery that he had disposed
along his front. Lord Wellington was not long in

preparing for the attack; but the hour, unfortunately for him, was very late.

It was half-past seven when the sixth division, under General Clinton, was ordered to advance a second time and attack the enemy's line in front, supported by the third and fifth divisions. The ground over which we had to pass was a remarkably clear slope, like the glacis of a fortification—most favourable for the defensive fire of the enemy, and disadvantageous to the assailants, but the division advanced towards the position with perfect steadiness and confidence. A craggy ridge, on which the French infantry was drawn up, rose so abruptly that they could fire four or five deep; but we had approached within two hundred yards of them before the fire of musketry began, which was by far the heaviest that I have ever witnessed, and was accompanied by constant discharges of grape. An uninterrupted blaze was then maintained, so that the crest of the hill seemed to be one long streak of flame.[1] Our men came down to the charging position, and commenced firing from that level, at the same time keeping their touch to the right, so that the gaps opened by the enemy's fire were instantly filled up. At the very first volley that we received, about eighty men of the right wing of my regiment fell to the

[1] " The fire against them (the sixth division) seemed to be threefold more heavy than that sustained by the third and fifth divisions. . . . The hill was one vast sheet of flame. . . . Clinton's men looked as if they were attacking a burning mountain, the crater of which was defended by a barrier of shining steel. But nothing could stop the intrepid valour of the sixth division."—Lieutenant Grattan, *Adventures with the Connaught Rangers*, p. 253.

rear in one group ; the commanding officer immediately rode up to know the cause, and found that
they were all wounded.

Previously to the advance of the sixth division,
the light companies of the right brigade were
formed on the right of the line, and, as we moved
on, one of the enemy's howitzers was captured
by the light company of the 32nd regiment.[1] It
had been discharged once, but before the gunners
could load it again, it was taken by a rush. The
success of the attack was complete ; for as soon as
the sixth division got near enough they dashed forward with the bayonet, and another portion of our
troops acting on Clausel's right flank, his army was
quickly driven from the position into the wood in
their rear ; but before this night had come on, and
to the convenient cover and the darkness alone were
the French, who fled in great disorder, indebted for
the safety of their whole force.

They retreated the next morning through Alba de
Tormes, followed by our cavalry, who came up with
their rear-guard, and threw them into confusion.
Three battalions of their infantry, being deserted by

---

[1] Thomas Ross-Lewin, lieutenant of this company, in a letter written on
the field of battle to Mrs. Ross-Lewin, says : " Our Division has suffered
very much. . . . It was, my dear Anne, a glorious day for Old England.
The 32nd behaved in a most gallant style. We charged up a steep hill and
carried it, and then advanced to another, which our Brigade also carried,
driving the French Columns before us and taking Five pieces of Cannon.
Our Light Company had the honor of taking two Guns . . . their Army is
compleatly (sic) broken. I do not suppose you will be able to make this
scrawl out. I write it on the grass. I am much Fatigued, not having had
rest or a change of Cloathes (sic) for Eleven days. A more decisive Victory
was never gained over the Enemy. Marshal Marmont will ever remember
us ; he has lost his arm and wounded through the body."

their cavalry, formed square near the village of La Serna. They were charged with great spirit and promptitude by the 1st and 2nd regiments of heavy German horse, led on by Baron Bock, and broken; many of them were cut down, and about 900 taken prisoners; but although they had surrendered, some irregular firing continued for a short time, by which several of the dragoons were killed and wounded.

Three French generals were killed in the battle, and three more wounded, besides Marmont, who had to undergo amputation of one arm. Their loss in killed, wounded, and prisoners is computed at 14,000 men. Eleven pieces of cannon were taken, and brought into Salamanca on the following day. It was considered an odd circumstance that the 32nd regiment in this engagement recovered their big drum, which they had lost on their retreat to Corunna. Two eagles were also among the trophies of the fight. It is stated that 5100 British and Portuguese were killed or wounded.[1]   Among the killed was the gallant Le Marchant, and among the wounded were Marshal Beresford, and Generals Sir Stapleton Cotton, Leith, Cole, and Alten. The 61st, which was by far the finest regiment in the sixth division, was almost annihilated in this severe action, and was formed into a battalion with the 53rd and another regiment. The Spaniards lost only two men.

[1] The 32nd's losses were Ensigns Seymour, Newton, and 15 men killed; Captains Ross-Lewin, Toole, Lieutenants Greaves, Eason, Robinson, Bowes [Boase?], Butterworth, Ensigns Newton (second of that name), Blood (volunteer), and 111 men wounded.—Colonel Swiney, *Historical Records, Duke of Cornwall's Light Infantry*, p. 88.

In the last advance of the sixth division, I had
nearly reached the French position when a musket
ball struck me,[1] and, from the loss of blood, I soon
found it requisite to go to the rear for surgical assistance ; but, as it was already dusk, I wandered about,
ignorant whether I was or was not taking the right
direction for a village. I had walked on for some
time in this state of perplexity, when I suddenly
heard the trampling of horses, and, on calling out to
know who went there, I found, to my great satisfaction, that the party belonged to my own regiment, and
that my batman was one of their number. They
conducted me to the village of Arapiles, where we
found the men breaking open the houses for the
admittance of wounded officers, seven of whom were
of my regiment. All the habitations and outhouses,
even to the very pigsties, were speedily filled with
wounded men, whose cries to have the dead taken
away from them were incessant throughout the
whole night.

The next morning I went into Salamanca, where
I was received in the kindest manner by the good
people at my old billet. The family soon gathered
round me, and, after the proper inquiries concerning my wound, the battle, &c., began to detail
the circumstances that attended a violent explosion
which took place there in a neighbouring street since
our departure, and to show how miraculously their
house escaped, two large shells having fallen into the
courtyard without bursting. It appeared that, after

[1] This, fired at a very short distance, passed through the left arm just
under the shoulder, inflicting a very severe wound.

the reduction of the fortified convents, the powder
found in them was removed into another building
in the city, and over it was placed a guard of fifty
Spaniards; but a priest, who was desirous to see
the quantity, obtained from the officer permission to
visit the chamber in which it lay, and both of them
entered together, the latter incautiously smoking a
cigar. In two or three minutes after, the powder,
beyond a doubt ignited by a spark from the cigar,
exploded, blowing the priest, the officer, and the
guard to pieces, and laying many houses in the
vicinity in ruins. A great number of lives were lost
besides those of the soldiers who occupied the temporary magazine, and heads, legs, and arms were
scattered in every quarter of the city.

Shortly after I reached my billet, two English
ladies were brought in: one very young and beautiful, whose husband, a captain, fell in the battle;
the other, wife to a subaltern who was known to
have been very badly wounded, and of whom no
further account had been received. The faculties of
the first-mentioned female were to all appearance
totally overpowered by affliction; and her companion, while striving to bear up against her own
misfortune, also exerted herself to restore departed
reason to her friend. For some time the young
widow remained perfectly motionless, and her eyes
had settled into a vacant stare, but at length she
began to exhibit symptoms of returning recollection,
and made some signs to her countrywoman. "It is
her husband's watch that she wants," said that lady.
The watch was found fastened under her habit, and

as soon as it was placed in her hands she kissed it repeatedly, and then laid it in her bosom. The worthy old miller, whose house we occupied, melted at this touching spectacle ; neither could any of his family, from the oldest to the youngest, restrain their tears. I myself, even, though no stranger to scenes of woe, testified that my bosom had not yet become callous. The mules that were turning the mill wheels came to a full stop ; and even the brown muleteer who crossed the yard participated in the very general sympathy that the misfortunes of these afflicted ladies excited, and blubbered outright. The first paroxysms of the fair mourner's grief were succeeded by violent hysterics, and then a flood of tears came to her relief. When I found that reason began to resume her empire over her mind, I sent in my name with an offer of my services. I had previously provided their servants with rations, and, on receiving a promise from the good family of the house that every attention should be paid to them during the night, I retired to my room.

When I rose in the morning, I heard that a carriage had arrived, and that both the ladies had gone off in it to another billet. A few days after I walked out to the great square, and judge of my surprise, when the first object that arrested my attention was the lady who had caused us so much uneasiness, leaning on a young commissary with two gold epaulettes, and evidently enjoying excellent spirits. She set off with this gallant on the following day for Rodrigo.

The Irish College, being better calculated for an

hospital than any other building in Salamanca, was immediately converted into one, and the wounded were removed thither with the greatest possible expedition. When all our own wounded had been taken off the field, the French were, of course, removed ; but forty-eight hours had elapsed before this task could be completely accomplished, and the vaults of the College were the only parts of the building that remained free for the reception of these poor fellows. There, in those dismal dungeon-like lodgings, their mangled bodies and broken limbs were laid on cold, damp flags. Still, nothing that could be done for them was neglected, and the moment that the wounds of our men were dressed, the attention of the medical men was given to theirs ; and, uncomfortable as their present situation was, they would have accounted themselves fortunate had they been permitted to remain in it, when its disadvantages were compared with the miseries which they were yet to endure, for an order was issued to move the French wounded to the rear, and the only conveyances that could be procured for them were Portuguese carts, the most uneasy vehicles ever invented. It was most distressing to hear the groans and cries of those unfortunate men, as the cars jolted over the bad roads, and caused them excruciating torture and often the second dislocation of fractured bones that were in the first stage of knitting. Numbers of them expired before the train reached Rodrigo.

Our wounded officers and men recovered very slowly, a circumstance attributable either to the

influence of the climate, or the state of the blood,
impoverished by bad living. When a few of us
were able to mount our horses, we rode to the field of
battle, having been told that the pigs were uprooting
the graves, and being unwilling to suffer those of
brother officers who had fallen there to be so treated.
As we approached Arapiles, we were shocked and
astonished at the extraordinary want of feeling and
delicacy that the Spaniards betrayed. They left the
naked bodies of the dead to lie unburied, close to
their very thresholds ; and I remarked one house in
particular, which no one could enter without stepping
over a human corpse. We found a long line of
vultures on the battle - ground ; these ill-omened
birds stand quite erect, and might be mistaken by
a distant spectator for a regiment drawn up in a
single rank. Here was a fine field for them ; the
bodies of men and horses, which an attempt had
been made to burn, lay everywhere in heaps, only
half consumed. After the action, wherever the car-
case of a horse was found, such human bodies as
had fallen near were collected and thrown over it,
and these again were covered with branches of
trees, which, being quite green, made too weak a
fire to reduce them to ashes ; consequently the air
had become very offensive, and the whole scene was
extremely revolting. A vast number of pigs, which
had been driven hither by their owners, also roamed
about the field, and shared the loathsome feast with
the vultures. We were enabled to discover the
grave of only one officer—the same who led the
forlorn hope at the successful assault of the forts at

Salamanca.   A knee and a hand appeared above
the ground, and we knew whose corpse it was from
the shape of the fingers, which were remarkably
long, and from the colour of his pantaloons.   We
gathered all the stones that we could find in the
vicinity of the grave, and raised a rude heap over
the remains of our gallant friend.   The cairn would
at least have served to secure them from the attacks
of the pigs and vultures ; but the Spaniards removed
all such impediments to their ploughing before many
days had passed.

¹ Ensign Newton.

CHAPTER XII

AFTER the action at Salamanca, Lord Wellington,
driving King Joseph before him, moved upon Madrid.
The citizens received the allied troops with loud
acclamations, and nothing could surpass the enthusiasm with which Lord Wellington was greeted
by all classes. Don Carlos de Espana was named
Governor of the city, but this reminds me of one of
my anecdotes.

A surgeon, belonging to one of the British regiments at this time in Madrid, paid a visit to the
tombs where the remains of the kings of Spain and
many of their descendants repose ; and among them
his attention was directed by the sacristan to the
head and trunk of the ill-fated Don Carlos, whose
tragic story once excited so great interest throughout
Europe, and has since been revived by Alfieri, who
has taken it for the foundation of one of his dramas.
The doctor, who was curious in skulls, wished to
examine the Spanish prince's more minutely than
was practicable while it continued in its present
abode ; he, therefore, watching his opportunity, laid

N

irreverent hands upon it, contrived to conceal it under his cloak, and walked off with it to his quarters. But the disappearance of the head was soon remarked, the depredator was followed, and no persuasions could induce the guardians of the precious relics to suffer this portion of them to remain in his possession one moment longer. However, the doctor secured two of this celebrated prince's teeth before he yielded the remainder of his plunder to his inexorable pursuers. We were afterwards in the same regiment together. I recollect going to his room one morning at an early hour—a skull was placed on his breakfast table. "Stay and breakfast with us," said he. I had no objection to remain at the table with his then dumb companion; the only effect which the presence of this *memento mori* could have had on me would be my feeling it to be immaterial whether I took tea or coffee, as it would be all the same a few years thence. "Sit down," added the doctor, "I will give you a basin of soup; one of the band died last night with a most extraordinarily shaped head, and it is there on the fire boiling." This was rather too much, and, taking up my cap, I left the worthy son of Esculapius to breakfast without my company.

On the 1st of September Lord Wellington quitted Madrid with four divisions, and marched through Valladolid in the direction of Burgos. He was joined on the way by 12,000 Spaniards, called the army of Gallicia. The enemy retired before the allies, and passed through Burgos on the 17th of September. Lord Wellington, though unprotected at the time with heavy artillery, determined to lay siege to that place, a fortress of great strength and well garrisoned. It was invested on the 20th by the first and sixth divisions and two Portuguese brigades, the rest of the army taking up an advanced position to cover the besieging force.

My wound being now skinned over, I took charge of a party of two hundred and fifty men, and set out on the 29th for Burgos. At every stage I met wounded men returning to Salamanca from the siege. It was the time of the vintage, and the peasants were busily employed gathering the grapes into vaults outside the villages. These vaults were considerable excavations, into which the grapes were thrown through holes at the top, and they communicated with the houses by long subterraneous passages.

I halted one day at Valladolid, a very ancient town ; it commands both the roads leading to Lisbon and Madrid. The line from Irun through Madrid was kept in good repair by the French, and, in order to preserve the communication along it, they erected blockhouses at short intervals, and fortified some of the villages through which it runs. The blockhouses might contain from two to four hundred men, and some had eight guns mounted on them ; they were entered by means of ladders, and were impregnable to the irregular Spanish troops. Still, such was the activity and boldness of the guerillas, that they were constantly cutting off detachments of the invaders, when marching between these posts. The enemy could not send a letter without an escort, which was

the source of a very harassing duty to their troops.
The Plaça Mayor at Valladolid is surrounded on all
sides by a broad piazza, under which the inhabitants
promenade in great numbers during wet weather.
The ladies at my billet denied that they had any
acquaintance with the French officers, and declared
that on no account would they hold any intercourse
with the enemies of their country ; but, soon after
this parade of patriotism, I found in a table-drawer
several cards of invitation that they had received
from the now disowned militaires—evidence that
militated sadly against the sincerity of their expressed
sentiments, and the reality of their abhorrence of a
gay and sprightly son of Mars, though his sword
might be a little stained with the blood of their
countrymen.

Both the officers who accompanied me, and I
myself, experienced considerable difficulty in pre-
venting our party from plundering ; but we reached
Burgos in fourteen days, without leaving one of our
men behind, or hearing any serious complaints preferred against them by the natives ; which, the
Adjutant-General said, were circumstances highly
creditable to the officers, as no such instance of
regularity had occurred before. On the road my
wound broke out afresh, and became very troublesome ; when three days' march from Burgos, we met
an assistant-surgeon of the Guards with some wounded
men of his corps, but he could not give me a bit of
plaister. I could not help thinking it very strange
that he should be so unprovided.

The siege was not advancing. The castle stood

on a steep and rocky eminence, but the principal part of the works were constructed by the French. At the top of the hill an old tower had been altered to a formidable battery; there were, besides, three distinct lines of defences, well provided with cannon. The garrison was about 2500 strong.

On the evening of the 19th of September, a detached work in a commanding situation was carried by assault. Here batteries were erected, but Lord Wellington had only three eighteen-pounders and five howitzers. On the night of the 22nd an attempt to scale the outer wall failed. Then two of the three eighteen-pounders were dismounted by the superior fire of the castle. The besiegers next tried the sap and the mine, but with considerable loss of life on their part; and, when a breach was effected in the first wall on the 29th by the explosion of a mine, the troops directed to storm lost their way, and the garrison, in the space of a few hours, repaired the damage done.

On the 4th of October another breach was made, and a lodgment was effected by the assailants; but a sortie of the garrison on the following day caused considerable mischief, though they obtained only temporary possession of the post. A parallel was then commenced toward the second line of defences. Throughout the siege the workmen had to contend with many difficulties and great danger; it was nearly impossible for them to cover themselves, as they had to work on rock, barely concealed by the surface of clay, and so hard that it required extraordinary labour to make the slightest impression on it. When our troops had established themselves within the outer wall, the enemy placed shells in long scoops, and, lighting the fuses, lifted them from the ditch to the crest of the glacis, whence they rolled down the slope, and exploded among the working parties. The musketry of the besieged was also very galling.

During the night of the 8th, another desperate sortie of the garrison was attended with much loss and damage on our part. Ten days after, the howitzer battery, five twenty-four pounders, breached the second line ; but the assailants, consisting of detachments from the Guards and the German legion, were repulsed by the heavy fire of the defenders, though they had succeeded in clearing the breach.

The city of Burgos, once the capital of the kingdom of Castile, lies close under the castle ; but, notwithstanding this rather undesirable proximity to the formidable object of contention, the citizens remained in their houses, and the market was open as usual. To get to this repository of the necessaries of life, we had to cross a particular street, which was commanded by the castle, and whenever we appeared in it musketry was fired at us, so that we generally traversed it at our best pace. The cathedral is a large and very ancient structure, built magnificently in the Gothic style, and it is said to bear a close resemblance to York Minster. An immense chandelier of solid silver is suspended before the altar, and it was a matter of surprise to us that the French should have allowed it to hang

there so long. My regiment had very comfortable
quarters in a convent ; but other corps were not so
well lodged.

A staff-surgeon, who looked upon an hospital
waggon as a much better thing than his billet, had
removed his bed to one, and between the hours of
dinner and rest, he was in the habit of playing a
cool rubber with three of his friends in this his
new tenement. One wet night the old party had
assembled : a jug of hot water, a magnum, whose
contents were never purchased at the apothecary's,
and glasses which never remained empty long,
graced the board, while the pattering of the rain on
the staunch tilt of the waggon served to increase
their comfort by continually reminding them how
very different they would feel were they exposed at
that hour, as so many of us were, to all the inclem-
ency of such weather; in short, no set ever enjoyed
themselves more. But what can be so fleeting and
unstable as the happiness of the short-sighted beings
that inhabit the surface of this revolving globe ?   A
lieutenant of the corps of drivers,[1] whose spleen very
probably was out of order, suffered himself to be
nettled by what he considered the unceremonious
occupation of his waggon, the doctor not having
thought proper to ask his consent ; and he therefore
resolved upon playing the gamblers a slippery trick
in the midst of their enjoyment. Full of his un-
charitable purpose, he ordered out a pair of horses,

---

[1] This is said to have been " Tom " Ross-Lewin, who was then on
temporary duty with this corps. On the occupants complaining of their
numerous injuries, he exclaimed, " Sure, hadn't they *a doctor* with them ! "

had them harnessed to the waggon with the least possible noise, and whispered to the driver to proceed as hard as he could to headquarters—a drive of two miles over a very rugged road. The order was faithfully obeyed.

" Smack went the whip, round went the wheels,"

and head over heels went the tenants of the vehicle, all losing their equilibrium by the sudden jerk at starting, together with table, hot water, bottles, glasses, punch, and lamp oil, nor could they recover from their uneasy and prostrate postures, before they had jolted over ruts and stones every foot of the way to headquarters. There they arrived with a pleasing confusion of ideas, but without injury, if we except a few slight scalds, cuts, and contusions, which, indeed, were hardly worth mentioning, as the travellers carried their surgeon with them.

But, in the meantime, more serious matters were in agitation at headquarters. While we at Burgos were thinking of making a fresh assault on the castle, Soult had formed a junction with King Joseph, and their combined force amounted to no fewer than 60,000 men. General Souham, having joined Clausel and assumed the chief command, had remained during the siege at a convenient distance from the covering army, but was afforded no opportunity of interrupting the siege. It was only on the 18th of October that any very menacing demonstrations proceeded from the enemy, who had been strongly reinforced. They were followed by some movements of the allied troops, and headquarters were changed.

On the 20th, our outposts were driven in by the French ; but they were soon compelled to abandon the ground they had gained, and they did not renew their efforts.

On the 21st, Lord Wellington, threatened on more than one side by superior forces, decided, of course, on raising the siege without delay. Our retreat commenced after nightfall. We passed over the Bridge of Burgos, which was commanded by the castle, on a still dark night, with the utmost caution ; not a word was spoken, and no sound was heard save the tread of the numerous troops marching past, while the garrison threw blue lights at short intervals over the ramparts, that no enemy might approach unobserved. There was something peculiarly awful in this night march of so great a body of men—the cautious silence, the dead hour, and the consideration that in an instant the guns of the castle might send death among us. Some of the last troops had a few shots fired at them ; but altogether this clever movement was so well conducted, that the garrison were ignorant of it until it was too late for them to cause us any serious annoyance. The army was at this time sadly reduced by sickness ; my regiment did not muster more than one hundred and fifty men, although it had seven hundred and fifty in the country.

The French army followed us, and on the 23rd some skirmishing took place between their van and our rear-guard. They were greatly superior to us in cavalry. We marched from the Douro under circumstances of severe privation ; only one pound of biscuit was served out to each man for his six days' provisions. All the bridges were blown up as soon as the last of our men had passed over, which of course checked the pursuit ; but the enemy's advanced guard contrived to come up with us in the evenings, when a show of resistance would be made on our part. In the mornings we continued our retreat some hours before daybreak. We had to ford a number of small rivers, which, having become much swollen by the late heavy rains, contributed to render our march still more uncomfortable. One day that it had rained incessantly, the colonel and I got in late to our bivouac, and were waiting with impatience for the arrival of our baggage-horses, when the colonel's batman staggered in, quite drunk, and bringing the pleasing intelligence that they were lost. It was evident that he in the first place had opened the panniers and drunk our stock of spirits, and that then a party of Spaniards who had crossed our route, finding the horses without attendants, had taken the liberty to make them their own : the deplorable consequence was, that neither the colonel nor I had left us a single article, whether of clothes or of comforts, besides what we chanced to carry about us.

Having crossed the Carrion, we took up at Duenas a very strong position on rising ground, with the stream in our front. Some of our troops occupied a large convent before the town, and we had some guns masked there, which were intended to open on the enemy as soon as they should approach sufficiently near. With better management this battery would have done much execution, but, very foolishly, the guns were discharged on the first few dragoons that came within range, and consequently the ruse failed of its desired effect. A village in front of our left was seized by the French ; some Spaniards and Brunswickers were sent to retake it, but did not succeed until after a long and rather hot contest. An uncommonly level plain, extending before our position to a considerable distance in every direction, afforded us an opportunity of viewing the whole French army, and so great did their numbers appear to be, that report makes Lord Wellington declare, on this occasion, that he had never seen at any former period so many Frenchmen in his front. They showed a splendid body of cavalry, and a formidable array of infantry formed in contiguous columns, and certainly they presented a most imposing military spectacle. After halting here for one day, we continued our retrograde movement.

I rode a tired mule on the march the day that we left Duenas, and, to add to my enjoyment, the sorry jade fell in crossing a river, and soused me well. After this preparation, I passed the night on some wet chaff, and in the morning I found that the curtains of my eyes had become so stiff that they could not raise themselves ; and whenever I wanted particularly to take a peep at what was going on, I was obliged to employ my fingers to keep them open.

Upon our crossing the Douro, the bridges were blown up, and, as the river was not fordable, and the French were endeavouring to repair the bridge at

Tordesillas, we rested for two days in front of this place. Here we ascertained that several men had deserted, and that some sick, who were unable to keep up, had been made prisoners.

The retreat was still conducted under very disastrous circumstances. Our light cavalry were done up, and the artillery horses nearly so. Men, spent with fatigue, fell into the enemy's hands, and desertion continued. The roads were in dreadful condition ; the streams to be forded, many and swollen ; the bivouacs wet, and almost without fires ; and food was as scarce as fuel ; many of the troops had neither bread nor biscuits, and only rations of carrion-like beef. The excessive dread that seemed to be felt, lest any part of our commissariat should fall into the enemy's hands, proved very injurious to the troops, whose physical strength was exhausted through want of the necessary supplies.

The Spaniards turn their pigs into the woods when young,[1] having first put private marks on them, and in this manner they are reared without any further trouble on coarse grass and acorns. Some straggling Spanish and Portuguese followed our column, shooting these animals, and bringing the flesh to the officers for sale. One day, after a total abstinence from food for the forty-eight hours preceding, I bought a piece of what I supposed to be pork from one of these fellows, and broiled it on some embers ; but, having neither bread nor salt, I became so unwell soon after I had finished my un-

[1] Lieutenant Grattan gives a most amusing description of a desperate onslaught upon these animals made by the 4th Division.

savoury meal, that I with difficulty kept up during the remainder of the march; and the discovery that those ruffians, when disappointed by not meeting pigs, had sometimes cut off the flesh of dead men and sold it for pork, had no tendency to diminish the nausea that I already felt. Two officers of the 28th regiment, having clearly ascertained that they had been imposed on in this way, were taken very ill, and, for years after, the bare mention of pork was sufficient to make them shudder.

We reached our old position in front of Salamanca on the 8th of November, and halted there for four days. Sir Rowland Hill, who had broken up from his position on the approach of Soult and the usurper in the beginning of September, had effected his junction with Lord Wellington three days before. Ballasteros was subsequently banished to Ceuta for his disgraceful inactivity and obstinacy, in not entering into the views of the British leader. The light division had been a good deal engaged during the retreat. The loss occasioned to us by fatigue and desertion was considerable, and some baggage fell into the hands of the enemy.

The junction of the French armies, which had been advancing against us from two points in overwhelming force, was now effected. Soult took command of the whole, and a very pretty command he had, not fewer than 90,000 men and a formidable artillery. Our force mustered only 52,000 strong, of all nations, and the French cavalry were nearly as three to one, compared with ours. The British general was always crippled by his weakness in this arm. Of course, we could make no stand in our position at San Christoval against the pursuing armies. We crossed the Tormes by the bridge of Salamanca, marching through the town; but how different were our sensations at this time from those that we experienced on our first entry! Then we felt elated and confident of victory, now we were completely crestfallen; then we were hailed as deliverers, but now regarded as persons who brought ruin in their train; for the French would inevitably enter the city, and perhaps take revenge for the enthusiastic reception that we had met with a few months before. The moment that our rear-guard had issued from Salamanca, the sign-boards at the coffee-houses were turned; for on one side was painted, " *Caffe de los Tras Nationes,*" in compliment to the allies, and on the other, " *Caffe de l'Imperador,*" to please the French; thus they were always prepared to receive either party. However, I will not do the inhabitants the injustice to impute to them such indifference that they were not more inclined in favour of the British than the French; on the contrary, I am certain that their conduct, as regarded the latter, was only the result of fear; and, as regarded the former, of patriotism and good feeling. No *vivas* hailed the arrival of the French; coldness and silence, or, at best, a forced civility, were all that they met with, or had any reason to expect from the people in general. I felt confident, as I passed through, that my old host, the miller, would still have been ready to receive me, though marching in a retreating army, with a hearty welcome, and I regretted that I had not time to call on him and his honest family.

We passed one night on the ground where the battle was fought. The enemy did not seem to be desirous to force us into an action, and when the British commander gave them an opportunity of engaging, they compelled him, by threatening his communications with Ciudad Rodrigo, to set his army in motion without loss of time, and take the roads leading to Portugal.

So much rain had fallen latterly, that the roads were in a most wretched condition, and in many places knee-deep, and we had, as usual, various deep streams to ford. All this was dreadfully distressing to men who were already nearly worn out by long marches, want of rest, bad living, and the weight of their arms and accoutrements ; and several, sinking through weakness, were smothered in the mud. On one spot I saw the wife of a Portuguese soldier lying dead with an infant at her breast, from which the little orphan vainly tried to extract its accustomed nourishment. A little further on, there was a poor fellow stretched by the roadside, with his mouth full of mud, and evidently at the point of death ; and, as we passed, a Spanish muleteer stooped down to him, and said jestingly, in his language, for he was his countryman, " It is very cold, sir."

Such tents as we had began now to be left standing on the ground that we had occupied for the night, as we no longer possessed the means of carrying them. The heaviness of the rain, and the chilliness of the air, induced me to sacrifice appearance in some measure to comfort, for I was desirous, if possible, to escape a fit of the ague ; I therefore unrolled my blanket, spread it as a mantle over my shoulders, and fastened it in front with a skewer, somewhat after the manner in which a Moor wears his haick, and then flapping my cocked hat behind, I rode thus attired on the flank of my company. This alteration in my costume was neither very becoming, nor very military, but it was very comfortable ; and although at first it excited much laughter at my expense, a long row of white mantles was visible on the next day on the line of march. But I am not the only person of inventive genius who has first been ridiculed and then imitated.

One of the queerest figures observed on this retreat was an eccentric subaltern of my corps ; besides enveloping his form in a blanket, and wearing the hinder flap of his cocked hat down, he was mounted on a cast dragoon-horse, sixteen hands high and gaunt and raw-boned in the extreme, and he always rode with a gridiron slung over the shoulder of his hungry steed. When we took up our ground at night, he used to stretch himself at full length on the grass, and direct his servant, a Kerry mountaineer, to proceed forthwith to thatch him ; this was done by first bending twigs over him, so as to leave him just sufficient room to roll from one side to the other, and then covering the arch thickly with straw or sedge. In this manner, through the ingenuity of his thatcher, he contrived to keep himself perfectly dry and warm, while we lay cold, wet, and comfortless. Neither did he feel the want of money so sensibly as his brother officers did, for he made it a

rule never to listen to petty scruples, nor to spare a
Spaniard's hen-roost as long as it had a single tenant
remaining. He always said that a dinner was the
least he might expect from the people for fighting
their battles ; but, as he was not sure that his logic
would satisfy them, and at the same time wished
to prevent them from preferring complaints against
him, he took care to pick his birds near some other
officer's hut or quarters, and generally at the door
of one particular captain, whose sense of propriety
was remarkably nice ; of course the last-mentioned
person, in consequence of this trick, was repeatedly
accused of plundering poultry by angry complainants
besetting his dwelling in the mornings, and vehe-
mently using the provoking argument, *ecce signum*,
as they pointed to the circumjacent feathers.

On the 16th and 17th of November there was
some trifling skirmishing, and on the latter day Sir
Edward Paget was taken prisoner ; he was alone,
and did not suspect that the enemy's cavalry was so
near—they spread out in every direction to take him,
and he, being well mounted, made great exertions to
effect his escape, but was so completely hemmed in
that he was at length forced to surrender.

As we drew near to Ciudad Rodrigo, the French
began to desist from the pursuit, and disturbed our
rearguard no more ; but although we had got rid of
them, many other annoyances remained, and had it
not been for that active partisan, Don Julian Sanchez,
who mounted about eight hundred helpless men of
ours behind his guerillas, and conveyed them in that
manner to the above-mentioned fortress, we must

O

have lost them, in addition to the many others who perished in this disastrous retreat.   My regiment lost fifty men ;[1] the 82nd regiment two hundred ; and every corps in the army had their casualties to a greater or less extent.   The thirty-first day from the date of our departure from the position in front of Burgos saw us arrive under the walls of Ciudad Rodrigo.   In the neighbourhood of that place we found some very extensive cabbage gardens, with the produce of which our batmen took the liberty to feed our half-famished cattle.   An order immediately appeared to the effect that the different regiments on this march should pay for the damage so done, and the Spaniards were directed to furnish an estimate of the value of their plundered vegetables, which estimate, as it may be supposed, was not very moderate.

Lord Wellington also issued a very angry order, accusing the army of great relaxation of discipline during the retreat, and denying that the marches were either so long, or so harassing, as in any degree to palliate such disgraceful irregularity.   It is very true that no circumstances can ever render desertion justifiable, and all who were guilty of a crime so discreditable to the character of a soldier merited the severest censure and punishment ; but to blame the men who left their ranks only when their physical strength no longer enabled them to keep their places on the march was the height of injustice ; and the chief reason why so many did break down was the

[1] During the operations before Burgos the 32nd lost one man killed, together with Ensign Quick, and three men wounded.

absence of the necessary supplies that should have
attended the troops. It is acknowledged that it
would be very galling to see an enemy's bulletin
puffed up with accounts of captures of a portion of
our commissariat ; but I leave it to others to decide
whether, in such a case, it is more advisable to incur
the risk of losing a few mules, in order to secure
to the troops a proper supply of provisions, which
would make them equal to greater fatigue, or to
send forward the commissariat, a course which,
while it really gives the army in pursuit a larger
number of prisoners, may deprive them of the
boast that a part of our stores have fallen into
their hands. The decision will, of course, depend in
a great measure on the comparative value of mules
and men in the estimation of the arbiter.[1]

One of our captains, on the evening of our arrival
at Ciudad Rodrigo, met with an adventure which an-
noyed him not a little. This officer had a strong
and unconquerable aversion to remain in the same
house with a dead person, and his servant, Murphy,
cherished a similar antipathy to such fellow-lodgers.
Now the Spaniards take very little trouble with their
dead ; they merely dress them in their best suits, lay
them on biers without coffins, and in the course of a
few hours see them removed to the place of interment
by a couple of men each, a priest walking on in front,
and a bellman preceding him again by a few paces ;
and even before these unostentatious funeral arrange-

---

[1] All regimental officers who shared the dangers and hardships of this
retreat were greatly incensed, and justly so, by the tone of Wellington's
orders. Grattan devotes several pages of his narrative to this matter.

ments are commenced, the corpses are left to lie
unwatched in the courtyards or lumber-rooms. This
preface will serve to account for Murphy's exclama-
tion, soon after he and his master had taken possession of their billet, " Holy Biddy ! Here is a
corpse, sir, in the inside room ? " " You don't say
so ? " exclaimed the captain. " My hand to you,
sir, but there is," added Murphy in affirmation ; " a
fine old lady as dead as a herring." " Then go off
directly, Murphy, for the mule," rejoined the captain, " put up the baggage, and follow me to the
alcalde's, for I will not stay a moment longer in this
billet." Accordingly, he repaired to the magistrate,
and obtained a much better quarter than the first.
The mule was quickly unloaded there, and everything promised well for the captain's enjoying a
bon repos. " Go into that closet, Murphy," said he ;
" they tell me that there is plenty of wood in it ;
make a good fire. Bring out more of it ; this is
something like a billet." He was proceeding in this
manner, alternately giving directions and expressing
his satisfaction, when he was suddenly interrupted by
Murphy's roaring out, " Blood an' turf, sir, here is
another corpse, standing against the wall as stiff as
the leg of a pot ? " It was then too dark and too
late to think of procuring other quarters ; our captain, therefore, had no alternative but to remain *in
statu quo,* and he sat him down dejected by his fire,
ever and anon casting a jealous eye on the closet
door. His billet was the residence of a very ancient
family, one of whose ancestors, having followed Guy
Lusignan from the Holy Land to the kingdom of

Cyprus, had died in that island, and his body, being embalmed, had been sent to his native country and to the head of his honourable house, in the possession of whose descendants it had since remained for centuries, nor had it ever occasioned the least annoyance to any person previously to the arrival of Murphy and his master.

From Ciudad Rodrigo we marched to Barquilla, where we made a halt of three days before we crossed the border. We entered Portugal drenched with rain, as Jupiter Pluvius was the deity of the day, and we took up our ground in a ploughed field. The green wood was so wet that it would not burn, and those who had provisions could not cook them ; consequently it was hardly possible to conceive anything much more wretched in its way than was our situation. Nevertheless, an aide-de-camp arrived from General Clinton to inform us that the general had no objection to our making ourselves as comfortable as circumstances would permit !

The army, with the exception of Sir Rowland Hill's corps, which returned to Estremadura, now went into cantonments in the province of Beira. We took up our winter quarters, on the 3rd of December 1812, at St. Jago. This village is situated in the midst of beautiful and romantic scenery : the mountains are covered with pine, cork, and chestnut trees ; and the valleys yield in abundance all such productions of the earth as are requisite for the support of man. Previously to the invasion by the French armies, it had been a happy retired spot, affording an agreeable abode to the wealthy hidalgo

as well as to the humble peasant; but, since that
event, the best houses had been destroyed, and the
principal families had fled to seek elsewhere a more
secure place of refuge from the horrors of war.
The colonel's billet, which was also mine, was a
large house divided into spacious rooms, but none
of them had a fireplace. In consequence of the
want of so great a comfort in their proper apartments, the Portuguese families retire to their kitchens
in the very cold weather, and sit there in company
with their domestics round the fires, which are
kindled on raised platforms, such as may be seen in
a blacksmith's forge. They do not use grates, and
their victuals are cooked in deep earthen pans called .
panellas ; these utensils are ranged in a circle, the
enclosed space being occupied by the coals. Our
large sitting-room would have been most uncomfortable, had it not been for some charcoal embers
that we kept in a pierced earthen vessel of the kind
used by the natives for roasting chestnuts. We sat
round this fire for a few evenings without experi-
encing any inconvenience from the fumes of the
charcoal, until an officer, who was in delicate health,
happening to pass a day with us, fell from his chair
in a kind of stupor, while we were at dinner ; this
we ascribed merely to debility ; but shortly after, on
rising from the table, and walking across the room,
I also dropped down, to all appearance lifeless,
although, on recovering, I could not recollect that
I had felt any unusual sensation before the attack.
Still, as smoke was never visible in the room, we
did not suspect the real cause of those fits, until the

colonel was suddenly seized, some days afterwards, with strong convulsions, and did not recover for several hours. We were then convinced that those attacks were the effects of the charcoal, and of course we used it no more. From that time we drank our wine mulled in order to keep up the heat of the body internally, as the means of doing so externally were denied us.

The woods near St. Jago afford coverts for hundreds of wolves, and the Portuguese have frequently offered young ones to our officers for sale, at half a dollar each. A commissary belonging to our army succeeded in making one of these animals so tame that it followed him like a dog wherever he went. The old wolves were constantly seen at daylight, feeding on the offal in the places where the cattle were slaughtered.

Now that the army had taken up its winter-quarters, and not even a report of any intended movement was heard, I obtained leave of absence, as I had some private affairs to settle at home, and proceeded to Lisbon. For a month after my arrival in the Portuguese capital, no vessel sailed from thence for England; consequently I had time to visit some places which I had neglected to see on former occasions. One of these was the chapel of St. Roch, which really is a superb place of worship. There is a recess in it dedicated to St. John the Baptist, and adorned with a representation in mosaic of the saint baptizing in Jordan, which is the *chef-d'œuvre* of the art. When the sacristan drew the curtain that stretched across the niche and gave me

a full view of this wonderful piece of art, I thought
it a most beautiful painting ; but to convince me of
my error, my conductor furnished me with a ladder,
and thus enabled me to examine it more closely, and
to perceive the joining of the stones. The Portuguese say that it is invaluable, and Junot would have
transported it to Paris, had its removal been practicable. The representation of the water flowing over
the Baptist's feet was so exquisite an imitation of
nature that you would almost fancy you heard the
rippling of the current. So great a proportion of
the wealth of this country is in the possession of the
ecclesiastics that the decorations of the principal
churches and monasteries are everywhere on the
grandest scale.

The chief attraction at the theatre was Vestris,
and it was much frequented by the admirers of the
ars saltandi. The British officers spun out the night
at the faro tables. The gambling-house most in
vogue was kept by a dignitary of the Church, who,
with his black cross hanging from his neck, did not
scruple to sit as banker between his assistants. Some
of our people had been very successful in play, and
they made known their system to others of their
countrymen, who readily agreed to adopt it. But
the clerical manager of the hell proved too deep for
them ; he discovered the plan of the confederates ;
and, one night, having set a few packs of cards in a
particular way, he left their purses in deplorable
emptiness.

The billet assigned to me was a very good one.
The family saw a vast number of visitors—all well-

dressed persons, and among them several girls of large fortunes were pointed out to me. I made some inquiries respecting the nature of their portions, being desirous, though quite disinterestedly, to learn whether they were to be paid in cash, land, or in wine, like that of the Cadiz merchant's daughter ; [1] and I was told in reply that they consisted of jewels, and that when a Portuguese damsel gave her hand to her lover, she gave him with it perhaps ten thousand pounds in rings. The ladies here take as much pride in the smallness of their feet as the Chinese ; but very few of those whom I have seen had good legs or well-turned ankles. Their figures are generally ungraceful, indeed I may say clumsy ; but I believe that *embonpoint* is admired in Portugal, and that the belles leave no means untried to preserve their fair forms from the sin of leanness. The most remarkable point in their evening dress was the profusion of jewels that adorned their persons, and of artificial flowers that they wore in their hair. When the company assembled at the soirées, each guest was presented with a glass of water, and the gentlemen handed their snuff-boxes to one another. I cannot say that I approved very much of those water-drinking and snuff-taking *conversazioni;* for I have no particular predilection for the pure beverage of the fountain, and I never make a soot-bag of my nose.

One of my Lisbon acquaintances was Dr. O'C——ll; he had been settled in that city for the twenty years preceding, and he was very civil to a brother officer

---

[1] This refers to an attachment formed by a handsome young subaltern of the 32nd to a lady whose entire fortune consisted of 130 pipes of wine.

of mine as well as to me. During the occupation of
Portugal by the French, he had been thrown into
prison by Junot's orders, because he had happened
unluckily to say that one of that Marshal's aides-de-
camp rode a very handsome horse—a remark that
was construed into a hint that the horse, as it was
very probable, had been stolen. The doctor, it was
said, had acquired a good fortune, and kept a comfortable establishment ; and my companion, who was
rather a *bon vivant*, seemed to wish to partake of his
hospitality by means of an invitation to dine, and
even told me that he would give him a hint the next
time they should meet. He kept his word ; for,
encountering Mr. O'C——ll the day following, he
began to say, after some commonplace remarks,
" Pray, doctor, should an English officer become
acquainted with a Portuguese gentleman in Lisbon,
just as we are now, for instance, what sort of attention should be paid to the stranger ? " The wily
doctor replied without a moment's hesitation, " Everything in Portugal is done by snuff—if the parties
desire to be intimate, a reciprocal, temporary ex-
change of boxes takes place—an appointment is then
made to meet in the evening at some coffee-house,
and they wish each other a good morning for the
present ; in the evening the appointment is punctually
kept, each takes a cup of coffee and a glass of liqueur,
and, after spending an hour or two in conversation,
they take a parting pinch and return to their respective homes. Such, sir," added he, with a grin,
" is our system of friendly intercourse." The *militaire*,
half-tickled, half-chagrined by this reply, putting on

something like "a smile through a tear," and pulling
off his hat, began to scratch his head rather violently.
I could not altogether stifle a most untimely laugh,
and the doctor, remarking that he had a visit to pay,
wished us a good day.

At length a transport was directed to sail for England with convalescents from different regiments, and
I embarked in her as senior officer. She was a large
vessel, mounted ten guns, and had on board a considerable supply of small arms, which were distributed amongst such of the soldiers as were able
to use them. When we got to sea we kept a good
look out for privateers, but continued our voyage
without interruption until we entered the Channel.
A thick fog came on then, and, while it lasted, a brig
ran close under our stern, her bowsprit being over
our taffrail before we observed her. We hailed, but
received no answer. This looked suspicious, and
the cook was immediately ordered to apply the poker
to the touch-hole of one of our stern-chasers; the
gun, however, did not go off, which was a fortunate
circumstance for all parties, as the supposed privateer
proved to be one of our own Channel cruisers.

On the same night we had another alarm. The
watch called out, "A suspicious sail ahead," and all
hands were soon at their quarters; but, after a sus-
pense of some moments, the cook suddenly exclaimed, "A fine landfall! the old Eddystone." He
was perfectly right. We had mistaken the lighthouse
for a ship—a mistake that may easily occur in thick
weather.

Not long after the fog cleared off, and we entered

Plymouth Sound, which, together with Mount Edge-combe, presented a beautiful prospect at sunrise. Another hour saw us landed once more on the happy shore of old England, the land of liberty and sterling worth, for the maintenance of whose glory and safety we had cheerfully endured the fatigues and privations of a soldier's life, and perilled life and limb in more than one bloody field ; and on the Patrick's Day following I reached my ultimate destination in Ireland.

CHAPTER XIII

Return to Spain—Fortress of San Sebastian—Bravery of Lieutenant Edward Ross-Lewin—His death—Bayonne—Surprise of a French picket—A fair prisoner—Battle of Orthes—Defeat of Soult—French Connaught Rangers—Wellington and the Ranger—A ragged regiment—Ball at Toulouse—A military musician—The kilts prove offensive to French delicacy—Lord Keith—A judge of claret.

Note—Losses of the 32nd regiment, July–December 1813.

In the middle of October, 1813, I proceeded to Dublin, on my way to Portsmouth, and sailed from our Irish capital on board a Holyhead packet. The weather was very bad, and we lay-to for forty-eight hours in a heavy gale of wind. The nights were dark, and on the second, the mate suddenly heard an unusual rustling in the water ; he instantly rushed into the cabin, seized a lantern, and hurrying on deck, held up the light. The next moment two brigs scudding under bare poles passed close to the cutter, one at either side, and but for the activity of the mate, would in all probability have run us down.

On my arrival at Portsmouth, I found that the fleets bound for the north of Spain and the Mediterranean were detained by contrary winds ; a circumstance which was lucky for me at least, as it gave me an opportunity of proceeding with them to my destination ; but the continuance of the delay prevented me from joining the army in time to be present at the first operations which followed the surrender of Pampeluna.[1]

On the 27th of November the whole weighed under convoy of the *Indus*, seventy-four, and the *Garland*, sloop of war. On the 4th of December we encountered a tremendous gale, such as no person on board had ever experienced. The fleets were dispersed in all directions, and my ship lay-to for several days. When the storm had somewhat abated, we fell in with a portion of both fleets and the seventy-four. The latter took us all into Corunna, and leaving the Mediterranean ships there, convoyed the rest thence to St. Andero, where we cast anchor on the 14th, having been in all eighteen days at sea. We found this town very dismal and uncomfortable ; the mud in the streets was ankle deep, and the houses were filled with British sick and wounded. Mules were not to be had, unless at a most exorbitant price ; and the army was one hundred and fifty miles off. The run from St. Andero to Passaes is generally of no more than four-and-twenty hours, and the latter port was the nearest to the army where the supplies, with which the ships were freighted, could conveniently be landed ; accordingly I decided upon proceeding thither in the transport.

We sailed, and were off the harbour of Passaes on the 17th of December. The entrance to it has at first sight the appearance of being an artificial

[1] During the course of these operations his brother, Lieutenant Thomas Ross-Lewin, was twice (once severely) wounded. Between July and December 1813 the 32nd had lost Colonel Hinde, Lieutenant-Colonel Wood, Captain Toole, Lieutenants Boaz and Ross-Lewin, Ensigns Lloyd, and O'Brien Butler, and about 150 men killed and wounded.

strait cut through a steep mountain, and is danger-
ously narrow for large vessels in bad weather.   As
it was quite calm, we stood off until daylight, and the
next morning, having fine clear weather, the fleet
made for the harbour.   Some of the ships ran close
to St. Sebastian, from which place guns were fired,
and signals made for the fleet to anchor there, but
they were misunderstood on board, and supposed to
be intended to prevent us from entering.

The sight of the fortress of St. Sebastian naturally
awoke in our minds proud recollections of the
prowess displayed there by British troops, in the
triumphant assault of the 31st of August ; but sorrow
unavoidably mixed itself with my feelings, for on that
memorable day I lost an intimate friend, Lieutenant
Ross-Lewin of the 9th,[1] who had been appointed only
a few days before to the adjutancy of his regiment,
and was a very promising young officer.   He received
a musket shot in the belly, as our troops were driving
the enemy before them through the town ; and Mr.
B——y,[2] assistant-surgeon of the 9th, afterwards
told me that when he found him, he was seated on a
step in one of the streets, had replaced the bowels,
which had protruded through the wound, and was
calmly stitching up the aperture with needle and
thread, articles which officers on service often carry
about them.   As the last stitch was completed, he
fell back and expired in B——y's arms.   His two

---

[1] Edward Ross-Lewin of Cornfield Manor, Co. Clare.   He entered the
army as Ensign, 12th May 1808, and was promoted to a Lieutenantcy on
3rd October 1811.   He had displayed great gallantry during the assault.

[2] Surgeon Thomas Bulkeley, M.D., afterwards in the 32nd Regiment.

latest predecessors in the office of adjutant had met
their deaths within very short intervals—one fell at
Vittoria—and the same horse and trappings passed
from one to the other of these three officers.

All the ships made for Passaes ; but as none of the
masters had ever been in that harbour, there was
some hesitation as to who should be the first to lead
in.   A fresh gale sprang up in the meantime, and a
heavy murky cloud was seen to rise threateningly
astern.   Our ship lay-to ; the sky became overcast ;
and the dark cloud shortly after burst over us.   The
rain now fell in torrents ; the passage remained no
longer discernible ; and the gale increased to a
hurricane.   Some of the fleet went to leeward of the
port, and my transport was very near going too ;
indeed had she drifted but ten minutes more, she
must inevitably have been dashed to pieces against
perpendicular rocks, and every soul on board must
have perished.   The master and crew with the
exception of the man at the helm, a young Scotch-
man, lost all presence of mind, and gave up the
vessel as hopeless of escape.   The military officers
ran to the master, and seizing him by the shoulders,
endeavoured to shake him out of his stupor, and at
length they succeeded so far that he desired the
helmsman to wear the ship.   The only sail that we
had left, all the others having been blown away, was a
close-reefed fore topsail, and on the stoutness of this
piece of canvas all our lives depended ; fortunately
for us it bore the blast, and we gained the entrance
of the harbour.   As we ran in between the tall, black,
and frowning cliffs, the ship was not more than a

pistol shot from the breakers. We found the admiral inside, with the boats of the ships of war ranged in two lines beginning from the farther end of the entrance, and we sailed between them, each ship anchoring by the stern. A few days after, I observed several of the ships that had drifted far to leeward of the port, embedded in the sand off St. Jean de Luz.

Finding it impossible to procure a billet at Passaes, I went on to Ranteria, another village about a league from it, up the country. There I found several of our officers, who were on their return home in consequence of ill-health or wounds, and among them Colonel Hinde[1] of the 32nd regiment. This officer had had the command of a brigade of the sixth division, and it was generally said that, by a masterly movement of the 32nd and 36th, he had prevented the entrance of a French column into Pampeluna, and occasioned the enemy a severe loss, by engaging them in a narrow pass before they had time to debouch on the plain. The Colonel had received a severe wound in the leg.

I procured two horses at Ranteria, and proceeded the next day to join the army, which was then investing Bayonne. My route lay through Irun, the last Spanish town toward the frontier. The Pyrenees slope away from it very gradually, so that the ascent is perfectly easy. It was occupied by Spanish troops, among which I saw three very fine regiments, that were commanded by General Alava. The country was generally deep, flat, bleak, and altogether uninteresting, except as far as it had been the scene of

[1] See page 150.

some sharp fighting, and it was frequently intersected by streams which, rising in the mountains, are much swollen in the winter, though almost dried up probably in the summer.

When I got into the small seaport, St. Jean de Luz, the rain was falling in torrents, and the place was so crowded with our people, that at first I could find no shelter for myself, batman, and horses. Colonel Barnard of the 95th,[1] happening to perceive my situation, came up to me and said, that although he was much stinted for room, he would still share his accommodation with me. Nothing could have been more obliging than such an offer, but I could not think of taking advantage of it. At length I succeeded in establishing myself in a wretched loft, where I passed a most uncomfortable night.

I also passed through Ustaritz, a town on the Nive, and on the third day of my journey entered Villa Franca, where I found the sixth division. They were occupying farm-houses, and communicating with General Hill, whose right was on the Adour, while our left was on the Nive. Both rivers unite about four miles from the Bay of Biscay, into which they fall. The extreme left of our army rested on the sea. The right wing of the French army continued to occupy their entrenched camp before Bayonne, that city so celebrated in a military point of view as being the place where the first bayonet was made—

> Cette arme que jadis pour depeupler la terre
> Dans Baionne inventa le demon de la guerre.[2]

---

[1] Afterwards Sir Andrew Barnard, K.C.B.
[2] *Henriade.*—H. R-L.

This city, which is well fortified, is situated at the conflux of the Adour and the Nive, and has bridges over both of them. The latter river, though narrow, becomes very deep and rapid near Bayonne; the former is of considerable breadth, and navigable; and the anchorage is commanded by the citadel, which stands upon the right bank. The entrenched camp was on the left bank of the Adour, and in front of the ramparts of the town, that are terminated at either extremity by that river. Here Soult had the power of making a sudden attack on the allied army when and where he pleased, with the advantage of a compact position, and a secure retreat under the guns of Bayonne; while our force was distributed along a deep curve, which was crossed by a river, and afforded very inconvenient communications between its different points. By these circumstances the Marshal had endeavoured to profit, but, owing to the firmness and gallantry of his opponents, without success.

In January, the Duke d'Angoulême arrived at headquarters at St. Jean de Luz, and distributed addresses through the country; but, as matters stood then, he could only be treated by the British commander as a private individual. The people of the country, generally speaking, were almost tired of Napoleon, and the decided royalists, among whom the clergy were included, were very numerous in some districts; but the French-born soldiery were still warmly attached to the cause of their warlike Emperor. The spirit of a great part of the foreigners in the French service was not so much to be relied on, and some anxiously desired an opportunity to return to their homes. Of this the conduct of a considerable proportion of those posted at Bayonne afforded ready proof; for two battalions of Nassau troops, when their turn of outpost duty came on, deserted to the allies, that they might be sent to their own country.

A considerable inundation extended along our front; the ditches were all full of water, and passable only by means of planks laid over them. The enemy threw a picquet across the Nive nightly, and at length we determined on making an attempt to surprise it. The execution of this design was entrusted to Captain Gually, of the 11th regiment, and a party of that corps. On the day appointed some men were sent forward after dark to lay planks across the intervening ditches, while an athletic Irishman, armed with a heavy club, was directed to approach the spot where the enemy's advanced sentry was posted; to say when challenged, that he was a deserter, and having thus lulled the French soldier's suspicions, to watch an opportunity to strike him unawares, knock him down, and disarm him, before he could give the alarm. All this was cleverly performed, and the captain, without delay, led up the armed party to the picquet house. There was a sentry at the entrance, who made an effort to close the door; but it was instantly forced in, and before the Frenchmen had time to think of resistance they were prisoners. Their officers were, when surprised, in an upper apartment, together with the owner of the *bateau* in which they had been ferried across the river, and a remarkably fine Spanish woman, the *chere amie* of the captain who commanded the picquet. I was on the most advanced of our picquets that night, and the prisoners were brought to the house where I was posted. The weather was severely cold, and the Spanish woman, who had fallen off a plank into one of the ditches, was in sad plight. The appearance of this poor creature, dripping wet and bareheaded, with her long black hair hanging dishevelled on her shoulders, excited universal sympathy. My drummer exerted himself to keep up a blazing fire ; and she soon became so far reconciled to her new situation, that she evinced no inclination to proceed when an order arrived for the removal of the prisoners further to the rear. The French captain was excessively nettled by her conduct, and, in a peremptory tone, desired her to accompany him—a command which she obeyed, but evidently with extreme reluctance.

*   *   *   *   *   *   *

*   *   *   *   *   *   *

Having directed Sir John Hope to invest Bayonne, and having driven Soult beyond the Gave de Pau, Wellington now resolved to attack the latter at Orthez. On the 26th the third division and the cavalry forded the Gave de Pau below Orthez, and the fourth and seventh divisions at a point still farther down the river. It was intended that Sir Rowland Hill's corps, and the sixth and light divisions, should force the bridge of Orthez ; but it was afterwards thought advisable not to make the attempt.

On the morning of the 27th I saw Lord Wellington for the first time during this campaign; he had been reconnoitring the enemy, and, seating himself on the grass in his well-known short white cloak, he took out some paper, and began to write; but some drizzling rain that was then falling incommoded him. Another officer and I, perceiving the inconvenience he suffered, immediately procured an umbrella, which my companion fixed near him so as to shelter the paper, and retired, his lordship having thanked him for his attention. As Sir Rowland Hill was seen crossing the river above Orthez not long after, we conjectured that the orders were written for him.

The sixth and light divisions had already moved down to the point where the third division had forded the day before, and crossed by a pontoon bridge that had been laid down for the guns. The Pau is a very difficult river to cross by wading, as the fords are deep, and the current flows with considerable force.

Soult occupied a range of hills, which formed a curve concave to the front, his left resting on Orthez, and his right on a steep declivity behind the village of St. Boes. He had also a strong reserve posted on high ground that commanded the road by which he should retreat, if dislodged from this strong and well-chosen position.

Marshal Beresford, with the fourth and seventh divisions, and a brigade of cavalry, commenced the battle by attacking the enemy's right; but, after carrying the village, he failed in the attempt to drive the enemy from the height, owing to the very disadvantageous nature of the ground for the assailing force, and the tremendous fire both of artillery and musketry. Had this attack succeeded, Sir Thomas Picton, with the third and sixth divisions and a brigade of cavalry, supported by the light division, was to have moved against the enemy's centre and left; but an attack on the centre could not be hazarded while the enemy's right were firm. When we had gained the summit of the high ground facing the enemy's position, some guns opened on us, and, a ricochet shot striking in front of my regiment and passing clear over, I turned round to watch its course through the large field in our rear. It bounded along towards the spot where a solitary British soldier was in the act of searching a knapsack, and struck him lifeless in an instant.

The plan of attack was now quickly changed; the seventh division under General Walker, and a brigade of the light division under Colonel Barnard, were led up the height on which the enemy's right stood, but at a point nearly contiguous to the centre; and the third and sixth divisions advanced at the same time under Sirs Thomas Picton and Henry Clinton respectively. A heavy fire opened from the position as these troops moved forward, but the enemy suddenly retreated; for Sir Rowland Hill had passed the river, and was marching for the main road to St. Sever to cut off their retreat, according to his instructions. This movement was made with sufficient rapidity to cause the retreating army, who at first moved off in good order, to break their ranks and run, lest they should be intercepted. Their loss is said to have exceeded 6000 killed, wounded, and taken ; the proportion of prisoners taken during the pursuit was very great. Their loss in killed and wounded must have been less than ours, as they had greatly the advantage of ground, and by their sudden retreat did not suffer the infantry to come to close quarters. The brunt of the battle was borne by the third and fourth divisions. It was here that a soldier of the 88th, one of the regiments of which the third division consisted, observing on the uniform of a dead Frenchman the same number that was on his own, exclaimed in astonishment, "Sun burn me, but the French have *Connaught Rangers* too!"

My division did not go farther than Orthez that night. The next day we continued the pursuit to St. Sever. The enemy, after crossing the Adour, which runs below that town, broke down the low wooden bridge that was over it, and consequently we were obliged to ford. The part of the river to which the sixth division came was nearly five feet deep ; it was necessary, therefore, to throw ropes across for the men to hold by, and these were attached to two field-pieces placed in the stream for that purpose ; at the same time dragoons rode into the river to pick up any men that might lose their hold, and in this manner we effected the passage on a cold morning.

St. Sever is a neat town, beautifully situated on rising ground, and commanding a most extensive prospect. There was a military school here, and the pupils came out to see us, dressed in uni-form, and wearing cocked hats with the national

cockade. The people with whom I had any conversation seemed to be indifferent with respect to
the final result of the war, provided they could have
a clever man at their head and peace. At several
villages we were met by the inhabitants, bearing
green boughs in token of amity ; and no instance of
treachery or ill-usage on the part of the peasantry
toward our men occurred at any place through
which we passed, although, had they desired it, they
might have found many opportunities of cutting off
straggling soldiers. This may be attributed partly
to the fact that the people were growing tired of
war and a military government, and partly to the
good conduct and conciliatory demeanour of our
troops. Numbers of the French soldiers now
quitted their ranks and returned to their homes.

Soult threw some troops into a wood on our left
to check our advance; but they were soon driven
from it, and from a village beyond it, by the light
companies of the regiments composing the sixth
division.

The disposition of the people in the south of
France became daily more favourable They certainly had good reason to think well of the allied
army, from whom they expected much better treatment than they usually received at the hands of their
own soldiery at this period. Some instances of
injury done to property would unavoidably occur
now and then where the allied troops were stationed ;
but that they were not infinitely more numerous,
notwithstanding the excellent precautions taken to
prevent them, must seem extraordinary, when it is

considered that Lord Wellington's force did not consist solely of his own countrymen, and that the Spaniards and Portuguese under his command had fresh in their recollection the atrocities committed by the French during their invasion of the Peninsula.

On entering France, very strict orders had been issued to prevent plunder of any kind. A provost-marshal was appointed to every division, whose duty it was to ride round the bivouacs, to take up all stragglers found plundering, and to punish them on the spot, should he think fit. His guard of cavalry were distinguished by white scarfs, worn round the arm. The vigilance of the provost-marshal had, of course, an excellent effect; but it is not in the power of man totally to put a stop to plundering in any army while stationed, during war, in a foreign country. One day, as Lord Wellington and some of his staff were riding down a lane somewhere in the vicinity of Orthez, they suddenly saw a soldier running up with a hive of honey under his arm. His lordship immediately directed one of his staff to speak to him; but the man, who belonged to the 88th, no sooner perceived this unlucky encounter, than he assumed an air of the greatest simplicity, and, before the officer had time to open his lips, looked up in his face, and cried out in the true accent of a Ranger, "Hurry, hurry, or they're all all gone from yez." This completely disarmed Lord Wellington, who could not suppress a smile, and rode off without taking further notice of the ready-witted Irishman's transgression.

My regiment marched with the army until it

arrived within twenty leagues of Toulouse, when it was ordered back to St. Jean de Luz for new clothing. No one who had never before seen British troops could possibly have discovered at this period the original colour of our clothing ; for it was so patched with a diversity of colours, and so bespoke a variety of wretchedness, that, with regard to this part of our equipment, we must have borne an undesirable resemblance to Falstaff's ragged regiment. We reached St. Jean de Luz in eight days, and, having exchanged our tattered raiment for the new uniforms, set off again on the 18th of March to rejoin the army.

It rained incessantly as we returned, until, on the seventh day's march, we entered Tarbes ; but once arrived there we made ourselves very comfortable.

On the 10th of April we were directed to proceed from Tarbes to Toulouse with the battering train, pontoons, and boats. It was impossible to have this portion of the *materiel* in superior order ; the French declared that it formed the most complete exhibition of the kind that they had ever seen. After a march of ten days, the train moving slowly, we joined the sixth division at its station about six leagues beyond Toulouse. The battle had been fought ; the white cockade was worn generally ; and Marshal Soult had submitted.

The day after my regiment had rejoined, the Commune of Toulouse gave a grand ball to celebrate the return of peace. Each regiment in the allied army received two invitation cards ; one of those sent to mine was given to me, and accordingly I attended the festive scene. The rooms of the Capitol were thrown open at nine o'clock; they form a suite of seven, of which four were devoted to Bacchus and Ceres, and three to Euterpe and Terpsichore. At ten martial music announced the arrival of Lord Wellington, at the great staircase; and on his approach, accompanied by the mayor of Toulouse, the company rose, and formed a lane, through which he passed to the octagon room, the last of the suite. Here the royal throne was placed under the picture of Louis XVIII., and on one side a seat was prepared for the British commander, over which his portrait was in like manner suspended. The ceiling of this room is finely painted, and it has a high gallery, in which the vocal performers took their station. The acclamations of the company were for some time so loud as absolutely to drown the music that proceeded from a splendid band, which began to play as his lordship entered. This first piece of instrumental music was followed by a vocal display—a song which was sung in fine style, and of which each verse terminated with the word Vellinton, or as the French witlings would have it, Vilainton—a poor pun. The concert ended with "God Save the King," in full chorus. His lordship returned to the great dancing-room with the same forms as had been observed on his first entrance; and he seemed to be in excellent spirits, and much pleased with the attention paid him. Waltzes and other dances then commenced; and really, any spectator of the scene, who did not call to mind the innate levity and volatility of the French, would

with difficulty have been able to persuade himself of
the fact, that those dancers, who were merrily
spinning and swimming through those gaily-decked
apartments, had so recently beheld their territory
violated, their troops vanquished, and their national
pride humiliated, by the very men to whom this
entertainment was given. However, I feel bound to
add, that I did not see there a single officer belonging to the regular army of France.

The doors of the supper rooms were thrown open
at 12 o'clock, and the pressure of the crowding
guests toward this new scene of attraction quickly
became excessive, the ushers exerting themselves
to prevent it in vain. "*Sauve qui peut*" seemed to be
the general cry. The tables were well covered and
tastefully ornamented. The wines were admirable,
particularly the claret, which seemed to be the
favourite supper wine. The number of persons
present was, I should think, about eight hundred.
The civic guard, composed of respectable citizens,
did duty at the different avenues leading to the
Capitol; they acted ill as soldiers, but wisely as *bon
vivants*, for, when supper time approached, they
requested to be relieved by English sentries, and
were among the first to rush to the loaded tables,
on whose contents they did extraordinary execution.
The politeness said to be natural to Frenchmen was
either temporarily forgotten, or was out of date since
the days of the old *régime*. It is true they told the
British officers that everything was for them: "*Pour
vous, Messieurs, pour vous*," were their words, but their
actions strangely contradicted them; for they de-

voured all the good things that came within their reach;
even Marshal Beresford for a considerable time was
unable to procure a place at the table.   There were
several handsome women in the rooms ; but the then
prevailing mode of dressing the hair was very un-
becoming.   The greater proportion of the fair dames
and damsels of Toulouse that appeared at this ball
were arrayed in white, in honour of the occasion.
The "presence" of the lion, miscalled the "leopard,"
which had been pronounced to be "frightful" four
years before, was now considered sufficiently agreeable, and hailed with every appearance of satisfaction.

As an accompaniment to these proceedings, and
the display of *drapeau blanc,* the *fleur-de-lis,* and the
white cockades, all memorials that had been erected
in compliment to the ex-Emperor, were now dis-
placed and demolished.   There was a pleasing
novelty in the long-disused but now revived cry of
"*Vive le Roi!*"   The very parrots and starlings were
to be starved till they could give utterance to these
three magical monosyllables ; and everything was to
be royal and *à la Bourbon* for another year.

I left Toulouse the morning after the ball, and in
the course of the day the sixth division marched to
Auch, the principal town in this part of Gascony, the
department of Gers.

There were some genteel families in the neighbourhood of Auch, and one of our officers became
very much attached to a nice girl who resided at
a chateau not very far distant.   However, in one
respect at least the accomplishments of the fair lady
and her admirer did not keep pace ; the latter was

profoundly ignorant of music, while the former was passionately fond of that fashionable science ; and accordingly, she one day expressed to him a wish to obtain some specimens of English music. Of course the *inamorato* was delighted to have an opportunity afforded him of gratifying her, and promised to pro- cure them by the following day. As soon as his visit had terminated, he hastened to a brother officer, who was a good musician, but also, unluckily for him, a great wag, and requested that he would give him some music for the lovely inmate of the chateau. The request met with a ready compliance, and at the appointed time the lover set off breast-high for the abode of his mistress, with the " Pioneer's Call," neatly written, in his pocket ; for his waggish friend had given him this charming composition, gravely assuring him that it was a favourite English air, and promising that it should be followed by others, also much admired. Some of the neighbouring *dilettanti*, who, like the fair enslaver of the Briton's heart, were desirous to hear our national music, attended at the chateau to enjoy the expected treat, and waited im- patiently for the arrival of *Monsieur le Militaire Anglois*. At length his approach was announced, he entered, presented the unlucky paper, and received a thousand thanks. All drew near to the pianoforte, and the fair musician took her seat at the instrument. But what was the astonishment, the dismay, the horror of the ill-starred suitor when he heard her play off the first notes of the " Pioneer's Call ! " A murmur of surprise and disappointment ran through the assembly, and the pianiste in amazement let fall her hands,

exclaiming against the taste of the London com-
posers. It is almost superfluous to add, that the
principal sufferer by this cruel practical joke had no
sooner recovered from the first effects of the shock
caused by the discovery of his musical blunder, than
he sought relief from his embarrassment in a precipitate retreat.

The sixth division remained in cantonments in
and about Auch until the 2nd of June ; it then broke
up, to move to the camp occupied by the troops that
had preceded us, on the banks of the Gironde, three
leagues below Bordeaux.

We were eight days on the march ; the weather
was unusually sultry ; but the country through
which we passed was beautiful—indeed, it was one
continued garden. The towns were neat, and the
inhabitants polite and obliging. The citizen and the
villager were alike struck by the martial and uncommon appearance of the Highlanders, and often
exclaimed—"O! les Ecossois, qu'ils sont fiers !—qu'ils
ont l'air imposante !" but in some places the ladies
would only look at them through their fans. In one
town the young girls were all shut up. It was made
the headquarters of a brigade, and the General had
for an orderly a serjeant of the 79th, a man of very
large stature ; it happened that the said Highland
Goliath, soon after the arrival of the General at his
billet, was lying asleep on a table in the kitchen,
which was adjoining to and communicated with the
chamber of one of the aides-de-camp, and this officer,
hearing the lady of the house enter the cook's labo-
ratory, had the curiosity to peep through the

keyhole. He saw her approach the unconscious sergeant softly, and gaze at him with surprise for some time ; she then withdrew, but only to return with her two daughters, who seemed equally to enjoy the curious spectacle. So much for the reality of the delicacy of some French ladies.

We reached the encampment on the 10th of June. The regiments destined to reinforce Sir George Prevost in Canada, and those selected for the expedition under Sir Edward Pakenham, had already embarked.

The Duke of Wellington, who had left Paris on the 10th of May, and Madrid on the 5th of June, arrived at Bordeaux on the same day that we joined the troops in camp, and on the 13th he came out to take his leave of the army. We were five hours under arms, and the heat was excessive. When the review had terminated, his Grace was saluted by the whole line with hearty cheers, which never ceased until he was completely out of sight. He sailed the next day for England, took his seat in the House of Peers for the first time on the 28th, and received the thanks and congratulations of Parliament, expressed in the most complimentary and enthusiastic manner. He deserved them.

At Bordeaux the shops are handsome. I had an opportunity of inspecting all the best assorted, as I had a variety of purchases of shawls, scarfs, lace, gloves, &c., to make for some of my female friends, and I found them also admirably provided in every respect. As I was looking over some finery at the establishment where some of the most important articles were to be obtained, a tall English gentleman,

Q

whom I found there, recommended me not to make any purchases before his lady returned from the warerooms above stairs. When she came down she immediately proceeded, in the most obliging manner, to make the required selections, and, on the completion of her task, added that she had no doubt that my friends would be well pleased with her choice. I afterwards ascertained that the persons to whose civility I was so much indebted were Lord and Lady Keith. His lordship's flag was then flying in the river on board the *Queen Charlotte.*

A very extensive brevet came out this month, and I became a Major in the line, 4th June 1814; but, as the regiment had embarked at Blancfort at the time that I visited Bordeaux, I was compelled to limit my stay to two or three days, although my recent promotion was an excellent preparative for enjoying its gaiety. A few other officers, who had been deputed to cater for those on board the transports, took a boat and dropped down the river; and I accompanied them. In the first tide we only got as far as Blaye, a distance of seventeen miles. This is but a small town. The inhabitants have a pleasant promenade shaded by trees, leading from the water to the barracks, which are within fortifications. I was not permitted to enter the fort; the ramparts are high and planted with cannon, and as the country is low on each side of the river, they command an extensive prospect. Upon landing we repaired to the principal inn, where the officers of a French demi-brigade, the garrison of the fort, messed, and we ordered dinner to be laid in the room adjoining that

which the military occupied ; but the landlord, who
suspected that they were not well disposed toward us,
removed us to a more distant part of the house lest
any unpleasant collision should occur between the
two parties. The landlord was right in his surmises ;
for, upon my walking out with another officer, both
unarmed, to take a turn on the public walk, a French
officer came up to my companion and said," D——n
you Englishman, will you fight ?—I was prisoner at
Portsmouth—you will fight ? "   We returned to the
inn, thinking that the man was decidedly insane ; but
still we consulted the rest of our party concerning the
course that we should adopt. They were unanimously
of opinion that it would be absurd to take any further
notice of the matter. We remained at Blaye for the
night, and in the morning we went to the market to
purchase a few things, when the person who acted
so outrageously on the preceding evening approached
us and renewed his insulting attack on the officer to
whom he had before addressed himself. Several
other officers of the French corps were within sight,
and my friend instantly went up to them, and represented to them how he had been insulted by their
brother officer, without the slightest provocation from
him or any of his party; and then requested to know
whether such a proceeding had received their sanc-
tion. They declared that it had not, and immediately
took away their troublesome comrade, seeming to
remonstrate with him strongly. We experienced
no further molestation ; but, as some drunken men
of their corps followed us, saying that they also had
been prisoners, we thought it prudent to get to our

boat without delay. This demi-brigade had not yet consented to wear the white cockade, and evidently bore us no goodwill. Had the insulted officer been so ill-advised as to resent the provocation he received it is most probable that the consequences would have been very unfortunate.

When we reached our transports they were on the point of getting under weigh, and France was out of sight the next morning. We had a fine passage of ten days to Cork.

The small town of Middleton was our first quarter; and Clonooney, a wretched, isolated barrack, standing in the middle of a bog, our next; but after a short stay at both these places, we marched to Fermoy, a very pretty and pleasant town. There we remained during the greater part of the winter of 1814, and in the following spring we were removed to the "beautiful city of Cork."

The inhabitants of Cork are remarkably sociable and hospitable, and also very musical; no people pay more attention to the military and naval officers; the dinner parties are particularly numerous, and at them our heroes were wont to fare sumptuously. A wine merchant invited the officers of the 36th regiment to one of these entertainments, and their commanding officer, amongst others, went to it. Colonel B., though a gallant soldier, was extremely diffident, and seldom mixed with any society besides that of his own officers. His nose had grown to a much greater magnitude than was necessary, and seemed of itself to be tormented by *mauvaise honte*, and perfectly ashamed of its remarkable dimensions and Dutch-bottle shape; for it was constantly suffused with a deep blush, approaching pretty nearly to the hue of that generous beverage which the peasant on the banks of the Douro presses from the purple fruit of his vines; and all allusions to this prominent feature were particularly offensive to its sensitive proprietor. When the cloth was drawn, which was not then considered unfashionable, the finest wine passed quickly round. "Now, gentlemen," said the host, "I wish particularly to have your opinion of this bottle; it is different from anything we have been drinking, and should you prefer it, more shall be ordered up. Hand it to the colonel; he has the nose for claret!" Nothing could have been more unfortunate than this remark; and, in a few minutes after it had been uttered, the colonel left the room.

CHAPTER XIV

NAPOLEON'S sudden return to France from Elba, the
revolt of the French soldiery in his favour, and the
consequent expulsion of the Bourbons for the second
time, set the armies of Europe in motion once more.

My regiment embarked at Cork on the 1st of May
1815, and sailed immediately ; we touched at Dover
for a few hours, and then proceeded to Ostend.   As
at that port large vessels have not sufficient water to
get up to the pier at ebb tide, which it was when we
arrived off it, we could not land before the return.
The pier, which is built on piles, runs out to a considerable distance, but landing is troublesome in
boisterous weather.   When we had disembarked, we
marched after a short delay to the canal, where we
found, about a mile from the town, the boats that
were to convey us to the interior ; they were covered
and very large, but, being drawn by only two horses,
they moved slowly.

We left Ostend at 9 P.M., and did not reach
Bruges before morning, the distance being twelve
miles.

We arrived at Ghent, which is twenty-eight miles from Bruges, on the 12th of May, having been two nights in the boats. We found Louis the Eighteenth here; he had with him a number of French Royalists, and deserters from Napoleon's service, among whom were Marshal Victor (the Duke of Belluno) and General Clarke. His Majesty held levees constantly, and was much gratified by the attendance of British officers. He seemed to suffer a good deal from gout, as his velvet shoes indicated; but it had made no alteration in his countenance, which was always expressive of placidity and bene-volence. He attended to his devotional duties at the cathedral with pious regularity; but the possession of piety and devotion does not exalt a monarch in the eyes of the French people.

I was billeted at the house of a very old gentleman who kept four carriages and a most respectable establishment; he desired me to use his house as if it were my own. His domestics dressed him every morning at six; they then drenched him with sugar-less tea; at seven a regular breakfast of hot rolls, cakes, radishes, cheese, coffee, and white wines was prepared; we dined before one, soup and fish, never-failing dishes, and a second dinner was served at seven in the evening, at which his best wines and beer were produced. I was fortunate in standing high in the old gentleman's good graces, and as an evidence of this, he said to me one morning, " I will now show you a sight that my countrymen shall never see," upon which he took my arm, and we proceeded to a spacious room that did not appear to have been opened for some time. " Now," said he, as we entered, " I will lay before your eyes the works of the great painters of the Flemish school." The paintings were not hung on the walls, but were merely laid against them, and rested on the floor, and were thus disposed all round the room—an arrangement which did not permit of their being viewed to advantage. " Here," said he, pointing to one of the first that we came to, " is a piece worth 1500 pounds English—a perfect *chef d'œuvre;* the subject is Rubens and his wife at the chase of the wolf, and it is the work of that great master. Here is another by the same hand," he added, as we advanced another step, " which is valued at 1000 pounds—the subject, Rubens and his wife at the time of their marriage. This is one of Vandyck's," continued he, pointing to another, " it is worth 800 pounds." So he went on, but I did not see one-tenth of them, the exertion of taking me round them all would have been too great for him. The window-shutters were again closed, the door fastened, and most probably, if the old gentleman lives to this day, that room has never been opened since he did me the honour to show me its treasures; for his nephew also told me that I should consider this an extraordinary compliment, as the repeated solicitations made by persons of rank and importance for permission to see this collection had been invariably rejected ; neither had any artist ever been suffered to take a copy of a single painting contained in that valuably furnished chamber. What circumstances had caused the old gentleman to come to a resolution which was so unfriendly towards his countrymen, and to which he so inflexibly adhered, I never could learn. His disposition seemed to be quite the reverse of ill-natured, and I could hardly prevail on myself to think that he acted in a manner apparently so selfish through mere whim. Perhaps confidence betrayed, or pride deeply wounded by the acts of some individuals of his nation, had given that anti-national tinge to his sentiments, which in the present instance influenced his conduct in so strange a manner.

The fifth division, to which my regiment belonged, being now ordered to Brussels, I took leave of my kind old host, on the 27th of May, with much regret. We arrived in that fine city on the 29th, the distance from Ghent to it being thirty miles. As we approached Brussels the ground began to undulate a little, which caused an agreeable variety in the face of the country; as, for more than sixty miles from Ostend, we could not perceive the slightest inequality of surface.

I was received at my billet with much politeness by the family, who were Germans. They were commercial people, and as such of distinction, the head of the house being president of the Chamber of Commerce. My new host was very curious in wines: one day we would drink still champagne; the next, claret; the third, perhaps sparkling champagne; and, in warm weather, fine hock that had come of age twelve years before. A residence under the roof of such an entertainer, while campaigning, made some amends for privations endured in the Peninsula.

The Duke of Wellington being appointed to the

command of the British, Hanoverian, and Netherland troops, had been at Brussels since the month
of April.   He had come last from Vienna, where he
had attended the Congress in the capacity of pleni-
potentiary for Great Britain.   His whole force may
be estimated at 80,000 men ; but it was composed
principally of foreigners, a great number of whom
were mere militia.   The native British troops, among
whom there were also many young and untried
soldiers, consisted of about 7000 horse and 27,000
foot.   The German legion comprised some thousands
of all arms, and they were well disciplined ; but the
Hanoverians were all new levies.   The remainder
were Brunswickers, Dutch, Nassauers, and Belgians.
The British artillery consisted of thirty brigades—
six guns to each brigade ; they were in admirable
order.

This army was divided into two corps—the first
commanded by the Prince of Orange, and the second
by Lord Hill.   The cavalry were placed under the
orders of the Earl of Uxbridge.   The Duke of
Wellington's headquarters were at Brussels, but the
numerous troops now assembled in Belgium, in
addition to the national army, could not all be
maintained conveniently in Brussels and its immediate
neighbourhood, and accordingly they were distributed in different parts of the country.   The Prince
of Orange was at Braine le Comte, about fifteen
miles to the southward of Brussels, and Lord Hill
at Grammont on the Dender.   The British cavalry
were stationed in the villages along the banks of the
Dender.   The greatest part of the artillery remained

at Ghent. The guards were at Enghien; the fifth
division at Brussels; the Brunswickers about the
palace of Lacken; and a considerable portion of
the Netherlanders in front of Brussels.

The Prussian army, which was about 100,000
strong, occupied the line of the Sambre. The
headquarters of Marshal Blucher, who commanded
it, were at Namur, about thirty-five miles south-east
of Brussels, at the confluence of the Maese and the
Sambre, and his right communicated with the British
left.

This disposition of the allied armies, however, was
such as to afford the Duke of Wellington and Prince
Blucher the means of speedily combining their forces
in the probable event of a sudden advance of the
enemy. It was necessary for each of these generals
at the same time to keep open their communications
with their respective countries; it was also of importance to cover Brussels and Ghent; and the
British commander had to watch the roads leading
from France by Tournay and Mons, while the
Prussian guarded the approaches by Namur and
Charleroi.

Another grand object was to gain time, as the
Russians and Austrians were advancing against
Napoleon from the east. On the other hand, it
naturally was the usurper's aim to bring us to an
action with the least possible delay, since, in case
of a decided victory, he might be enabled, by one of
those rapid movements which he knew how to make,
to throw himself suddenly on the other hostile
armies and beat them in detail. Besides, a battle

gained over us would have been the signal for a general rising of the people of France, to repel the threatened invasion by the Emperors of Austria and Russia.

Napoleon, possessing so many fortresses on his own frontier, behind which he could secretly assemble large bodies of troops, had it always in his power to make an irruption into the Netherlands at an unexpected moment, and his position also secured to him the choice of the point of attack. Consequently, the allies had to contend with the serious disadvantage of being attacked in very superior force at partial points, when perhaps their advanced troops might not be able to keep the enemy in check for a sufficient time.

During our stay Brussels was the scene of much gaiety ; war seemed to be totally forgotten. The Duke of Wellington gave a grand rout on the 8th, at which the Prince of Orange, the Duke of Brunswick, and all the British and foreign nobility, then resident in Brussels, attended. Four cards of invitation were received by each regiment, and one of those sent to mine fell to my lot. The company passed through an illuminated garden to the reception-rooms ; the Duke of Wellington stood, distinct from all present, near the entrance, to receive his guests, and looked very well. Dancing was kept up to a late hour. The Prince of Orange led the Duchess of Richmond to the supper-rooms, which were in the apartments of the middle story. The rooms were excessively crowded considering the time of the year, and not one half of the guests could find places at supper-tables.

The Duchess of Richmond gave a grand ball on the 15th. That day I dined with Sir James Kempt. Coffee and a young aide-de-camp from the Duke of Wellington came in together. This officer was the bearer of a note from the Duke, and while Sir James was reading it, said: " Old Blucher has been hard at it; a Prussian officer has just come to the Beau, all covered with sweat and dirt, and says they have had much fighting." Our host then rose, and, addressing the regimental officers at the table, said : "Gentlemen, you will proceed without delay to your respective regiments, and let them get under arms immediately."

On my way I found several of our officers sitting at a coffee-house door, and told them Sir James Kempt's orders. They seemed at first to think that I was jesting, being hardly able to credit the tidings of so near and so unexpected an approach of the French ; but they soon perceived that I spoke seriously, and dispersed each to his own quarters. In a few minutes, however, the most incredulous would have been thoroughly undeceived, for then drums began to beat, bugles to sound, and Highland pipes to squeal in all quarters of the city. The scene that ensued was of the most animated kind : such was the excitement of the inhabitants, the buzz of tongues, the repeated words of command, the hurrying of the soldiers through the streets, the clattering of horses' hoofs, the clash of arms, the rattling of the wheels of waggons and gun-carriages, and the sounds of warlike music. The different regiments of infantry closed up in Place Royale ;

and at daylight the whole were in motion towards Waterloo, the Duke of Wellington and the generals riding on béfore us.

We, the fifth division, halted for some time near the village in the forest of Soignies, which some suppose to be a part of the immense one of Ardennes, so celebrated for its extent, and the deeds and adventures of which it was the scene, as well in the classical as in the middle ages. It now answers the useful purpose of supplying Brussels with firewood. When the bugle sounded to fall in again, one of our captains exclaimed: "That is my death-warrant!" The poor fellow's prediction was soon verified; for he was killed a few hours afterwards.

From Waterloo we marched to Genappe, a league and a half farther on. Genappe is nearly five leagues from Brussels; it has only one street, but the houses are large and comfortable; the country about it is quite open, and continues so for the whole distance between it and les Quatre Bras, a small inn so called because the road from Brussels to Charleroi, by which we advanced, is there intersected by that from Nivelles to Namur, passing by St. Arnaud. The Prussian right rested on the latter place; and it was an essential object with the allies to keep open both these communications; we therefore halted at les Quatre Bras a little after 2 P.M., there to dispute this important point with the advancing enemy.

Between 10th and 14th of June, Napoleon had assembled the first, second, third, fourth, and sixth

corps of his army close to the frontier, between the
rivers Sambre and Maese.   Here, including the
Imperial Guard and the flower of his cavalry, he
found himself at the head of an effective force of
130,000 men,   His artillery consisted of 350 pieces.
The army was formed into three great divisions, led
by Marshals Ney and Grouchy, and Jerome Bona-
parte.   Under these leaders, Generals d'Erlon, Gerard,
Reille, Lobau, and Vandamme, commanded the infantry ; and Generals Kellerman, Pajol, Excelmans,
and Milhaud, the cavalry.   Napoleon's major-general
was Marshal Soult.

On the 15th, at daybreak, he attacked the Prussian
posts at Thuin and Lobez on the Sambre.   His
attacks were successful ; and General Ziethen, whose
corps had been at Charleroi, retired upon Fleurus.
Upon this, Prince Blucher concentrated his forces
upon Sombref, occupying also the villages of St.
Amand and Ligny in front of his position.

On the evening of this day the enemy, advancing
from Charleroi along the high road to Brussels,
drove a brigade of the Netherlanders, under the
Prince of Weimar, from Frasne, and compelled it
to retire to les Quatre Bras.   The Prince of Orange
immediately sent to its aid another brigade of the
same division ; and early in the morning of the 16th
some of the lost ground was recovered, so as to
secure the command of the communication with the
Prussian position.

The fifth division was followed by the Duke of
Brunswick's corps, and these again by the con-
tingent of Nassau.   The whole force in the field,

after the arrival of the last-mentioned troops, did not exceed 19,000 men; we were without artillery;[1] not a single British dragoon appeared, and the Duke of Brunswick's cavalry, though very fine men, were badly mounted.   Our position was of no strength; and all that, under Providence, we had to depend upon in the endeavour to maintain it against a very superior force, well provided with cavalry and artillery, was the skill and presence of mind of our generals, and the courage and discipline of the troops — and the God of Battles ordained that none of these should fail us.

The ground we occupied for the most part swelled into gentle slopes, and extended from the Namur road on the left to a thick wood on the right, called the Bois de Bossu.   The Charleroi road ran through the position, and in front there were some fields of amazingly tall rye.[2]

When we came up the firing had almost ceased, but it soon increased again; and shortly after we were hotly engaged with the second corps of the French army, led by Marshal Ney.   A heavy column advanced against the fifth division, the

[1] That is, at the beginning of the action; five batteries came up and were engaged during the day.

[2] "The rye in the fields was so high that to see anything beyond our own ranks was almost impossible.   The enemy even, in attacking our squares, were obliged to make a daring person ride desperately forward to plant a flag, as a mark, at the very point of our bayonets; on this they charged, but were invariably repulsed" (Colonel Llewellyn, 28th Regiment.   Siborne's *Waterloo Letters*, p. 348).   All officers bear striking witness to the coolness and devoted gallantry of the French cavalry.   They would appear to have been veterans, "old grey-headed devils," as one writer calls them.   They showed no mercy to such of our wounded as were within their reach.

officers marching in front, flourishing their swords and encouraging their men ; but they were quickly driven back, and forced through the hedge at the bottom of the slope on which we had been drawn up. They had to cross a long narrow field and a second hedge before they could get under cover from our fire, and an admirable opportunity of taking a number of prisoners was lost here, while they were making their way through a small opening. Indeed, numbers of them had ordered their arms in the expectation of being pursued and taken ; but they escaped with inconsiderable loss, as our troops were halted at the first hedge. The French, when they had all passed to the other side of the fence, lined it, instead of retiring, and commenced from behind it a most destructive fire on our division, which was so much exposed on the side of the hill ; in consequence, the regiments were ordered to fall back, and lie down on the reverse slope. My regiment, while retiring thither, suffered severely from the fire of the troops that lined the fence. Such attacks were continued with little intermission, but we maintained our ground, invariably repulsing all the enemy's efforts to gain it.

As we had no British cavalry up, owing to the shortness of the notice that the Duke of Wellington had received when Napoleon advanced, and as the Brunswick dragoons were unable to make head alone against those of the enemy, it, of course, became necessary to throw the regiments on the left into square to resist the charges of the French lancers and cuirassiers, and to re-form line to meet the

R

attacks of infantry. When the hostile cavalry were
seen moving up to les Quatre Bras, the 32nd formed
a square on the Namur road, as did the 28th, who
were on their right and a little in advance; and the
42nd, who were still more to the right, were forming
square when they were suddenly charged by lancers,
whose approach was concealed by a fence and some
tall rye, before they could complete their formation.
Two companies were nearly all cut to pieces. Colonel
Macara was killed, and Colonel Dicks, who succeeded
him in the command, was badly wounded. About
the same time the enemy's cuirassiers galloped up
the high road to Brussels; the Brunswick hussars
attempted to check their advance, but were over-
whelmed by superior numbers and weight of men
and horses, and retired in confusion, pursued by the
enemy, toward les Quatre Bras. The cuirassiers had
gained the crest of the slope on which the house
stands, when the 92nd, who had been placed there
in reserve behind a ditch, rose and threw in a volley
so sudden, so well directed, and so deadly in its
effect, that the cavalry wheeled round and fled with
precipitation, leaving many of their number[1] killed
or wounded on the spot; and, as they returned,
suffering from the fire of one or two British regiments that they had passed in the charge. The 28th
distinguished themselves highly by the intrepid and
successful manner in which they resisted repeated
charges of cavalry.

During the action, the Duke of Wellington was

[1] The 92nd afterwards cooked their suppers in the cuirasses stripped
from the French cavalry! See Siborne, *Waterloo Letters.*

reinforced by the third division under General Alten, and the Guards under General Cooke. The 69th regiment had hardly taken up its ground, when the French cavalry got in amongst them, and caused them considerable loss in killed and wounded, but made no prisoners.

The Belgians held the wood for some time, but at length gave way, and the French were in possession of it when the Guards arrived. General Maitland's brigade were immediately directed to dislodge them. The possession of the wood was of much consequence to the French, as they could debouch from it on the Brussels road, part of which it skirted; and if they had a chance of beating our troops anywhere, it ought to have been when General Maitland endeavoured to recover the wood. The Guards, on their advance, were exposed to a deadly fire from an enemy that was hid behind trees, bushes, and banks, and knew well how to take advantage of all such means of defence; still they dashed on boldly, and finally remained undisputed masters of this important point, after three hours' hard fighting. Whenever the Guards emerged from the wood, and attempted to form, they were charged by the French cavalry, and obliged to fall back to the cover.

Early in the day the Prince of Orange was surrounded, and very nearly taken prisoner; but a regiment of his own troops saw his danger, and, rushing forward with much spirit, rescued him from the enemy. The steady conduct of a battalion of Hanoverians elicited the praises of all who witnessed it; they were sent out to skirmish with the enemy, and sustained a severe loss ; nevertheless they continued the contest with undiminished gallantry.   I afterwards heard German officers say, that it was hardly fair to send troops who were quite ignorant of this species of warfare, and had no idea of taking advantage of the ground to oppose the experienced French tirailleurs.

Marshal Ney, alarmed by the failure of all his efforts to overcome the obstinacy of our troops, sent off in haste for the first corps ; and he was dreadfully disappointed on receiving the unexpected intelligence that Napoleon had employed it to support the attack on the Prussians at Sombref.   He had then only to bring the reserve of the second corps into action. He did so, and the contest was renewed, but with continued ill success on his part.   At length the first corps, which had not yet fired a shot, was despatched to Frasné by Napoleon, but it did not arrive before 10 P.M., too late an hour to permit of Ney's making any use of this reinforcement.

The firing ceased as the evening closed, and at that time the British occupied a more advanced position than that which they had taken up in the morning.   We slept on the ground that night.   In the course of it the cavalry came up from Niouve.

The loss of the allies in killed, wounded, and prisoners is estimated at 4000 ; and that of the French is said to have exceeded this by two hundred. Ney's force, during the action, was at least 30,000 men, and besides his numerical superiority, he possessed a great advantage over us in having a fine body of cavalry, to which we could only oppose a few squadrons, and they not British. It was also much in favour of the French generals that they commanded none but their own soldiers, while the Duke of Wellington was at the head of an army composed of most heterogeneous materials, some of which undoubtedly were excellent, but on others little reliance could be placed.

The gallant Duke of Brunswick was killed in the act of rallying his hussars, after they had been charged and thrown into confusion by the French cavalry. A captain of my regiment, toward the close of the day, was remarking what a number of escapes he had had, and showing how his clothes had been shot through in several places, when a musket-ball entered his mouth and killed him on the spot. Two more of our captains died of their wounds the next morning. One of them had had the misfortune some years before to kill in a duel an officer of cavalry, from whom he had received an unprovoked insult, too gross to be left unnoticed. The recollection of this affair always affected him most sensibly, and never after could he bear to hear the subject of duelling broached in conversation. From the time of his removal wounded from the field of battle, until the moment that he expired, he remained perfectly collected, though suffering acute pain, and almost the last words that he uttered were in allusion to the fatal termination of his private quarrel. "Whoso sheddeth man's blood," said he, repeating the passage of Scripture, " by man shall his blood be shed." It was thought rather singular that the only officers of my regiment who lost their lives at

Quatre Bras should have been three captains,[1] successive in seniority, a leash of Irishmen, and the greatest friends, generally messing together. Over their honourable grave it might well have been written, "They were lovely and pleasant in their lives, and in their deaths they were not divided."

During the whole of the 16th, the Prussians, under Blucher, had been hotly engaged with Napoleon's army. The position occupied by the former was very strong, and defended by three out of the four corps of which their force consisted; Bulow's corps had been stationed at too great a distance to admit of his joining in sufficient time. The villages of Sombref, Ligny, and St. Amand were included in the position, they were built upon uneven and difficult ground, and Blucher planted at them several pieces of artillery. The Prussians stated the force immediately under Napoleon's command at 130,000; but, including the first corps, it could hardly have exceeded 100,000 men. The engagement was very obstinate and sanguinary; the same ground was taken and retaken several times; and neither party gave or took quarter. But the fighting terminated to the disadvantage of the Prussians, who retreated during the night, having lost 15,000 men and some pieces of artillery. The gallant veteran,

---

[1] Jaques Boyse, Thomas Cassan, Edward Whitty. See page 18.

Col. Swiney, in *Historical Records of the Cornwall Light Infantry*, p. 115, quotes a long letter bearing date June 25, 1815. "In the second charge a shell burst right on the colours, took away the silk of the regimental colour and the whole of the right section of the fifth company, amongst whom was my lamented friend Captain Whitty; his head was literally blown to atoms. M'Conchy, who held the colour that suffered, was only slightly wounded."

Blucher, in leading a cavalry charge in person, fell with his horse, and was in imminent danger of being made prisoner by the French cuirassiers, who advanced past him ; but fortunately they did not observe him as he lay on the ground, either then, or when they returned. The retreat of the Prussians was made leisurely and in good order. They were not followed until the afternoon of the 17th, when Napoleon directed Marshal Grouchy to pursue with 30,000 men, the third corps.

The loss of the enemy fell short of that of the Prussians by perhaps 3000 or 4000 men ; but with the want of candour so observable in the statements of French officers, it was estimated in their bulletins at only 3000 killed and wounded. By this success the enemy gained the important advantage of destroying the communication between the allied armies ; and Napoleon resolved, by uniting with Ney, to make every effort to overwhelm the Duke of Wellington's army while unsupported by our ally.

On the morning of the 17th, tidings of the retreat of the Prussians were brought in by a British patrol, Blucher's aide-de-camp, who was directed to be their bearer, having been killed on his way. The Duke of Wellington now found himself compelled to abandon all idea of maintaining himself at les Quatre Bras, as he had intended, and to withdraw his army to some point nearer to Brussels.

Accordingly, at 10 A.M. our army was in motion, and fell back leisurely towards Waterloo. As we marched past several wounded cuirassiers who had lain on the ground since the preceding day, some cried out, *Vive l'Empereur !* and others, "The Emperor is coming, you will see him soon." I saw seven of their horses lying in a heap, near the spot where the 92nd brought them up.

We were followed by a large body of cavalry. After we had passed through Genappe, and as they debouched from it, the Earl of Uxbridge directed the 7th hussars, his own corps, to charge them ; the British regiment made the attempt twice, but was each time repulsed with loss.   It was decidedly an error to oppose these hussars to the lances of the Imperial Guard, who were superior in weight of men and horses, as well as in numbers.   The officers of the 7th also rallied their men too soon after the failure of the first charge.   The Earl,[1] finding that the 7th could make no impression on their opponents, then brought up the first Life Guards ; and the difference between a light and a heavy regiment became quickly apparent ; for this fine corps bore down all opposition, and drove back the French cavalry in great confusion.   After this affair no further attempt to molest us was made by the enemy ; all that we suffered from was the weather, as the rain fell in torrents.   It seems rather unaccountable that the French should have permitted us to retire in this manner, since Ney was then at the head of two corps, and Napoleon was about to follow him with a similar force.

We halted between Genappe and Waterloo, it

[1] The Earl of Uxbridge subsequently addressed a letter to the 7th hussars, acquitting them of all blame for their conduct in this affair.— H. R-L.

being the Duke's intention to make a stand about half a league in front of the latter place. Each regiment took up its ground without the least confusion ; and the fifth division passed rather an uncomfortable night, lying among high grass and corn, " in thunder, lightning, and in rain."

During this day Marshal Blucher had retreated without interruption to Gembloux, where he was joined by his fourth corps under Bulow ; and, proceeding thence to Wavre, he had taken up a good position there, and re-opened his communications with the Duke of Wellington.

CHAPTER XV

As morning dawned on the 18th, the men procured
some wood and made large fires ; biscuits and spirits
were served out ; and our clothes were nearly dry
when the enemy appeared on the heights opposite to
us, standing to their arms. Our men immediately
began to rub dry their firelocks, put in new flints,
and make all necessary preparation for the day's
work. The ground occupied by us extended, it was
supposed, about a mile and a half, and was exactly
calculated to contain an army of our strength.

Lord Wellington's force was, considering his loss
on the 16th, about 75,000 British, Germans of the
Legion, Hanoverians, Brunswickers, Dutch, Nassauers, and Belgians, and he disposed these troops
as follows : on the right, under Lord Hill, were the
second and fourth British divisions, the third and
sixth Hanoverian divisions, and General Chasse's
division of Netherlanders. Lord Hill's right was
thrown back on a deep ravine toward Merke Braine,
and the village of Braine la Lende, beyond this

hamlet, was also occupied. And here between 4000 and 5000 British and Belgians were placed in observation, wholly out of the line, on a cross-road which led to Brussels. The centre was composed of the corps of the Prince of Orange. The village of Mount St. Jean, where the roads leading from Nivelles and Charleroi to Brussels unite, was at some distance in his rear, and both these roads passed through his ground. In front of the right centre and near the Nivelles road, was the chateau of Hougoumont, which was surrounded by a grove of tall trees, an orchard, and walled gardens ; this post, which was at the angle where the right wing was thrown back *en potence,* was of the greatest importance, and held by three companies of the Guards, the remainder of General Cooke's division being drawn up on the slope behind it. A light Nassau regiment also was detached from the centre to occupy the grove and orchards.

The left wing consisted of the fifth division,[1] commanded by Sir Thomas Picton, a British brigade under Major-General Lambert, and some Hanoverians and Netherlanders. Its right was on the main road from Charleroi to Brussels, and its left on a height above the hamlet of Ter-la-Haye, where the ground became woody and broken. The Prince of Weimar's brigade of Nassauers held Ter-la-Haye and some houses and farms on the extreme left. On the right side of the road, and at the bottom of

---

[1] The 32nd, together with the 1/95th, the 28th, and the 79th, formed the 8th Infantry Brigade under Sir James Kempt. Out of a total of 145 officers engaged, the 8th Brigade lost 95 killed and wounded.

the hill, stood the farm-house of la Haye Sainte, in which and the court-yard two companies of a light battalion of the German legion were posted. These were a detachment from General Alten's division, whose left flank rested on the Charleroi road.

The cavalry were, for the greater part, in rear of the left centre, and the artillery were disposed along the front of the whole line.

The ground from above la Haye Sainte, nearly to the extreme right of the position, sloped gently down, and was quite clear of all impediments. A long lane, with a quickset hedge at either side, ran by the entire front of the left wing, and here also the ground lay in an easy slope. Our front formed an irregular curve, convex toward the enemy. The extensive wood of Soignies was in our rear, and would have been of great importance to us, had we failed to maintain our position at Waterloo.

The Duke of Wellington's force, in the line, did not exceed 70,000 men. Thus Napoleon had skilfully contrived to make all his attacks with superior forces. His headquarters were at Planchenoit, a small village in rear of his right. His position extended about two miles along a ridge opposite, but rather more elevated and uneven than ours. The distance between both armies varied from one thousand to fourteen hundred yards. The intermediate space consisted of uninclosed cornfields.

The right wing of the French army was now commanded by Count Lobau. The veteran infantry of Napoleon's celebrated Guard were in reserve, as usual, on a plateau, near a detached farm-house.

After a few minutes past ten in the morning of the 18th the enemy sent forward a swarm of tirailleurs to the attack of Hougoumont ; they spread over all the ground in front of the house and plantations, and advanced, firing, without any seeming system. This irregular attack only preceded the advance of columns of infantry. The Nassauers were quickly dislodged, but the three companies of the Guards were more stubborn. These last were occasionally reinforced, and the enemy constantly sent fresh troops to the attack, being determined to carry this post at any cost. A great part of the artillery from the hostile position was also directed against it, and thirty pieces of ours continued to play on the assailants : our artillerymen received instructions not to fire at the enemy's guns, but on the masses of cavalry and infantry. The attack and defence were equally spirited. The roof of the château was set on fire by howitzers, and the enemy got possession of the plantations and gardens ; but the building, though in flames, was defended from the lower story so gallantly that the French could never enter it, and were finally expelled from the gardens and grove by the brigade of Guards engaged, and some Black Brunswickers, who were sent in support. Our troops maintained this post during the rest of the day with perfect success, displaying a degree of spirit and intrepidity commensurate with its value, for it certainly was the key of the position.

At the same time that the attack on Hougoumont commenced a heavy cannonade was kept up by the enemy upon our whole line, as a prelude to the advance of masses of cavalry and infantry. Several pieces of artillery were drawn by the enemy from their right down the slope of the hill that fronted the left wing of our army. The fifth division were then in columns of regiments, and a body of Belgians, with some of their field-pieces, occupied part of the lane, while the 95th and light companies were extended more in advance, with their right on a sand pit that lay opposite the gate of la Haye Sainte. As soon as the above - mentioned portion of the enemy's artillery were in position, the limbers were removed to the rear ; a few men remained at each gun, and they began to throw their shot into our columns with great precision. Their practice was undoubtedly very good, and the Belgians adopted a perfectly intelligible, although not very soldier-like method of expressing the high opinion they entertained of its excellence ; for only one or two shot had passed through them when they faced about, and went in a body to the rear, artillery and all. This little circumstance did not encourage us to place excessive reliance on the support to be expected from our new allies, *les braves Belges.*

There was also some skirmishing on our extreme left, between the tirailleurs and the Nassauers ; but the latter soon lost ground, and abandoned the hamlets and farm-houses which they occupied at the beginning.

The action now became very general. Columns of French infantry and cavalry, preceded by a formidable artillery, moved from every point, advanced up the slope, and precipitated themselves on the centre regiments of our army. The light troops that were in front of our line were driven in rapidly by the advancing enemy, the foreign cavalry that were to have supported them breaking and galloping off in all directions; but our regiments in square resisted the onset with the utmost intrepidity.

The enemy had advanced their artillery on the right side of the Brussels road to within one hundred and fifty paces of the crest of the hill, and every discharge made sad gaps in our squares. This was a most trying time for the young Hanoverian levies; nevertheless they stood firm. I have since heard their own officers say, that during the whole day they never evinced any disposition to give way, but that, at first, when openings were made in their squares by the enemy's artillery, there was some hesitation before they were filled up, as the men fancied that the shot would always strike at the same spot; however, when the officers explained to them the absurdity of this notion, they readily closed the breach.

Our artillery also made dreadful havoc in the ranks of the enemy in all their advances, yet the cuirassiers would ride up to the very muzzles, and at one time had possession of a great part of our guns, although they could not remove them, the limbers being in the rear. Whenever the cuirassiers found it necessary to retire our artillerymen advanced from the squares in which they had been compelled to take refuge, and renewed their fire. There were intervals during the day, in which we of the left wing had time to look about us; and it became a source of surprise to many that the French officers should be permitted to ride between the squares, as we saw them, while an immense column of our cavalry stood unemployed in the rear.

After making the most desperate efforts in other parts of the field, and especially at Hougoumont, the enemy turned their attention principally to the left and left centre. A strong body of French infantry advanced against the left wing,[1] and pressed on to the lane. Sir Thomas Picton instantly placed himself at the head of his division to meet the attack, crossed the lane, and charged the French, who, firing a volley, faced about and retired. Here, I must say that, upon the advance of the enemy, I observed some of our light troops fall back rather too soon.

The attack cost us a gallant leader, for Sir Thomas Picton received a ball through his right temple, and fell dead from his horse. His body was borne off the ground by two grenadiers of the 32nd regiment, and not, as painters incorrectly have it in their representations of this sad scene, by Highlanders. During the charge a French officer seized a stand of colours belonging to the above-mentioned corps,[2] but he was

---

[1] Sir James Kempt wrote (Siborne's *Waterloo Letters*): "I met D'Erlon's attack at the charge with the 28th, 32nd, and 79th regiments in line, and completely repulsed the enemy's column, driving it in a state of the greatest confusion down the slope." Lieutenant-Colonel Calvert remarks : "From 12.30–3 the 8th Brigade had to sustain repeated attacks from, I believe, the entire first corps of the French army."

[2] "The 32nd was formed in six divisions in consequence of its reduced numbers. In the attack of the French infantry on the left centre of the line the brigade advanced in line to charge. Immediately on passing the narrow road which ran along our front, the ensign carrying the regimental colour was severely wounded. I took the colour from him until another ensign could be called. Almost instantly after, the brigade

instantly run through the body by a sergeant's pike, as well as by the sword of the ensign who held the colour. And after the attack was repulsed two Frenchwomen were found dead on the field. I saw one of them; she was dressed in a nankeen jacket and trousers, and had been killed by a ball which had passed through her head.

Our troops pursued the retiring column down the slope, and would inevitably have closed with them, had they not begun to fire, and thereby retarded their advance. However, a good account was given of this column shortly after; for Sir William Ponsonby's brigade,[1] consisting of the Royals, the Scotch Greys, and the Enniskillen dragoons, galloped in at the corner of the field, and took more than 2000 of them prisoners, driving them out on the

still advancing, and the French infantry getting into disorder and beginning to retreat, a mounted (French) officer had his horse shot under him. When he extricated himself we were close on him. I had the colour on my left arm, and was slightly in advance of the division. He suddenly fronted me and seized the staff, I still retaining a grasp of the silk. At the same moment he attempted to draw his sabre, but had not accomplished it when the covering colour-sergeant, named Switzer, thrust his pike into his breast, and the right rank and file of the division, named Lacy, fired into him. He fell dead at my feet. Brevet-Major Toole, commanding the right centre division at the moment, called out, 'Save the brave fellow,' but it was too late."—Captain Belcher in Siborne's *Waterloo Letters*.

[1] "Very soon after reaching the spot where the 32nd was in position, a volley and a charge of bayonets caused the French to recoil in disorder, and with a heavy loss; and it was at this moment of fire, smoke, and excitement that the heavy cavalry of the army suddenly appeared among us, and instantly charged that infantry which the fire and charge of bayonets from Picton's division had previously shattered and broke" (Lieut.-Col. Leach, C.B., in Siborne's *Waterloo Letters*). It was presumably during this charge that Lieut. Ross-Lewin was "trampled into the mud."

S

road. The dragoons also captured two eagles, one belonging to the 45th and the other to the 105th French regiments of infantry. The prisoners were at once marched off to Brussels, where their appearance served to convince the inhabitants of the falsehood of the reports spread by the runaway Belgians, who had declared that the battle was lost, our army nearly cut to pieces, and the speedy entry of the victorious French inevitable.

After the repulse of our assailants we resumed our former position, and Sir James Kempt took the command of the division. The French cavalry, cuirassiers leading, then fell upon Sir William Ponsonby's brigade in very superior force, and a sharp and well-sustained, though unequal, combat ensued. Some Polish lancers, who charged from a different point, came suddenly upon Sir William Ponsonby at a moment when he unfortunately was separated from his men, and, owing to the weakness of his horse, which stuck fast in the mire, he could not effect his escape, and was killed on the spot.

Shortly after, a division of cuirassiers, who were sent to support the infantry then engaged under the direction of Marshal Ney in a pertinacious attack on the farm of la Haye Sainte, were charged by the household brigade, under Lord Edward Somerset, and very roughly handled. About this time, too, the captain who commanded at la Haye Sainte ran across the road to my regiment, and requested that we would direct him where to procure ammunition, as his was nearly all expended, and he feared that he should not be able to defend his post much longer.   He was advised to go farther to the rear, where some might be had ; but he was unsuccessful in his search.   Consequently, the French at length carried the farm-house, and bayoneted its defenders,[1] who had not a single cartridge left.   It was either through an oversight or through want of time—most probably the latter—that a passage had not been opened in the back of the house, by means of which a communication might have been kept up between the troops occupying la Haye Sainte and those posted behind it.   Had this been done the lives of many of those brave men would have been saved, as they might either have retired, or have been reinforced ; and, had the gateway which was to the front been built up, and the house and the wall of the farmyard been loopholed, a most galling fire might have been kept up from them on an enemy advancing by the Brussels road.   There was a sort of back-door to the house, but it was very small, and there was a descent of several steps from it, which made it almost impracticable for any of the men to escape by it, had they made the attempt, after their ammunition was expended.

After the enemy's success at la Haye Sainte, which occurred a little before 3 P.M., their fire from it was very annoying, and my regiment suffered a good deal.   At length the 27th (the Enniskillen foot), which had not been previously engaged, was led

---

[1] The pioneers which should have accompanied the garrison had been withdrawn, and it was only with the greatest difficulty that the infantry succeeded in making rough loopholes in time to meet the French attack. A vivid account of the loss of La Haye Sainte is given by Major Graeme in Siborne's *Waterloo Letters*, p. 407.

up by General Lambert, and occupied the ground on which we had hitherto stood. My regiment retired a few yards, formed square, and lay down ; but even in this situation some of our officers were wounded, and we lost several men. The 27th had not been long in their new position before they lost 400 men [1] without firing a shot, thus affording a fine example of steadiness, discipline, and passive courage. The possession of that farm-house was a great advantage to the enemy. It not only exposed a portion of our troops to a very destructive fire, but it also afforded a convenient and sheltered point where masses of theirs, both cavalry and infantry, might be collected, preparatory to fresh attacks. In the hope of victory, Napoleon now made the most strenuous efforts, and employed every kind of force, artillery, cavalry, and infantry, to overwhelm the brave but weakened battalions of the centre. Their ranks were thinning fast ; the partial charges of our cavalry, however gallant, afforded them little respite from the repeated assaults of cuirassiers and lancers, as well as of infantry ; and the fire of the British artillery could not reply sufficiently to that of the French ; yet all the energy and pertinacity of Napoleon, the fury and enthusiasm of his troops, and the superiority of his numbers, cavalry, and artillery, prevailed not over the firmness and discipline of those exposed and ill-supported squares. This

---

[1] This regiment (Inniskilling Fusiliers) is said to have lost 15 officers and 463 men out of a total strength of 698. In Dalton's *Waterloo Roll Call* only 9 out of 19 officers are returned as killed and wounded. Sir Harry Smith in his autobiography speaks of the "27th regiment lying literally dead in square."

furious and sanguinary conflict was long maintained ; but about five in the evening it suddenly slackened.

At this time two of Lord Hill's brigades were brought up and placed in the first line of the centre, and dispositions were made to meet an expected attack on the part of the position above la Haye Sainte. The cannonade still continued without intermission, and there was every indication that the pause in the close fighting would not last long. It was then that the Prussians first appeared. Bulow had come up with a small body of infantry and cavalry, rather to the rear of the enemy's right. The fire of his guns was discernible from our position ; but it soon ceased, as it was compelled to retire again. The French must have felt surprised, as well as disheartened, when they saw Prussian artillery opening on them while the British army still bade them defiance ; but they did not forget themselves, and with admirable alacrity showed a front to their new antagonists, whose opposition was then temporarily discontinued.

It was now evident that the arrival of the Prussians in force could not be delayed for any considerable time. The loss of the French, especially in cavalry, was already very severe, to say nothing of the discouraging effects of their repeated repulses ; and neither Hougoumont, nor any point in the main position of the British, had been carried. Napoleon, therefore, must have felt from this moment, if he did not think so before, that a complete victory was no longer within his grasp, and that all he could hope for was such a success as might enable him to avert the calamity of a total defeat. He had yet a strong reserve, composed of the infantry of the Imperial Guard, the flower of his troops, and with these he determined to make a desperate effort. Accordingly, between six and seven in the evening, he placed himself at their head, directing the attack, supported by cavalry and artillery, against the centre of the British army ; but he himself did not proceed beyond a pit at the foot of the slope, where he took his station, sheltered from the fire by a small mound. It is said that the countenances of those brave men were strongly expressive of chagrin and indignation as they marched past that spot, and saw their emperor there, at a moment when they expected him to be still at the head of the column, resolved to throw the die boldly, desperate as was the game, for victory or death—for an imperial throne or a soldier's grave. Their chief seemed to have forgotten Lodi ; and in the record of this, the last of his fields, history has placed a blot on the name of Napoleon-le-Grand. It is true that one or two of his generals implored him not to expose his precious life ; and disappointment, verging on despair, may have momentarily enfeebled his naturally powerful mind, and caused him to vacillate between the entreaties of mistaken friends or artful courtiers, and the dictates of honour and duty. The old and the middle guard, being about 10,000 strong, and led by Ney, still continued to advance in two columns, with their wonted gallantry : light troops and a portion of the first corps moved upon their right by la Haye Sainte, while the remains of the second corps, which had been princi-

pally engaged at Hougoumont, aided in the attack on
the outer flank. The troops from la Haye Sainte
beat back a brigade of Brunswickers who attempted
to arrest their progress ; but the Duke of Wellington
quickly rode up to the battalions which had given
way, and succeeded in rallying them.

To meet the attack of the Imperial Guards on the
right centre the Duke depended on two British
brigades, one of which belonged to the Guards, and
the other consisted of the 52nd, 71st, and two very
weak battalions of the 95th. The four regiments of
Sir Colin Halkett's brigade, which had already sustained a very severe loss, were placed between those
troops and the Brunswickers. The British battalions,
formed four deep by our sagacious commander's
directions, held their fire until they could give it with
full effect, then poured in a deadly volley that caused
the whole right column of the Imperial Guards,
which was the most advanced, to waver, and followed
it up with rapid and unintermitting discharges.
Within fifty yards of them, the enemy, who had
approached the position in fine order, attempted to
deploy, but in vain ; they could do nothing under
such a fire. They fell suddenly into inextricable
confusion, and facing about, retired precipitately in
broken masses, followed by the nearest British
infantry, and Sir Ormsby Vandeleur's and Sir Hussey
Vivian's brigades of light cavalry, of which the latter
were comparatively fresh. By this repulse the
fortune of the day was decided. Napoleon had
made his last effort—"*la Garde avoit donné*"; and all
that remained for him was retreat.

During this part of the day, between seven and eight o'clock, Sir James Kempt was on the right of his division, watching with perfect coolness the progress of the attack; and soon, taking off his hat, he cheered us on towards the enemy.[1] The British commander, now seeing that Bulow was again engaged on the enemy's right flank, and that Ziethen's corps was issuing from the woods on the left, ordered his whole line to advance. This inspiring order was received with a general shout, and the movement was made with all the alacrity of which troops so long and so harassingly engaged were capable. The Duke then crossed the main road with his glass in his hand, and galloped down the slope in front of our left to the spot where the remnant of the 27th regiment had halted. This handful of brave men gave him three hearty cheers, and I am confident that there was not a man in the army who did not feel elated at the sight of their victorious chief, safe and unhurt after this perilous and bloody day. Never did any general share the dangers of a battle in a greater degree than did the Duke of Wellington on the field of Waterloo. He was frequently in the hottest of the fire; almost every individual in his staff was either killed or wounded, and even he himself took

---

[1] A young officer of the 32nd writes: "We had not a single company for support, and the men were so completely worn out that it required the greatest exertion on the part of the officers to keep up their spirits. Not a soldier thought of giving ground, but victory seemed hopeless, and they gave themselves up to death with perfect indifference. A last effort was our only chance. The remains of the regiments were formed as well as the circumstances allowed, and when the French came within about forty paces, we set up a death howl, and rushed at them. They fled . . . in the greatest confusion." Quoted in *Historical Records of 32nd*, p. 127.

refuge at one time in the midst of a square, when charged by the enemy's cavalry. One would have thought that, throughout this memorable conflict, the commander vied with his troops, and the troops with their commander, in giving evidence of their mutual confidence.

The French army now abandoned all their ground, and a total rout ensued. The reserve of the Old Guard, with a gallantry becoming the high character of these veteran battalions, formed in squares, and, with some guns and a small body of cuirassiers, attempted an orderly retreat. They preserved their formation for a short time, resisting with steadiness the united efforts of the British horse and foot that assailed them ; but they suffered considerable loss, and of course were ultimately compelled to relinquish the unequal contest, and, disencumbering themselves of their knapsacks, to swell the fugitive mass.

The British and Prussian marshals met at the rear of the French position, near the farm of La Belle Alliance, and embraced each other with cordiality. Some Prussian regiments marched close to the spot where the fifth division was drawn up, and halted for a few minutes, their band playing "God Save the King," in compliment to us. Our hearty ally, Prince Blucher, immediately commenced an eager pursuit, and continued it throughout the night. Marshal Ney, like a true soldier, endeavoured with the aid of a few of his officers to rally some battalions of the Guard, and succeeded in some degree, but only for a very short time ; for the Prussians soon fell among them *pêle mêle*, and all was irretrievable confusion.

One hundred and fifty pieces of cannon were taken. The slaughter of the fugitive French by the Prussian cavalry was very great. Nothing could exceed the animosity that existed between the troops of these two nations ; and the victors unmercifully retaliated on the vanquished for former insults and injuries.

We remained on the field of battle during the night, our men being too much exhausted to follow the flying enemy any farther ; but the troops, to whom the pursuit was left, were well qualified to execute their task with vigour and effect. When the excitement of the fight was over, our people felt much oppressed by fatigue and want of refreshment ; still we contrived to make large fires, and to sleep very soundly for the remainder of the night round the hot embers.

One of the field-officers of my regiment having had his horse killed under him in the action, I consented to his replacing it with one of mine, and in consequence it became necessary for me to look out for another one. I repaired, as soon as I had risen from my heaven-canopied couch, to the park of artillery, where all captured horses were collected, and the officer commanding showed me one that had been shot in the chest. He was a fine young horse, four years old, and marked with the brand of the Imperial Guard, and, as the ball had not lodged, I determined to make trial of him. Though a little stiff, he was able to carry me, and I proceeded forthwith to ride over the field of battle. The mangled bodies of men and horses, broken gun-carriages, caps, helmets, cuirasses, arms, drums,[1] harness, accoutrements, pieces of battered uniforms, knapsacks, letters, and cards, that were strewed abundantly in all directions, and the crops levelled by the trampling of infantry and cavalry in the strife, plainly marked the extent of the field, and gave undeniable evidence of the fury of the conflict[2] that had raged there on the preceding day.

As I rode along, it was difficult to suppress those conflicting sensations of pride, exultation, and grief, which the remembrance of the events of the preceding day, and the sight of the present scene, had a natural tendency to awaken in the breast of any one similarly circumstanced. There lay, stiff and stark, many a gallant son of France or the British Isles, who had left their peaceful homes to meet as deadly foes, because their rulers had decreed to bide the stern arbitrament of war. How many a brave and generous spirit there quitted its mortal tenement, while the life-blood flowed from the wide sluices with which the manly form was gashed and disfigured! How many an affectionate heart was soon to become the abode of sorrow, when the tidings of the fatal yesterday should reach the ears of bereaved friends and relatives! How many a village in the victors' land had its bonfires, how many a city its

[1] The number of drums found on the field was particularly great, as the French drummers continue to roll during the charge, and consequently are much exposed. This was formerly the practice of our army also, but now the British drummers are employed in assisting the wounded.—H. R-L.

[2] Sir John Kincaid, then adjutant of the 1/95th, in his autobiography, remarks: "I had never heard of a battle in which *everybody* was killed, but this seemed likely to be an exception." And again: "The usual question after an action was to ask 'Who had been hit?'; on this occasion, 'Who is alive?' Meeting a very little fellow, I asked what had happened to them. 'I'll be d—d if I know anything at all, for I was all day trodden into the mud and galloped over by every scoundrel who had a horse.'"

illuminations, while the inmates of hundreds of their dwellings were to assume the sable garb of mourning for the fallen of their house, cut off in the pride of life, and fated to breathe their last on the chill, damp ground, far away from their own dear homes, and without one kind friend to comfort them in their dying agony, to wipe the cold sweat from the blood-stained brow, to receive the last parting wish or command, and to soothe the struggling soul with the hope of a happy hereafter! Such reflections are mournful, and will often suggest themselves, but there are others which diminish their effect.

It was a high and noble feeling that prompted the great Duke of Ormond to exclaim, when the body of his young, accomplished, and distinguished son, the gallant Earl of Ossory, was shown him, pierced with wounds, " My dead son, before any living son in Christendom ! "

Parties were busily employed on the field of battle in carrying off the wounded, and in burying the dead ; a great part of the latter were perfectly naked. A sergeant of the 12th light dragoons, who was with a burying party where our left had been stationed, had found, just as I came up to him, the bodies of two young cornets of his regiment, in search of which he had been for some time. I remarked to the sergeant that his regiment must have suffered dreadfully, judging from the number of bodies which I saw lying around me in the light cavalry uniform ; but he said that the dead at that spot were not all British, although the uniforms did appear to be very nearly the same. To be satisfied of this, I alighted, and had to examine the buttons before I could distinguish with any certainty between the dead of our dragoons and those of the French that lay mixed with them. This sergeant told me, that on the morning of the battle he rode up to a party of French light cavalry, which he had mistaken for some of his own regiment, they were clothed so much alike ; but a blow of a sabre, which wounded him slightly, soon convinced him of his error, and he owed his safety to the goodness of his horse. Is not this circumstance sufficient to illustrate the folly of our imitating so closely the costume of foreign troops ? At short distance the similarity of colour deceives, and at great, the difference of profile, especially of cap or helmet, is of great consequence. The postures into which some of the men had thrown themselves in their last agonies were not unfrequently remarkable. I saw a dead Highlander lying on his back, with his arms firmly bent in an exact boxing attitude, and near him one of the Enniskillen dragoons, whose hands were joined and elevated above his breast, as if he had expired in the act of prayer.

The total loss in killed, wounded, and missing of the British and King's German Legion, during the three days (not including that of the Hanoverian levies), exceeded 11,500 men, and that of the King of Netherland's different troops was stated at 4136. My regiment was reduced to one hundred and thirty, and my company to eleven men ; nor had we one reported missing.[1] Among the wounded were the

---

[1] The 32nd had numbered 674 officers and men on 14th June, of these 17 officers and 245 men had been lost at Quatre Bras, and 10 officers and 273 men at Waterloo. Ross-Lewin's company lost 49 men out of a total of 60.

Prince of Orange, and the present Marquis of Anglesey, then Earl of Uxbridge, who lost a leg. The two principal British officers killed were Sir Thomas Picton and Sir William Ponsonby. The latter was a very gallant officer, an amiable man, and much regretted. The former was a general of whom it may truly be said, he deserved well of his country, brave, energetic, and enterprising. Unsurpassed in spirit, zeal, and devotion, his example infused additional life and vigour into the troops who had the good fortune to be placed under his command ; what Ney was to the French, he was to the army that beat them. The motto of the Douglas seemed to ring unceasingly on his ear, and, wherever danger assumed its most terrific form, there he was to confront it. A noble specimen of the true soldier ; the compass by which he steered through life had honour for its pole, and knew no variations ; and proudly may the scions of the ancient race of Britons point to the page of history which the shining career of their countryman adorns, and bid their sons emulate the fame of their hero of Badajos and Waterloo.

The fighting at les Quatre Bras and Waterloo was of the severest character ; never were positions more furiously attacked or more obstinately defended. The French never fought with greater *acharnement*, as they express it; yet, at no moment during the two days was their fire equal to that with which they received us as we advanced to the attack of Clausel's position at Salamanca. Their artillery was admirably served, and the gallantry of their cuirassiers, though baffled by the intrepidity of our troops, was

most conspicuous, and merited the highest en-
comiums. They were chosen men, of tried courage
and experience, and formed really splendid cavalry ;
all behaved well, but several acts of chivalric daring
performed by individuals of their number, on both
these memorable days, were worthy of the olden
times of a Dubois and a Bayard. Victories gained
over such troops are indeed glorious. The conduct
of the infantry of the Guard at Waterloo, at the end
of the day, was also most heroic and devoted,
although their efforts were also unavailing. It is
needless to say with what determined valour the
greater portion of the different troops, composing
the Duke of Wellington's army, resisted and repelled
the enemy's most formidable attacks, and endured on
exposed positions a terrible and incessant artillery
fire ; the result speaks sufficiently to that point. At
the same time it may be mentioned that the practice
of our artillery was excellent, and also that our
heavy cavalry maintained a decided superiority over
the French force of the same kind in every charge
that was made. The household brigade, in particular, rendered themselves formidable to the
enemy's dragoons ; they were a very fine body of
men, and their superb horses were in the best
condition. Still it was a general remark in the
French army that their cavalry exposed themselves
too much, while we thought that our cavalry were
kept in reserve rather more than was necessary.
Perhaps the Duke wished to save them during the
action, in order to protect his rear with them, should
he have sustained a reverse sufficient to compel him

to make a retrograde movement. One of the consequences of the irrepressible ardour of the cuirassiers and other French cavalry was that their numbers were so diminished, and their horses so jaded, toward the close of the day, that they became ineffective when their army began to retire, and when their services were much wanted.

I cannot here pass over the conduct of a regiment of foreign hussars in our service. They were uncommonly well-appointed, clad in handsome scarlet uniforms, which were elegantly trimmed with white fur, and generally speaking selected from the middle or higher classes ; many of them, it is said, were members of the first families. Nevertheless, this corps of gentlemen did not fight ; whether through their setting too high a value on their gentle blood lightly to hazard the loss of any of it ; or through their feeling too proud of their local respectability to think of mixing in combat with men who, for the most part, were comparatively low-born soldiers ; or through their fancying themselves so ornamental that they were under no obligation to become useful, has not hitherto been ascertained : all that we know with certainty is, that every request made to them, with the view of inducing them to attempt a charge on some of the enemy's cavalry, met with a positive refusal. Some of the Belgian troops again, both cavalry and infantry, behaved in the most infamous manner, and numbers of them reached Brussels before the battle had well begun. It is my opinion that a want of heartiness in the cause was superadded to pusillanimity, so that both together strongly cooperated to dispose them in favour of retrograde movements ; and it is most probable that the Belgians in general were very indifferent as to the result of the campaign, provided that it did not tend to prolong the sojourn of the contending armies in their country. There was undoubtedly a numerous French party in Brussels at the time, and it is even said that many among the Brussellois had prepared suppers for the entertainment of the French, who, they confidently expected, would enter that city on the 18th, at an hour sufficiently early to admit of their partaking of the good cheer ; but, when the defeat of Napoleon was made known, they all appeared to be highly pleased, and they certainly paid the greatest attention to our wounded.

As we did not move off before the afternoon of the 19th, we heard, while near Waterloo, of the proceedings of the Prussians and the French during the night. The last stand was made at Genappe. The retreating troops found there some pieces of cannon that had been following their army during Napoleon's first advance ; they immediately placed them in position, and having upset some tumbrils and waggons, and having barricadoed the street and the entrances to it, seemed determined to make a vigorous resistance. Upon this, the Prussians brought up some field-pieces, and, after firing a few rounds, carried the town by storm. Had not the French been so completely disheartened, they might have checked the pursuit here for some considerable time, and enabled the rest of their army to continue their retreat so long unmolested, and partly

T

to recover from their confusion. Sixty pieces of cannon, with all Napoleon's *materiel*, were taken; and the Prussian and Brunswick horse charged furiously through the town, sabring indiscriminately all the fugitives they overtook. One of the Brunswickers came up with the French general, Duhesme, who earnestly called for quarter, but the reply he received was, "You killed our Duke on the 16th, and you shall not survive him;" and these words were accompanied by a sabre stroke that felled him to the ground. Napoleon's carriage was taken just as he had quitted it to mount a horse, on which he effected his escape. The French army then began to separate into small bodies; their cavalry sold their horses to the farmers; and their generals found it wholly impossible to rally the fugitives before they had crossed the Sambre, Napoleon himself having failed in an attempt to arrest their flight at Charleroi. It happened unfortunately for the runaway troops that we were not in a condition to pursue them, instead of being obliged, through weariness, to leave that duty to the Prussians, as undoubtedly more quarter would have been given, although they had treated some of the few British prisoners taken on the 16th and 18th with great inhumanity. The Prussians had not forgotten the French visit to Berlin.

We took the Nivelle road through Bavay, and halted for one day at the latter place. It is an inconsiderable town, but remarkable for its vicinity to the village of Malplaquet, where the Duke of Marlborough and Prince Eugene defeated the

French army in the year 1709. When passing through the principal street of Bavay, my attention was arrested by the uncommon appearance of the arms blazoned on the panels of a coach, which was drawn up at the door of a British general's billet: "Pray, sir," said I to a little man who wore a travelling cap and was standing near, "can you tell me whose carriage this is?" "It belongs to your humble servant," he replied, "Sir Sidney Smith." We entered into conversation. He had discovered Napoleon's cipher, and with it all that monarch's plans, from the papers found in the imperial carriage at Genappe. He also informed me that we would meet with no opposition before we reached Montmartre. Sir Sidney Smith carried his forage with him, and had a haystack raised between the hind wheels of his carriage; some wags intended to put a coal of fire in this cumbrous appendage to the vehicle as he was going to start, but were by some means prevented from carrying this mischievous design into execution.

The British and Prussian armies continued their advance on Paris almost without interruption. Sir Charles Colville was sent to the right to take Cambray; the walls of this town were fifty-eight feet high. The British general, in the name of Louis XVIII., summoned the garrison to surrender, but they refused. Upon this the inhabitants let down ladders from the inside, and the town was taken by escalade. The French soldiers retired into the citadel with the loss of 130 prisoners; but on the 23rd they acknowledged Louis XVIII., who was very well received at Cambray on the following day. On the 26th of June the first brigade of Guards stormed the outworks of Peronne, once La Pucelle, and immediately after its citadel surrendered.

A Prussian corps had preceded us on the march and plundered all the villages that lay along our route ; the most wanton acts of mischief had been committed ; windows were broken, handsome pier-glasses smashed, furniture of all sorts demolished, and the wells filled up. A palace of Joseph Bona-parte's was plundered of everything by our men ; sofas covered with white or green velvet became seats for our soldiers in their wigwams ; libraries of richly bound books were scattered about ; statues broken ; and, in short, every species of damage was done to the interior of the building. One morning on entering a chateau I heard the sound of a piano, touched by no skilful hand, in an adjoining room. The door was open and I walked up to it, when I found one of our pioneers seated at the instrument thumping the keys most unmercifully, and apparently much pleased with his performance. The stool on which he sat was covered with white velvet, and the marks left by his fingers on either side of it were very visible. The piano was afterwards broken up for the sake of the wires, which the men made use of for clearing their tobacco pipes. The Prussians, sharpsighted as they were in such matters, did not discover all the prog, for we were so lucky as to dig up a quantity of wine which had been buried in the gardens, and, besides, a great number of turkeys and hams were brought in to the bivouac.

We prosecuted our march to St. Denis without interruption ; but it had evidently been intended to arrest our progress there, as we found a breastwork raised across the road, and some guns planted behind it. On the 7th of July we bivouacked near Neuilly, which is only two miles from Paris. By this time I had effected a complete cure of my Waterloo horse. On the march a Prussian officer stole him out of my stable. This gentleman's camp was about two miles off, and, as soon as my charger was reported missing, I hastened thither, thinking it highly probable that he added one to the great number of horses which then followed the Prussian army. I soon found him, and the officer did not deny that he had taken him, but he assured me that he would have been the last person in the world to do so, had he known that the animal was the property of an Englishman.

The French were hotly pursued by the Prussians, and the latter, after some fighting, arrived before Paris on the 29th of June.

The Parisians had laboured with great energy at the various defences which it had been thought necessary to erect. St. Denis was well garrisoned, and every effort made to render the post defensible. The heights of Montmartre were strongly fortified and well provided with artillery. On the southern side of the Seine the defences were very weak—the French troops occupied there the village of Issy, the heights of Meudon, and St. Cloud ; but no attempt at strengthening them had been made, with the exception of the casemating some houses, and the digging one or two inconsiderable trenches. Accordingly, Blucher resolved to make the attack at this side, and, on the 30th, crossing the Seine, and occupying Versailles, he threatened the French position at the points already mentioned. The Duke of Wellington, in the meantime, having possession of Gonesse, was enabled to communicate with the Prussians by a bridge at Argenteuil. General Excelmans, however, contrived to surprise the Prussians at Versailles, and made some of their cavalry prisoners; but this success was speedily counterbalanced, for on the 2nd of July the French troops were forced to abandon their position and post themselves close to the city. The respectable inhabitants who had property at stake were now anxious to avert the horrors of an assault, for which the allies seemed to be preparing, while the soldiery and the populace were excited almost to madness, and it was hourly feared that some dreadful commotion would take place within the metropolis. However, on the following day Massena, who was commander-in-chief, made arrangements for a surrender, and terms were finally agreed to between him and the allies. At the time of the convention Marshal Davoust, say the French, had nearly 60,000 foot, 25,000 horse, and from four to five hundred pieces of cannon.

CHAPTER XVI

Surrender of Paris—Louis enters the city—Occupation of Paris by the Allies—I charge the Emperor of Austria—Remarks on the British, German, French, Portuguese, Spanish, Austrian, and Russian soldiers—Death of Ney—March to the coast—Ireland once more. *Note:* John Ross-Lewin, the author's youngest son.

IN the meantime the allied sovereigns [1] also advanced on Paris at the head of numerous forces, and established their headquarters at Hall on the 3rd of July. But the signal defeat of the French at Waterloo had already decided the fate of the common enemy ; and the allied sovereigns crossed the confines of France only to hear of the real termination of hostilities by the convention entered into at Paris.

The convention was received by the French army with violent indignation, which led to the commission of some excesses ; they even attempted to fall on the allied troops, who behaved with firmness and coolness, and calmly stood on their defence. During the whole of the 4th Paris resounded with cries of " *Vive l'Empereur !* " and the enraged armed bands of the populace fired from the bridges on several passengers. However, the generals succeeded in appeasing the soldiery, and the National Guard, which amounted to nearly 30,000 men, contrived to keep in awe their

[1] The Russian and Austrian emperors together with the King of Germany.

refractory fellow-citizens of the lower classes. On the 5th the troops of the Imperial Guard marched out, some crying "*Vive l'Empereur!*" and firing on the Prussian sentinels, who steadily refrained from returning the fire.

In the preceding year the victors had entered Paris in triumph, but all such display was avoided on the present occasion. The National Guards behaved with the best temper, and were relieved at the barriers in an orderly manner by the allied troops. On the morning of the 8th the tri-coloured flag was lowered in all parts of the city, and the lilied banner floated once more over the various public edifices. This was followed by the entrance of Louis le Desiré. When the restored monarch reached the barrier he found the prefect and the municipal body of Paris assembled to receive him, and surrounded by a dense crowd. The prefect inflicted on him a lengthy harangue, in which he dwelt on the miseries experienced by His Majesty's people during the Hundred Days, and the felicity again so confidently promised to them, and begun already to be so gratefully felt. The King replied in a few words; and then the royal carriage moved forward slowly, escorted by the Marshals of France and the municipal body, while kerchiefs waved from the windows, and the air was rent with acclamations. Louis had also with him a body of 8000 men, which had been organised at Ghent, and a few field-pieces; and the National Guards lined the streets through which the procession passed. When I said that the tri-coloured flag was lowered everywhere on the morning of the

8th, I should have excepted the Place Vendôme, for the King was entering it before the removal of the obnoxious ensign from the splendid pillar, which stands in the centre, and was formed of the cannon captured by Napoleon in different actions ; whether this circumstance was the effect of accident or design I cannot say, but it might easily have been construed as a slight to His Most Christian Majesty. The royal cortège reached the Tuileries about five o'clock.

Before that hour I stationed myself in the garden of the palace, and entered into conversation with some of the National Guards ; they spoke very disrespectfully of the King, and said that he would never have seen Paris again but for the Duke of Wellington, who was, in point of fact, King of France. The garden was filled with well-dressed people ; and some brought bands with them and danced under the windows, the ladies wearing garlands of lilies. Immediately after His Majesty entered the palace, he reappeared on the balcony, and made an attempt to address his congregated lieges, but his words were drowned in loud and reiterated cries of " *Vive le roi !—vivent les Bourbons !* " that proceeded from all parts of the densely-peopled area. The British officers who were mixed with the crowd did everything in their power to enforce silence. When, therefore, His Majesty perceived that it was in vain to expect a hearing, he had recourse to dumb show ; he first laid his hand on his heart to declare how gratitude for their expressions of loyalty, and affection for themselves, centred there, and then kissed his hand repeatedly, and retired. " Now," said a loyal Frenchman who stood near me, "he will go and eat four pullets for dinner ; the physicians will not allow him to take more."

King Louis seemed to be very unwieldy and in-active, but his countenance indicated a placid, benign, and benevolent disposition.   That he was an amiable, pious, accomplished, and polished prince no im-partial person will deny ; still he was not a monarch qualified by natural endowments, or by education and habits, to rule over such a people as the French of the nineteenth century.   Fortune, in raising him to a throne, marred the design of nature, which had fitted him to become a finished private gentleman.

The English newspapers containing the Duke of Wellington's despatches now arrived at our canton-ments.   Some regiments that had taken part in the battle of Quatre Bras were much hurt when they found that they had been overlooked, as they felt that their conduct had certainly merited particular notice.   The following are the six battalions that suffered the greatest loss during the campaign : the second and third battalions of the 1st regiment of Guards, the 27th, 32nd, the 79th, and the 92nd. On the 24th there was a grand review of the army under the Duke of Wellington.   The Emperors of Austria and Russia and the Kings of Prussia and the Netherlands attended to witness this military spec-tacle.   The troops were under arms from six in the morning until the same hour in the evening, and it was to them a very tiresome day, however enter-taining it may have been to the imperial and royal spectators.

To return to Paris and the camp. Our tents and huts were much infested by different kinds of insects, but specially by earwigs, which crawled up the tent-poles at night, and clustered there like a swarm of bees ; we often found also large black worms between our sheets. My tent was pitched close to the Seine, where its surface is covered with thousands of the broad flat leaves of the lotus ; such parts of the river attract the frog-fishers, as their prey congregate there in great numbers. Each of those anglers is provided with a long osier rod, from the smaller end of which a piece of fat meat depends by means of a cord ; he throws out this bait among the leaves until a frog pops up and swallows it, and then, by a sudden jerk, he whips the greedy animal over his head, and bags it if he finds the back free from speckles, but if it be not, the frog is flung away and the rod resumed.

Paris now became a scene of the greatest gaiety ; the streets and places of public resort were crowded with the militaires of almost every nation ; at every step something calculated to excite interest presented itself ; all exhibitions at national institutions, not excepting the Louvre, were open gratis to the inspection of strangers every day, and of the natives twice a week ; in this respect, besides many others, the French capital possesses a great advantage over the English. We required no introduction at Paris to enable us to pass a few months there agreeably. As far as regarded politics, the Parisians were, generally speaking, discontented with the present order of things ; the pink began to be seen frequently, and in crowds, the cry of "*Vive l'Empereur*," uttered with a loud voice, was occasionally heard, though the words "*de Russe*" or "*d'Autriche*" were repeated after it, in an under-tone, in order to protect the speaker from the charge of sedition, should any of the police be near him ; and it became every day more evident that the Tuileries would soon be vacant again but for the support afforded to the Bourbons by the allied powers. The sight of troops which they had so often vanquished, in possession of the capital of France, was galling in the extreme to the feelings of its inhabitants. They declared that the presence of the English, whose courage, generosity, and love of liberty were so congenial with their own sentiments, did not disturb them in the least ; but that they could ill endure to have a king forced upon them, after all their splendid military achievements, by Austrians, Russians, Prussians, Bavarians, Dutch, and Belgians.

The Prussian officers carried matters with a very high hand at Paris, being determined to teach the French how disagreeable such conduct as theirs in Berlin, in the days of Napoleon's triumphs, must be to all whose only choice is submission. Whenever officers of these two rival nations met in any public place of amusement, the Prussians insisted upon being attended first, behaved frequently with a rudeness little short of actual violence, and certainly they obtained ample revenge. The Prussian soldiery were not more conciliatory in their demeanour toward the people. A guard of British and Prussians mixed were constantly stationed at the Palais Royal, and one day a Prussian soldier when walking there got into a row with a mob, and was very roughly handled. An Irish grenadier of imposing altitude, upon hearing the affray, sallied out of the guard-room without his firelock, and, striding to the scene of action, quickly made a lane for himself by dividing the mob with both hands, as if he were swimming, which he did with the greatest ease and coolness, until he got within reach of the Prussian, who by that time was on the ground ; and then, stretching out his long neck and peering over the heads of the pigmies that yet intervened, he called out in the genuine Hibernian brogue, "Who is dat a-batin' of de allies ?" The whole formed a group that might remind one of the old war of the cranes and their diminutive antagonists. The rescue of the ally was immediately effected, and his stalwart liberator conveyed him to the guard-room without further molestation.

A second grand review of a portion of the allied troops took place, and was again attended by the four sovereigns. The French officers gave it as their opinion that the English troops had the advantage over the others, as well in appearance as in other respects, but our grenadiers would have looked better than they did, had they had their dress caps ; and, indeed, the rest of the British infantry were dis-figured by the small caps which they then wore, and for which the chaco has since been substituted. The Russian guards made a superb show, being not only a very superior body of men, but also well dressed and appointed ; and they marched past with the greatest steadiness and every appearance of perfect discipline. The principal defect that I could remark in them was the too great padding of their coats, and the unusual strength of their leathern gloves; the latter kept the fingers wide apart, and both gave the men an air of stiffness and inactivity which a soldier should never have.

The crowned heads seemed now to be thoroughly possessed with the *rage militaire.* They all went to Dijon to see the Austrian troops; and, on their return, the Duke treated them with a representation of the battle of Salamanca. I was not in the ranks on this occasion, but rode to the ground; my steed was very hard-pulled, and carried me alongside the Emperor of Austria; but, as his staff perceived that my intrusion among them was perfectly accidental and involuntary, it passed off with a smile. In one of the manœuvres the infantry opened to let the cavalry pass between, and while they were executing it the Emperor of Russia rode off from his staff and the Duke of Wellington, and galloped down to see the Household Brigade charge. The effect was very imposing, and the Emperor's attention seemed to be particularly arrested by the fine appearance of the Oxford Blues.

It may be permitted to make here a few observations that suggest themselves with respect to the qualities and character of the several kinds of troops with which I have met at different times. To begin with the British :—They are the best paid, best fed, and best clad troops in Europe; make the most brilliant and imposing appearance; and with equal

numbers, either cavalry or infantry, will beat any
soldiers in the world in an open country. In the
field our cavalry invariably showed themselves to be
superior in prowess to the French ; their chief fault
there, especially in the first campaigns of the Peninsular War, was an ill-restrained impetuosity, which
often led them into disadvantageous situations.
Witness the conduct of the 20th light dragoons
at Vimiera, where they galloped headlong, until
they were surrounded by vastly superior numbers,
and lost their colonel ; of the 23rd light dragoons
at Talavera, where they made a charge down a steep
ravine that has never been exceeded for reckless
daring, but occasioned them a severe and unnecessary
loss ; and again of the 13th light dragoons, who
dashed in a pursuit up to the very gates of Badajos,
and in the midst of the French forces. But, when
fighting was not so much required, the British cavalry
inefficiently performed various important duties, such
as the outpost, foraging, or convoying, and betrayed
much ignorance of the profession, and a culpable
want of vigilance and caution.

A considerable portion of the officers were care-
less young fellows, brought up in luxury, and unused
to anything bordering on serious application ; they
seemed to entertain the mistaken notion that all a
dragoon had to do was to make a dashing appearance, and to charge while his horse could carry him.
With the love of a handsome uniform and a showy
exterior, so common in all branches of the service,
but especially in the cavalry, I find no fault. In
the more degenerate days of ancient Greece, when

Spartan simplicity and Spartan determination were fast disappearing, the experienced and judicious Philopœmon found it necessary to give his soldiers of the League richly decorated and glittering appointments, in order to encourage a taste for the military profession among the dandified youth of his country. Our dashing dragoons then are very welcome to imitate in dress the "*beau sabreur*" of the French army, or the "golden lion" of ours, provided that they do not forget in the meantime to emulate their just reputation in war. The consequences of the inexperience or carelessness of the British cavalry were disagreeably manifested in certain surprises of their picquets by our alert foe ; till at length two regiments of German light horse in our service, that we had in the Peninsula, taught them something of the real duty of a soldier. Our cavalry horses, too, were frequently in the worst condition ; they are not so hardy by nature as those of many other countries, and they required better forage than they generally got in Spain or Portugal ; but I still think that they were not so well attended to as they ought to have been, and by such neglect the evil was materially increased. I never saw such wretched spectacles, such caricatures of the highboned Rosinante of immortal memory, as a brigade of our light cavalry were, that I observed on the retreat from Burgos at the time when General Paget was taken prisoner ; they appeared to be hardly able to crawl under the weight of their riders, and quite incapable of showing a front to the enemy's dragoons. The German hussars were very attentive to their horses, and almost lived with them ; I have often seen these men lying on the ground, fast asleep, while their horses stood between their legs, and, though the animals were tormented by flies and constantly stamping, their masters never apprehended any accident from them. I do not think that our light cavalry were well armed ; their carbines were too short and their sabres very bad.

The British artillery was in general very well served, though perhaps not quite so well as that of our enemy. With engineers, miners, sappers, &c., we were very indifferently provided ; and in the commencement of the war, nothing could have been more defective than the quartermaster - general's department.

Our troops of the line proved themselves to be the best heavy infantry in Europe, whether in the field of battle or in the breach. Their steady, confident, and unflinching courage, their discipline, and their physical strength, which no people know how to exert with greater effect, combine to give them this superiority, as a class of force which necessarily constitutes the main strength of every army, and on the conduct of which the hope of victory chiefly depends. There is no resisting an unbroken charge of British infantry.

Our German sharpshooters improved them considerably in the several duties of light troops ;[1] still

---

[1] With reference to the training of the German troops, Sir Harry Smith, in his Autobiography, vol. i. p. 26, says : " The men of the 1st German Hussars would often observe with the naked eye a body of the enemy which was scarcely discernible through a telescope, so practised were they and watchful."

they never attained to such a degree of perfection as might have been expected from a consideration of their natural qualifications. Our men, particularly in the beginning of the war, entertained very generally the absurd notion that the taking advantage of any sort of cover which lay in their way, when skirmishing, was an act of cowardice, and some of our commanders, strangely as the assertion may sound, seemed desirous to encourage them in this way of thinking. When we consider our soldiers, as such, we cannot approve of their yielding to this sense of shame ; but we cannot fail to admire them, as men, for preferring danger to what they considered dishonour. How differently the old Germans thought ! They were always to be seen dodging from tree to tree, or ensconcing themselves between rocks and fences, with admirable method and steadiness, while the British skirmisher would step out sturdily on the open space, and make a target of himself for the enemy. Still, in this irregular fighting, our men generally beat the French, and particularly when an opportunity presented itself for pressing forward rapidly, which their natural determination never suffered them to lose ; and the French infantry were seldom fond of coming to close quarters with our men, who, when they did, usually compelled some of them "to shrink under their courtesy." But it was on picquet that this disdain of shelter from the enemy's fire, so prevalent among our troops, was most likely to be injurious. It is the duty of a picquet to give warning of the approach of an enemy, and also to endeavour to keep him

in check as long as it is practicable, without danger
of being cut off. In order, therefore, to accomplish
their object in the most effectual manner, they should
neglect no advantage that the nature of the ground
affords, and steadily avoid exposing themselves more
than is absolutely necessary. If they do otherwise
they must expect to be well peppered, or quickly
driven in, and, indeed, it is most probable that both
these contingencies will befall them together. I
have known more than one instance in which
picquets that had been advantageously posted, have
foolishly abandoned the natural defences that gave
the few some chance of resisting the many successfully, and have, in consequence, received rather
rough treatment. I recollect particularly one affair
which occurred early in the war, and in which an
extensive line of picquets, composed of parties from
different regiments, were concerned. They were
posted most advantageously in a ditch, with a breastwork to fire over ; but when the enemy, who came
on in considerable force, appeared in their front, two
of our officers with their own men rushed out from
under cover into an open field, and in a few minutes
one of the two, and half of his men, were placed
hors-de-combat, without their having occasioned any
serious loss to the assailants. The rest of the
picquets maintained their favourable position, and
keeping up a rapid and well-directed fire, did great
execution; and they it was who really repulsed the
attack, as was evident from the numbers of the
enemy who lay killed and wounded in their immediate front ; yet, those officers who so thoughtlessly

and needlessly exposed themselves and their men, received almost the whole credit of this affair, and the senior of them was soon after promoted. Now what, may I ask, enhances the value of any success in war, in a greater degree, than the fact that it was achieved with the least possible numerical loss to the victors, and with a severe one to their opponents? Inasmuch, also, as courage is a higher quality than bravery, so the soldier, whose coolness and presence of mind enable him to seize every opportunity of fighting to advantage, becomes still more deserving of our approbation than the rash and hotheaded, who rush unmeaningly into dangers which the interests of the army require them to avoid, and whose ill-directed bravery reminds us of the description that Shakespeare makes Alençon give of English mastiffs, "Foolish curs, which run winking into the mouth of a Russian bear, and have their heads crushed like rotten apples."

I have seen some valuable officers of different regiments lose their lives by a display of indifference to fire at a time when no possible good could result from it. In battle regiments are sometimes ordered to lie down, to prevent an unnecessary loss of life, when their fire cannot be effectual; yet on such occasions some officers will continue to walk about, attracting the enemy's fire, which it were better to avoid, and exposing their own lives without benefit, but, on the contrary, with detriment to the service. This was particularly observable at Quatre Bras. My remarks on this point have reference only to officers in the ranks, for such as are mounted are usually occupied in observing the enemy's movements. The part of a good officer is never to court danger unnecessarily for the sake of display, but to be always ready to encounter it the moment that circumstances require him to do so. Such self-preserving considerations are forced upon us by the practice of the continental armies. If they will take every advantage of the nature of the ground on which they act, we must exert our utmost cunning to foil the enemy in their own manner: if they will revert to the old stand-up fight of our ancestors, we shall, I am confident, most cheerfully do the same; but until such a change of tactics shall be brought about it is mere foolhardiness in us to neglect advantages of which they avail themselves with effect.

With respect to intelligence, our men were certainly inferior to the French. Our troops are habituated to act by word of command, and not to think; the officers take all upon themselves; and, on service, when thrown into situations where he is left to his own discretion, the British soldier cannot be expected to act with so much confidence and judgment as those who are more accustomed to depend on their own resources. On the contrary, the French soldier knows everything that is going on, and consequently displays admirable sagacity and ingenuity. But there is another and a still more valuable quality which, in my opinion, is shared in a manner quite the reverse. The courage of the British soldier stubbornly adheres to the sticking-place without exhortations from his officers, while that of the French seems often to require an artificial stimulus. We may compare this quality in the former to a good bottle of our ale—always up—but the more so the nearer it is to the fire ; and, in the latter, to the sparkling champagne— quickly effervescing, but as quickly subsiding unless continually stirred.

The Portuguese army, after its reorganisation under the able superintendence of Marshal Beresford, became in most respects surprisingly effective. The cavalry, mounted on very light horses of the Spanish breed, were certainly indifferent troops, but the infantry behaved remarkably well, and some of the Caçadores particularly distinguished themselves by their spirit and daring on many occasions : of course, their confidence in their British officers and their hatred of the French were powerful ingredients to mix with and give effect to their natural desire to acquit themselves creditably. In general, the men were of rather low stature and narrow shouldered, though they had good legs ; still I have seen one or two very fine regiments of Portuguese infantry. They were not entirely free from a tincture of that gasconade so observable among the natives of most of the southern part of Europe, and seemed to affect a certain coolness of manner. When the balls whistled by their ears they would often exclaim, "The devil take the flies !" at the same time imitating the action of brushing them away from their heads ; and that they entertained no mean opinion of themselves is tolerably evident from the subjoined passage, extracted from a speech of one of their generals to his men upon the termination of the war in 1814 : "Valorous Portuguese, brothers in arms, conquerors of our enemies, liberators of our country!—in you are combined all the valuable qualities of the soldiers of Europe—the discipline of the Prussians, the subordination of the Russians, the attack and the fire of the French, and the firmness of the English—in short, one Portuguese soldier is in himself an army!" But, though not fully entitled to praise so unqualified, it must be acknowledged that they merited a great deal, both for their excellence as troops and their cordial co-operation with their allies.

The Spanish troops were finer-looking men than the Portuguese, but they were far from being so useful to us, or so much to be relied on in trying circumstances. The generals were, with some few honourable exceptions, rash, self-willed, and unskilful ; the regimental officers ignorant and inefficient ; the men individually brave, active, and hardy, but ill-armed, ill-clad, and ill-fed. They had no confidence either in their commanders or in their comrades ; and the cry of "treason" produced the same effect in their minds as that of "*Sauve qui peut*" in the French ; almost in the moment of victory sudden panics would seize them, and they would fly from the field in total confusion. The Spanish infantry also, in consequence of their imperfect discipline and bad formations, are most apprehensive of attacks from cavalry—a force whose very name cried by a few voices has sufficed to put them to flight. They were so slow and awkward in manœuvring that it was nearly impossible to execute any change of dispositions with them in the field ; and thus their unwieldiness was sometimes very perplexing to their allies. Nothing could be more uncertain, more capricious than their conduct when engaged ; at one time they would behave with extraordinary intrepidity ; at another, though equally well posted and in no greater danger, they seemed to have exchanged the hearts of lions for those of deer. The French officers used to remark that a Spaniard fought best at midnight and a Frenchman at noon. But the patriot troops deserve much credit for the persevering spirit and the readiness with which they constantly seized the earliest opportunities of re-assembling, after they had sustained the most disheartening and bloody defeats, and been totally disorganised and dispersed ; and, whatever may have been his unsteadiness in particular actions, the Spanish soldier, brave by nature, but half-starved, ragged, shoeless, ever ill-treated, and generally ill-commanded, claims from every impartial observer not censure and contempt, but pity and commiseration. The manner in which the Spaniards defended several of their towns and fortresses, had their gallantry in the field been still less frequently displayed, is alone sufficient to show that their disasters during the war ought to be attributed to causes independent of any deficiency of personal valour. Modern history affords few parallels to the heroic defence of Gerona, conducted by the brave and illustrious Don Mariano Alvarez, and that of Saragossa, when Palafox commanded there. The persevering and daring efforts of the spirited

Catalans in the field to free their country from
its invaders were likewise above all praise. The
patriots experienced a great loss during the war
by the early deaths of the sensible, judicious, and
patriotic Marquis de Romana, the truly noble
Duke del Albuquerque, and the intrepid and
energetic Reding.

The Guerillas—a partizan force, variously armed,
easily subsisted, and mounted on nimble and hardy
horses—were very zealous and active ; the desultory
warfare they maintained in a country of which they
had a perfect knowledge, was excessively annoying
and harassing to the French troops ; they were continually seizing convoys, intercepting couriers, cutting
off stragglers, surprising weak detachments, and causing alarms. Some of the bands consisted of several
hundred men ; others did not exceed twenty or
thirty ; but all were headed by vigilant and enterprising chiefs, among whom Don Julian Sanchez,
Mina, Longs, Porlier, and the Empecinado were
particularly distinguished. The giving of military
rank to the chiefs toward the close of the war,
and the attempts made to discipline the guerillas,
were very injudicious measures, and greatly diminished the utility of this force.

The Prussian soldiers, owing to rigid discipline and
a too frequent use of the cane, are mere machines ;
but they are fine men, and look well on parade, without the adventitious aid of showy uniforms. Their
artillery was very inferior in appearance to the
British. Blue and grey are the prevailing colours
in the Prussian military costume.

The Austrian army comprise a great variety of troops, regular and irregular, light and heavy, differing in personal appearance, uniform, language, and character.   Their regular troops are kept in strict subordination and severely drilled, but rapidity of movement is not their forte.   Their cuirassiers wear no back-plates, which has a tendency to make them lean forward when tired, and, in their conflicts with the French cavalry of the same class, who have a complete iron shell, they have generally been the greatest sufferers.   The officers, as well as those of the Prussian army, are theorists, still wondering how the tactics of Frederick the Great could be defeated, and depending too much upon the strength of their positions and the security of their flanks.   If an Austrian army only perceives one of its flanks turned, panic and general rout almost inevitably ensue.

The Russian soldiers are remarkably obedient, robust, and hardy.   Their pay is small, their rations coarse and limited, and they are liable to arbitrary corporal punishment for very trifling offences.   They possess a sort of stupid and obstinate bravery, and receive the warlike exhortations of their clergy with a superstitious reverence, which causes them to bear cutting up better than any troops in Europe, and, therefore, to use the language of the Fancy, they will always be found "troublesome customers."[1]

[1] The author's youngest son was killed at Inkermann.   John Dillon Ross-Lewin entered the army in 1847.   Bred up in the best traditions of the Peninsula, he was thoroughly trained in all the essentials of his profession, even before he received a commission.   At the Alma his proud and joyous bearing won the approbation of experienced veterans.   Sir John

The Russian Imperial Guard was an uncommonly fine body of troops ; and their cavalry were mounted on very good chestnut horses. Green is the favourite colour in their uniforms.

The Russian armies are preceded by hordes of Cossacks and Tartars, who serve without pay, but occasionally receive donatives. These irregulars are at all times ready to advance when called upon ; both horses and men can endure the greatest fatigue and privations ; they are of great service to an army by spreading alarms, cutting off small detached parties, and collecting provisions. As they subsist on plunder, they are no burden to the commissariat, nor are they any inconvenience to the Russian army. When in the vicinity of Paris, however, the war being over, all marauding was forbidden, and they were supplied with rations, like other troops. The Cossacks are headed by their Hetman ; this rank was held by Count Platoff. Their liveliness is strongly contrasted with the heaviness of the Russian regular soldier ; and their activity, indefatigability,

Pennefather, who witnessed his handling of light troops during the action of the 28th October, rode up and publicly shook hands with him, saying, "Well done, well done, you gave them a great slating. The 30th, sir, behaved like gentlemen." At Inkerman he was closely engaged with the enemy for nearly seven hours, and a contemporary writer remarked, "This gallant young Irishman held his diminished company before the enemy with an enthusiasm racy of the soil." On one occasion, being separated from his men, he was seen to kill three of the enemy with his sword, in quick succession, and to rejoin his company unhurt. He fell mortally wounded at the head of the last great charge. One brother officer wrote of him, "He was indeed Bayard, sans peur et sans reproche;" while another adds, "He was beloved and regretted by all ranks." His dying words were worthy of him. Turning to the group of sorrowing comrades by his bedside, he exclaimed, "Gentlemen, I am quite resigned, it was a glorious victory."

and perseverance have been at times most surprising. In 1814, 130 Cossacks were in possession of Ghent. Three thousand French troops were ordered to drive them from that city and its neighbourhood, but it took ten days to perform this duty effectually; for, though the Cossacks might retire twenty or thirty miles in the daytime, they would return at night, and by different approaches. They thus contrived to keep the French constantly under arms, and to harass them very provokingly, although not quite so fatally as on the disastrous retreat from Moscow. When they wanted information these wild cavalry would take up behind them some intelligent-looking Belgian boys, and, by way of encouraging them, would force into their mouths a piece of horse or other flesh, that had been kept soddening under their saddles.   Such of the Cossack women as I have seen were of low stature ; they can carry incredible loads of plunder, and will keep up with the men on their longest marches.   When a halt takes place, even for a short time, they erect a triangle, formed with three sticks, and suspend a pot from the top of it ; the fire is quickly made, a group surrounds it, and in a few minutes the parboiled viands are placed before them ; at these repasts, quantity, not quality, is the grand desideratum—it would be a rare thing to find a cookery-book in a Cossack camp.

In the seventeenth century the Dutch were the best troops in Europe ; but their military prowess has since experienced a decline.   They are hard fighters at home ; but heavy, stupid, and slow at manœuvring.

The Belgians are more animated and lively than

the Dutch ; but the celerity of their movements is more frequently observable on their retreat than in the advance. They are full of bombast and gasconade—perfect Pistols—and have all the faults of the French soldiers, with few of their redeeming qualities.

In the French army individual merit is more readily noticed than in any other. The French troops act for themselves with more confidence, and possess more quickness, more cleverness, more fertility of resource, than the soldiers of any other nation ; and they have also more men in the subordinate ranks that are fit for command than can be found in a similar situation in all the other European armies. The French soldier can dine, though an officer has not tasted his soup, and can sleep without being tucked in ; he is not worn out and dispirited by incessant drills and parades ; his officers do not think it subversive of discipline that he should have a little time for recreation ; and he has no cause nor temptation ever to look upon his uniform as if it were the habit of a slave. The French tirailleur, especially, is an admirable soldier ; he is most intelligent, most observant ; not satisfied with performing his own part well, his active mind neglects nothing that passes around him. The French artillery is always served in the most skilful and effective manner ; and the cavalry of all kinds are generally excellent soldiers, and in a higher state of discipline than the other portions of the army. In point of stature, the French troops are inferior to those of the great Continental powers ; but they are active and well-made men. They are liable to become suddenly disheartened upon encountering an unexpectedly obstinate and prolonged opposition ; nevertheless they recover and rally after signal reverses with much elasticity of mind ; and a French army that has fled in confusion and dismay from a field of battle will, within a surprisingly short time, become as effective as ever, and appear perfectly restored to its former confidence and spirit.

A deed highly disgraceful to a portion of the French people, and showing that the spirit of bigotry which instigated the actors in the horrid scene of St. Bartholemew's bloody day yet lived in the breasts of many, was perpetrated at Nismes, and imitated in other places—I mean the massacre of a number of unoffending Protestants ; and it is impossible to say how long and how generally such atrocities would have been committed but for the prompt steps taken to repress them ; the Duke d'Angoulême himself repaired to Nismes, and made every exertion to restore order and tranquillity. Accordingly, the lives of those Protestants who survived the first burst of sectarian fury were saved.

Some measures that the French government now adopted did not meet with very general approbation. Louis issued an ordonnance, by which twenty-nine peers were unseated ; and another, by which he proscribed twenty persons. Colonel Labedoyere was the first person who suffered death for his adherence to the ex-emperor, being shot soon after the proscription took place.

Ney was arrested on the 25th of August. The

council, before which he was called, not being composed of his peers, decided upon their incompetence to try him. His trial then commenced before the peers. His advocate, M. Dupin, stated that Marshal Ney was no longer a Frenchman, in consequence of the treaty of 1811, by which his birthplace had ceased to form a part of France, and was therefore not amenable to the laws of that country; but the marshal disdained to avail himself of this means of defence, and instantly exclaimed, "I am a Frenchman, and I will die one; hitherto my defence has been liberal, now they are narrowing it. I am grateful to my counsel for the devotedness that they have shown me, and will yet show me; but let them cease, rather than defend me incompletely. I appeal to Europe and to posterity!"

This was noble. Such language, at such a time, bespeaks the materials of which the man was composed. He relinquished his principal chance of safety rather than suffer his name to be struck from the roll of the sons of France, that land for which he had braved so many toils and dangers; and he was condemned to die. He was shot at half-past nine in the morning at the end of the grand alley leading to the observatory, whither he was conveyed in a coach, guarded by 200 Royalist soldiers. The people were led to expect that the execution would take place on the plain of Grenelle, and at a later hour. To the last moment his conduct was worthy of "*le plus brave des braves.*" He would not suffer his eyes to be bandaged, but, placing his hand on his left breast, he himself undauntedly gave the word of

command, " Comrades, right to the heart—fire ! "
Thus died, in the 46th year of his age, Michael Ney,
Marshal of France, Duke of Elchingen, and Prince
of the Moskwa.   His fate excited the commiseration
of most, and the indignation of thousands of his
countrymen ; and I knew no one in the British
army who did not regret it.   His conduct may have
been censurable, but all must acknowledge that
the landing of Napoleon placed him in a difficult
dilemma, and if he had escaped the charge of
treachery, he must almost inevitably have incurred
the imputation of ingratitude.   When he swore
allegiance to Louis XVIII. he could not have
thought of such an event as the return of Napoleon.
The king was a monarch against whom he had
fought, and for whom he could have felt but little
real regard.   The emperor was the prince of his
first choice, the chief under whose banners he had
stemmed the tide of many a battle, and the friend to
whom, conjointly with his own merits, he owed his
honours and exaltation.   Considering the stipulations
of the convention, I think that the proscription was
more treacherous than his conduct could be said to
have been ; and, with reference to the sentiments of
the French nation at large, few will now deny that it
was impolitic in the extreme.   If, then, neither justice
nor policy demanded his death, why did Humanity
prove so feeble that she could not silence Revenge ?

On the 30th of October our camp broke up, and
my regiment was moved to Carrier, a village on the
banks of the Seine, near St. Germains, and twelve
miles from Paris.

We passed a very dismal time at Carrier. The greater part of the houses were deserted by the owners, and no stranger ever came near it, as it was off the high road ; and we should have been in want of proper accommodation had not a part of the regiment occupied a neighbouring chateau. Some French regiments of the line had now marched into Paris, and the agitation of the public mind seemed to be gradually subsiding ; it therefore became probable that our stay in France would not be prolonged much further. Our anticipations were correct. It was finally decided that the Army of Occupation should be diminished to 150,000 men, placed under a commander who should be nominated by the confederated powers, and it was stipulated that they should hold seventeen frontier towns in France.

My regiment commenced its march to the coast on the 2nd of December, Calais being the port at which we were to embark for England. On our route we passed through Abbeville and Estaples. As we approached the latter place, our quartermaster was sent forward to procure billets there. After he had received his instructions from the commanding officer, and proceeded a short distance in front of the column, a mounted gendarme, who was evidently in a state of intoxication, overtook us, and one of our officers told him that the person riding on before us was a very suspicious character, whom the commanding officer wished to place under the surveillance of the police, until he could be delivered up to the Mayor of Estaples. The gen-

X

darme immediately drew his sword and galloped after the old quartermaster, with whom he soon came up. The Englishman did not much like his new companion, and crossed to the opposite side of the road from him, but the Frenchman quickly ranged alongside, accelerating or slackening his pace to suit that of his prisoner *de facto* if not *de jure*, and occasionally making use of threatening looks and gestures, which caused no slight uneasiness to the person to whom they were directed. "What can you want with me, sir?" the astonished and agitated quartermaster would ask. "*En avant, monsieur,*" was the gendarme's only reply, which was always accompanied by a flourish of his sword. In this manner the two fellow-travellers entered the town of Estaples, and rode through the streets to the *Hôtel de Ville*, where the gendarme handed over his charge to the mayor. The worthy magistrate soon discovered the real state of the case, and begged that the quartermaster would think no more of the matter, as it was clearly the result of a *mauvaise plaisanterie* of the English officers; but, while speaking, he was himself so tickled with the circumstance that he could not suppress an unseasonable fit of laughter. The quartermaster was sadly provoked, and sallied out of the hotel boiling with rage, and eagerly looking out for the arrival of the regiment to detail the vexations that he had been made to undergo.

A very severe frost had set in before our departure from Carrier and continued until our arrival at Calais. We embarked at that port in small craft, and landed at Dover on the 22nd of December 1815. We then marched to Sheerness, which became the quarters of my regiment for some time. As many officers as could be spared from the regimental duties obtained leave of absence for a few weeks, and I returned home to tell long stories to my friends.

CHAPTER XVII

The Channel Islands—I become Lieutenant-Governor of a Province—I preside in Court—Two veterans—A learned cleric
—The War Office and the broadsword.

WHEN I rejoined my regiment it was stationed at Gosport, and shortly after we embarked for Guernsey. When we landed on that island I was sent to Alderney with two companies. The coast of this island is subject to an extraordinary phenomenon, the causes of which no philosopher has as yet been able to explain; it happens frequently at quarter-ebb tide, though the weather may be perfectly calm, that vast ridgy waves will rise suddenly and roll toward the beach, either swamping or driving on shore above high-water mark every boat and vessel that they happen to catch in their course. Some time before my arrival four men in a boat were towing a sloop outside the pier on a calm day, when the swell arose unexpectedly; the great body of water that instantly came rolling on swept the boat over the sloop, and threw it and the men high and dry up the beach; the vessel sank, and, being carried by an under-current into deep water, not a vestige of her has ever been seen since. With regard to the strength of under-currents in this sea, I myself know that a small sloop, which went down near the Alderney shore during my stay, was carried to the coast of

Normandy. In order to form a secure harbour here, it was necessary to build a long pier, which in fine weather is a favourite promenade. On a bright Sunday morning in summer two Frenchmen were loading a boat with salt, and, though several females were walking on the pier, these fellows stripped themselves stark naked, that they might work with greater ease. Two or three custom-house sailors, who observed their indecent behaviour, determined to interfere, and, providing themselves with switches, made the boatmen smart for it; the latter were, as it may be supposed, much enraged by such rough usage, and in high dudgeon proceeded to launch their boat and pull out of the harbour; but they had scarcely rounded the pier when the quarter-ebb swell rose most threateningly, and the first surge broke over them. I was on the pier at the time, as well as many other persons, and we expected every moment to see them go down, without a possibility of giving them any assistance. The Frenchmen in their alarm seemed to have lost all presence of mind; they cried out, and pulled each his own way. However, before the next huge ridge reached them, the boat luckily turned round, and they managed to get once more inside the pier. Had not this happened they must inevitably have perished, as the boat was nearly full of water already, and the second wave, which far exceeded the first in volume, swept by the pier-head with tremendous force.

The civil government of the island is an heirloom of the Le Mesurier family, who are the chief proprietors of the soil. The military governor is the

general commanding at Guernsey, and the senior
military officer, resident, has the title and emolu-
ments of lieutenant-governor.   The laws in force
are the old Norman, and Alderney has its parliament
or assembly of the states ; this body hold frequent
sessions, but their decrees are subject to the Imperial
Parliament.   The principal judicial functionaries are
a judge and a procureur, who, however, have very
rarely a criminal case to employ their time, such
is the absence of crime from this little community.
The gentlemen to whom the care of the souls of the
natives and of the troops is committed are the clergyman maintained by Governor Le Mesurier and the
military chaplain ; they perform divine service in the
same church, but at different hours, as the first-
mentioned reads and preaches in French and the
other in English.   The people have no direct taxes
to pay, besides the tenth sheaf to the civil governor ;
but every boat that enters the harbour pays a shilling
to the lieutenant-governor, and another to the judge,
and its master, as soon as he lands, is obliged to
report his arrival to those functionaries, which gives
them an opportunity of having the first choice of the
cargo.   Every collier also pays at the rate of sixpence
per chaldron for all the coals discharged.   The gold
and silver in circulation is British, but the base coin
is for the most part French ; and there are some
pieces of it called doubles, so low as twelve to the
penny.

The military governor during the former part of
my residence here was Major-General Moore, an
officer whose friendly disposition and social qualities

rendered him a universal favourite both with the inhabitants and the garrison ; but after some time it was decided that Alderney should be no more the station of a general officer, and he was recalled, to our very great regret. The civil governor never paid his island a visit while I sojourned on it, and, as I became the successor of General Moore in the lieutenant-governorship, my pride was for this (the first) time gratified by the fact that I was the highest personage resident within the confines of a distinct state. There was undoubtedly a something of importance in the style in which all official communications were addressed to me : " His Excellency the Lieutenant-Governor, commanding the Troops and Militia in the Island of Alderney." Cæsar declared that he had rather be first in a village than second at Rome, but here I was first in a territory. I received my military reports and my marine reports—the latter from masters of colliers and foreign small craft ; I pocketed the shillings on boats and the sixpences on chaldrons of coal, which were conveyed to me at stated periods by the lynx-eyed harbour master ; I displayed my generosity by declining to take the fees for passports, as they were to be paid by the inhabitants ; I issued my proclamations for holding courts, which were composed of the judge, the procureur, and jurats ; and when they assembled I and the judge—I mention myself first as being the greater man—took our seats on two chairs placed in the centre of the court-house for our accommodation, and, while we presided, wore our hats by special privilege, which gave

us an air of extraordinary dignity, seeing that all
other persons were obliged to remain uncovered.
The jurats were ranged at either side, according to
their politics, for even this little state had its whigs
and tories, and very high did party spirit run among
them.   As soon as prayers were read the proposi-
tions for discussion were laid before the house, and
generally brought on a most animated debate.   Of
the oratorical powers of the speakers I regret to say
that I do not feel qualified to offer confidently an
opinion, as they always used their vernacular patois ;
but, if they followed the converse of Hamlet's direction to the players, and suited the word to the action,
I am certain that their eloquence must have been of
a very impassioned kind, as their gesticulation was
most violent ; their voices were also raised to a
pitch almost disagreeably high, and the frothing at
the mouth, while the tongue was in motion, was
considerable ; but, undoubtedly, whatever was thus
gained in energy was attended by a corresponding
loss of dignity.   Likewise, the fact that two orators
were frequently speaking at once, on opposite sides
of a question, was far from contributing to the
decorum, as it certainly must have detracted from
the intelligibility, of the debate.   One would have
thought that the assembly, always excepting both
the gallant and the learned presidents, were newly
imported from the land of Cadwallader.   As the
language in which the harangues were pronounced
continued to the last perfectly unintelligible to me,
I was unable to enter into the merits of the various
questions argued ; but, whenever we had a case of

plaintiff and defendant, I made a rule to decide in favour of the former, as it was a common saying of Lord Norbury's, that the plaintiff was nineteen times in the right for once that he was in the wrong. My demeanour was marked by imperturbable gravity while the business of the court lasted, as I have long been of opinion that gravity without is the best cloak for ignorance within, and I had the extraordinary good fortune, as a public man, to keep fair with both sides of the house, never having had the slightest disagreement with any of its members, except when I found it necessary, now and then, to suggest to the judge the propriety of his shaving himself oftener than once a fortnight.

Several persons of respectability resided here, and among them there were three or four retired military men. There are some situations into which individuals, forming the whole or a part of small communities, are thrown, where it would be to their mutual benefit that the utmost harmony should prevail, but unluckily it too often comes to pass that the reverse is the case ; so it was once at the Eddystone Lighthouse, when the two men stationed there fell out, and did not open their lips to each other for six months ; and so it also was in Alderney with two of the veterans, who, one would think, should have been the best company for each other, but were in reality nothing less, for jealousy, that bane of society, had crept in and effected a total alienation of good feeling between them. The one had been in the Guards when George II. was on the throne ; the other had been taken prisoner with General Burgoyne at Saratoga.

The circumstances on which jealousy had laid hold were the following :—The Guardsman had never been on service farther than the Bird-Cage Walk, but nevertheless looked down upon the other, who had not worn the red coat so long; while the Saratoga man considered that his having been on foreign service rendered him a very superior being to his rival ; but the Guardsman again had a great advantage on his side, for, though senior to the Saratoga man by ten years, he was hale and hearty, and knew old age without decay ; whereas his rival, whose constitution had been impaired by hardships endured in his younger days, was a martyr to sciatica. "Come, my dear," the old Guardsman would say to his wife, the third that he had had, "take down the fusee and let us go fowling. That is more than my neighbour, Lieutenant ———, can do." Accordingly, the gun would be removed from its position over the kitchen fireplace and the dust blown off it ; his loving spouse would next throw the old boy's handkerchief over the crown of his hat and tie it carefully under his chin ; and, when all other preliminary arrangements had been made, the ancient couple would sally down the lane, Mrs. ——— carrying the fusee, and also, as her sight was sharpest, looking out for game. If a starling or a lark was seen within range the gun would be handed to the venerable sportsman, and, having wiped his eyes, he would fire, though not always with a deadly aim ; should he happen to kill his bird he would bag it in triumph, as the event could hardly fail to reach the ears of his rival. But, on the other hand, the Saratoga man occasionally received an order from a friend, who lived near Southampton, to purchase an Alderney cow, an occurrence which always gave him much satisfaction ; the moment that the welcome letter containing the order arrived his uniform was taken out and aired, for on such occasions he considered himself on duty ; and when fully equipped he grasped his cane and went forth, swelling with military pride, and consciousness of an increased importance, and never forgetting to walk past the Guardsman's dwelling in order to excite that veteran's spleen. The animosity existing between these old officers was artfully encouraged by two or three other young ones, who took a malicious pleasure in going from one to the other, telling the Guardsman how lightly his neighbour talked of the Bird-Cage Walk, and how proudly he boasted of the service that he had seen ; and the Saratoga man how his rival sneered at hobbling invalids, and praised the soldier who could serve his fifty or sixty years without ever knowing what a day's sickness was. However, it was at length determined that the belligerents should be brought together, and an attempt made to smooth all asperities, and effect a permanent reconciliation between them ; but the task was one of no ordinary difficulty. These praiseworthy intentions were to have been acted upon on the 18th of June, as that day, being the anniversary of the battle of Waterloo, was to have been celebrated with a ball, to which the respectable inhabitants were invited, and, of course, the two veterans, who were to be mollified by generous potations of wine and punch before the mediators proceeded to make overtures of peace. But all our plans were marred by the Saratoga man's sending an apology, for, unluckily, he had found that his greatest enemy, the sciatica, had attacked him violently, and seemed resolved on maintaining its hold; while the Guardsman said that he and his lady felt much pleasure in accepting the invitation of the gallant officers, and concluded by subscribing himself, "A. B., Lieutenant Royal Veteran Battalion, fifty - six years in His Majesty's service. God save the King." Our ball went off very well; the rooms were very tastefully decorated; an excellent supper was provided; country dances, and even jigs, were kept up with much spirit to a late hour. As for some years no dancing-master had been induced to visit the island waltzes and quadrilles were not attempted, and gallopades had never been heard of.

The old clergyman at St. Anne's was a strange being; his manners and appearance were singularly simple and primitive; next to theology, his favourite study was that of languages, and he certainly was an uncommon proficient in several. A short time before I bade adieu to my government, I happened to tell him that it was rumoured that my regiment was soon to go out to the Ionian Islands; he instantly congratulated me on the probability that I should visit classic ground, " and, besides," said he, as well as my memory serves me, "what a desirable opportunity you will have of forming an acquaintance with a variety of interesting languages ! Of the soft and musical Italian I will say nothing ; but you may there meet with persons who can instruct you in Arabic, the most copious of all languages, and also in Turkish, which is certainly poor in respect of the extent of its vocabulary, but has the advantage of being easily acquired ; I think, too, that it will be worth your while to learn the Sclavonic, which is spoken by so many wild but interesting tribes ; of course, you will be anxious to learn Romaic, the language of the people among whom you are to pitch your tent—barbarous corruption as it is, of the divine Greek of the ancients. You may also study the Russian, which is far the finest of all European languages ; and to return to the Asiatic, I would recommend you not to neglect the Persian, the Hindoostanee, and, I may add, the Sanscrit, if you can find a proper instructor. You will never regret the time spent in making yourself master of any of them, and I must confess that I almost envy you the prospect which now opens before you."

When the time of my regiment's stay in those islands had expired, it was ordered to Hilsea, and I was obliged to take my final leave of Alderney. Before my departure, I received a polite note from Governor Le Mesurier, regretting my removal from the island ; and also a deputation from the worthy inhabitants, who expressed themselves as being very sorry to lose me, and wished to know if there was any chance that a memorial from them to Government would have the effect of obtaining me permission to remain still among them in the office of lieutenant-governor.

Hilsea barracks are an extensive set of cottage

buildings situated at a distance of three miles from
Portsmouth. After our arrival there an order from
the Horse Guards appeared, directing the officers of
all regiments to practise the broadsword exercise ;
this was considered very annoying by many, and
some went so far as to pronounce it perfectly ridiculous, since in all their experience they had never
known an instance in which the knowledge of it
would have been of any service to an infantry
officer in action. Sir Walter Scott's description of
the single combat between James Fitz-James and
Roderick Dhu, is supposed to have first suggested
the idea of making our officers " cunning of fence "
on the Scottish system ; and the next thing that we
expected was a second order commanding us to provide ourselves forthwith with targets, as Roderick
paid so dearly for throwing his away. If our military
directors were desirous that the infantry officers
should become expert swordsmen, why did they not
cause those to learn the use of the small sword, who
did not know it already ? For, who will deny that
this weapon is superior to the broadsword when
targets are not used ? My feelings respecting this
new plan were quite hostile to it, as I had increased
so much in pinguidity during my sojourn in Alderney,
that some of the first extension motions (for we had
to perform a variety of them in order to make us
supple) were very inconvenient to me. I had first to
extend my arms at right angles to my sides, next to
raise them gradually until my hands nearly met over
my head, and then, bringing them down with unbent
elbows, and inclining my body forward, but keeping

the knees stiff, to endeavour to touch the ground with the tips of my fingers. Owing to the rotundity of my figure, though it was still not quite aldermanic, and the consequent great resistance of the middle region, the executing of this extension motion was no easy task to me, and was almost sufficient to cause vertigo by forcing the blood up to my head. An additional annoyance was derived from the fact that a place was constantly assigned to me in the awkward squad ; though an older officer, and an older man than I, was raised to the first squad. The reason of this was that the radical heat of a tropical sun had so absorbed the radical moisture of his body and stripped his ribs of all their natural covering, excepting the bare skin, that he could touch the ground with his finger tips with considerably greater ease than I could. All this afforded much diversion to the younger officers. Some persons also went so far as to declare that an officer who could not learn to *stoop low* was unfit for the service ; and there was some truth in the remark ; yet, a British army had never before found it necessary to *stoop to conquer*. A stiff-necked brevet was voted a nuisance ; something more pliant was wanted. It was true that the old brevets had shuffled through the Peninsular and other wars ; but now they were in the way. Young men of rank were to get the command of regiments, the nation was at peace, and the army was considered a good school and likely to keep the younger sons of the nobility out of harm's way ; at all events, the command of a regiment at such a time would be an amusement. In order to make the army more agreeable to those scions of noble stocks, it was requisite to alter the uniforms, for they had seen foreign corps on parade during their continental tours that looked a thousand times better than any of our troops. Accordingly, the tailor's shop became the favourite lounge, and the honourable lieutenant-colonels were soon profoundly learned in all the arcana of gores and gussets, lace and trimmings, stitching and padding. Everything old was bad, and especially old officers. The cursed brevets marred everything. It was suspected that they were discontented on finding that no distinction was made between a brevet lieutenant-colonel and the rawest ensign, as far as regarded the frequency of the drills which each had to attend. "O! dear, no," a commanding officer of the new school would exclaim, as he sat in the tailor's shop fiddling with the shears and the measures, "why should there be any distinction? If they are not in the ranks they will be more at liberty to make their unpleasant remarks; and, you know, we must have all those drills for our own practice; besides, the more those old fellows are dissatisfied with the service, the sooner shall we get rid of them. Then there is another immeasurable bore—we command them regimentally, and they us in the line. What an absurd anomaly! Would it not be a splendid plan to send them agriculturising to Botany Bay, or at least to the American colonies? But if we can't dispose of them so, I know it is said at the Horse Guards that the poor devils will be bribed to quit the service, which will never be anything until cleared of such snobs. We shall no longer hear of General Fox, and his stupid notions respecting the comforts that the men should have." In this style the scions would talk of men, some of whom had entered the service before those carpet-knights were born, and whose seasoned constitutions would have still enabled them to bear the fatigues of a campaign with much less inconvenience than the younger but effeminate warriors, who were pleased to hold them and their services in contempt; still this was, perhaps, a circumstance of slight importance, as there was little probability of a new war, and less of such condescension on the part of certain holiday-soldiers as to expose themselves to the "vile guns." But they did not talk in vain; for, since length of service came to be considered rather in the light of a crime than in any other, the old hands were at length brought to a way of thinking on professional matters, in which at one time they never imagined that they could have indulged, and they began successively to decide upon quitting the army, in which their presence seemed to be no longer agreeable.

My regiment had not remained many months at Hilsea when it was intimated to us that we were certainly destined for the Ionian Islands.

It was subsequently arranged that I was to take charge of the depôt, and soon after the regiment embarked at Portsmouth, and sailed for the Mediterranean. I then went with the depôt to Winchester. My stay was very short, as only a few days had elapsed before my depôt was removed to

Y

Albany Barracks in the Isle of Wight, and the change was, in my opinion, much for the better ; for Winchester is not one of the most lively cities in the world, and military matters were very well conducted in my new station. The several duties were carried on with exactness, but things were so managed that no one experienced any feeling of restraint ; all that the service required was cheerfully performed, and Colonel Mainwaring, our worthy commandant, while he insisted upon that, demanded no more. It is much to be regretted that military men in command should so frequently seem ignorant of this happy method of uniting exact discipline with cheerful readiness.

When my sojourn had nearly occupied a twelvemonth, an unexpected order to embark for the Ionian Islands separated me from a circle of which I took leave with sincere regret ; nor could the expectation of visiting scenes that promised to afford so much interest reconcile me to the change.

CHAPTER XVIII

The Ionian Islands—Insurrection—Sir Thomas Maitland—Treatment of veteran officers—Case of Dr. Bulkeley—Military matters—Farewell.

I REMAINED in the Ionian Islands for two years. During my stay an insurrection of the peasantry took place in Santa Maura. Their chief ground of complaint was excessive taxation; they declared that they had no wish to act toward the English in a hostile manner, but they would resist the levying of the taxes imposed by the senate—by the Lord High Commissioner,[1] they ought to have said. Of course, the notion that the garrison would not interfere to put a stop to such lawless proceedings was perfectly absurd. The peasants were headed by their primates and priests, and well provided with fire-arms; and they soon appeared in force before the town. Major Temple, the British commandant, immediately called out the troops, consisting, I think, of two companies of the 28th regiment, and some artillerymen, and prepared to oppose the entrance of the insurgents into the town; but he found them so strong that he did not think it prudent to engage them in the field, and accordingly he retired into the fort until reinforcements should arrive from Corfu. His loss on this occasion was one artilleryman

[1] Sir Thomas Maitland.

killed, while endeavouring to spike a gun. As soon
as the rising was heard of at Corfu, fresh troops were
embarked there in boats, and sent off without delay
to Santa Maura. When they arrived Major Temple
again took the field, and discovered the insurgents,
strongly posted and in considerable force, near the
village of Specchiota, which stands midway up the
side of a steep mountain. Here they were instantly
attacked by a portion of the troops, and after some
firing were compelled to fly with precipitation, leaving
behind them several of their number killed, wounded,
or prisoners. The fire of the Santa Mauriotes was
very ill directed, as not a single soldier was killed,
and only two or three of the light company of the
32nd were wounded. Lieutenant Munro of that
regiment had a narrow escape, for, during the
advance, one of the insurgents suddenly sprung at
him from behind some brushwood, and snapped a
pistol close to his breast ; but it missed fire, and one
of our men knocked out the Greek's brains with a
blow of the butt-end of his firelock. Three priests
who had been active instigators of the insurrection
were taken, and gibbeted in chains. Some of the
heads of the villages were also executed; and the
disaffected, finding that they had miscalculated their
strength, relinquished all further attempts at rebellion.

When the priests were condemned to death, none
of the Greeks would act as executioners. It was
therefore proposed to a soldier, who was under
sentence of a court-martial, to discharge the disagreeable office of finisher of the law, with the
conditions, that his own punishment was to be

remitted, and that he was to receive besides a
pecuniary reward. When this offer was made to
him by a staff - officer, he unhesitatingly replied,
"Why then, indeed I will, your honour, and heartily
welcome. I'll hang as many of 'em as your honour
pleases for nothing, only I wouldn't like to do it
in my red jacket." The sole objection thus made
was easily obviated; he was disguised as much as
possible, and walked in a sack to the place of
execution; but his gait was so peculiar as to be
instantly recognised, in spite of every artifice, by his
comrades. This fellow, who knew the disposition of
the people and was determined to profit by it, cut
up the ropes with which the priests had been hung
into small pieces of about an inch in length, and
sold them as relics to the superstitious, who regarded
their executed pastors as sainted martyrs. The
military relic-vendor found a ready and profitable
sale for his wares, and to meet the increasing de-
mand for them, felt obliged to cut up other ropes,
that were perfectly innocent of the death of any
person, whether lay or clerical, and to dispose of
them as genuine to his credulous customers.

In the same year [1] there was a rising in Zante, but
it was quickly suppressed. Several persons, among
whom were Signor Martiningo and two or three
other men of the first respectability, were taken up
on suspicion, and incarcerated, or banished, by the
Lord High Commissioner; some because they had
presumed to complain of the manner in which affairs
were conducted by the government of the Ionian

[1] 1820.

Islands. However, Martiningo and others were liberated by order of the British Government, to whom a remonstrance had been made respecting the arbitrary conduct of Sir Thomas Maitland ; but the matter was not followed up by the passing of any censure on that functionary, except that implied in the reversal of his decree, although his proceedings would have led to his immediate recall had the feelings and wishes of the Ionian islanders been consulted.

The disturbances in Zante and Santa Maura led to the precautionary measure of disarming the peasantry of Corfu, as far as it was practicable, and this, though not altogether uncalled for, had no tendency to diminish the unpopularity of the Lord High Commissioner.

. . . . . .

I have already mentioned the maladministration of affairs, both military and civil, in the Ionian Islands, at least, for that period of which I am enabled to speak from my own immediate observation, rather than from hearsay ; but I find it necessary to advert to it once more. The Lord High Commissioner was undeniably a man of talents ; but he possessed one talent in particular, which he cultivated with perfect success, that of making himself unpopular with those who were placed under his authority. His enemies abounded in all the islands, and their dislike of him and his acts not unfrequently led to the indulgence of a similar feeling towards the state whose servant he was ; though, during the government of his British predecessors in office (whose conduct towards the governed was at least more conciliatory), the name of Great Britain was held in the highest respect by the islanders, and would now have been so regarded universally, had they had a De Bosset,[1] instead of a Maitland, in the capacity of Lord High Commissioner. The people of Zante, the most intelligent, industrious, and flourishing of the Ionians, desired to lay a statement of their grievances before the British Government. What was the consequence? Some of the most respectable individuals among them were arrested, and kept in strict confinement until they were brought to trial before the senate, who passed sentence of imprisonment or banishment on the most obnoxious. It is true that these unjust decrees were subsequently annulled by the British ministry; but was the man who, the people said, abused his trust so much to the discredit of his nation, punished for his arbitrary proceedings? No, no. In the first place, how could charges of oppressive and unjust conduct, preferred against so high an officer, be received at the Foreign Office? And, besides, what real foundation could there be for such an accusation? Was not the punishment of the offenders the act of the senate? And would it not be the grossest calumny to affirm that a body so patriotic, so enlightened, and so high-minded, would on any such occasion stoop so low as to suffer the pleasure of a British governor to influence them in their decisions

[1] Military Resident in Cephalonia. Major Ross-Lewin describes him as "too independent, just, and honourable, to be long regarded in certain quarters with a favourable eye."

to the prejudice of justice, and to the wounding of their tender consciences? Never believe it. It is not, therefore, matter of surprise or censure that Sir Thomas Maitland was not recalled, and remained to enjoy for a few more years the unmixed satisfaction of governing a people, all parties of whom, whether the Russian, the French, or the English, regarded him most sincerely—for here the Ionians certainly manifested sincerity—as an object of the same dark and deep-seated feeling that the Suliote, on the first day of his exile, entertained toward the Lord High Commissioner's old acquaintance, Ali Pacha. I was at Corfu during the incarceration in its citadel of Signor Martiningo, one of the wealthiest and most influential of the Zantiotes; he was so unfortunate as to be of the number of those who incurred the displeasure of Sir Thomas, and were punished by the award of the senate for the crime of attempting to petition against what, in their opinion, were no imaginary grievances. This person was imprisoned in a small apartment; a sentry was placed over him; all intercourse between him and his friends was forbidden; and he was subjected to the additional annoyance, that an officer on duty visited him at uncertain hours to see that he was properly secured. And all this preceded his trial. Such was the approved method of conducting affairs in the Ionian Islands, and, surely, it will not be surprising if a perseverance in it shall render the Ionians universally anxious for a fair opportunity of placing themselves under the protection of Russia, a state the religion of which agrees with their own; or of uniting themselves with the independent portion of Greece, when its Government becomes firmly established, and its power increased by further encroachments on the contracting dominions of the Porte. Let no man think it sound policy to stifle the complaints of the natives of these islands, and to keep them under with the bayonet. If their wrongs are imaginary, let them be discussed, and proved to be such ; if they are real, let them be redressed. It cannot be denied that very great improvements of various kinds have been effected in the condition of the Seven Islands since they came under our protection ; still much remains to be done, and one thing is certain, that while our general treatment of the people is illiberal, they will feel little gratitude for particular benefits of which we may be the authors. How sneakingly, too, was conciliation attempted, whenever it was thought expedient to make some atonement for harsh measures affecting the liberty and the property of the islanders ! One grand part of the system was a show of profound respect and veneration for the corpse, called St. Spiridione, in accordance with which the British military officers of all ranks were ordered to assist at those disgraceful exhibitions, the saint's processions. Never did I feel my profession more degraded than when I found myself walking bareheaded after that gilt and jewelled case in which the wretched plunder of a grave was carried ; when I beheld on every side such revolting scenes of folly and superstition ; and when I reflected that I, as well as my brother officers, was thus engaged in encouraging the idolatrous practices of artful and unprincipled priests, and their duped and erring flocks, but could not venture to disobey the orders that led us to act in a manner so offensive to our feelings. The officers and men have been compelled to neglect their own religious duties that they might perform their parts in the disgusting mummery of Greek processions. The thinking portion of the British army are justly indignant at being constrained so to lower themselves, and it is most sincerely to be hoped that the legislature will interfere and prevent the continuance of such a shameful proceeding.

Abolish all government monopolies in the islands ; let the people import the corn they consume ; and thus be enabled to eat cheap bread ; and leave their religious rites and ceremonies to themselves.

If the Lord High Commissioner was unpopular with the Greeks, he did not stand much higher in the estimation of a great majority of the military who happened to be stationed within the limits of his government. The minority, or those who held or pretended to hold him in respect, consisted in general, as might have been supposed, of the employés about the palace, and a few of those sneaking characters who are to be found in every profession, however honourable. Nor did his conduct toward the military evince any desire on his part to be on good terms with them ; for, with few exceptions, he paid them as little attention as he well could. Contrary to the custom of the service, the officers of the garrison, with a very few exceptions, were never invited to dine at the palace ; they made up a show at the balls which he gave at stated periods; and they were obliged to appear at his levees, which otherwise would have been thinly attended.

It also happened that several officers who were stationed here with their regiments, and had hitherto borne a fair reputation, were forced to quit the service. Different opinions were passed with regard to the actual culpability of those individuals, and some went so far as to think the conduct of the accusers quite as reprehensible as that of the accused; but it is a matter of difficulty to find, among a great variety of persons, a decided unanimity on any question; and men who did not know how soon their own turn was to come may have drawn prejudiced conclusions concerning the justice of the fate of the sufferers. The case of Surgeon B——,[1] of the 32nd regiment, excited a very great sensation in our military circles. He was a man who devoted his whole time to his professional duties; his attention to all who required his assistance was most unremitted; his disposition was eminently humane and feeling, and his liberality kept pace with his benevolence, as the soldiers, whose wives and children were constantly the objects of it, can well testify. In most places a man of such worth would have been regarded as an acquisition of great value—here it was unfortunately the reverse; he was not in favour; he either gave proof of some qualities which were not relished in certain quarters, or he was too intimate with those who were placed under the surveillance of particular employés. The several circumstances

[1] Thomas Bulkeley, M.D. See page 223.

which had led to his removal occurred at different
periods, with long intervals between ; and, did I feel
quite at liberty to mention them, the detail of them
would only prove tedious ; but, having said so
much, I feel bound to state that they in no respect
injuriously affected his character, whether general
or professional ; indeed, in the opinion of most
persons, they had a direct tendency to exalt him
in the esteem of every unbiassed and well-disposed
observer.   After the different charges had been
preferred against him, Sir Thomas Maitland issued
an order that no individual belonging to the 32nd
regiment should hold any communication with him ;
this prohibition extended to the wives and children
of the officers ; and a sentry, with his bayonet fixed,
was directed to attend the doctor wherever he went,
for the purpose of insuring the rigid observance of
the Lord High Commissioner's commands.   This
was taking a leaf out of Ali's book with a vengeance.
An Irish grenadier, of the 28th regiment, named
Fitzgibbon, was selected to be the doctor's escort ;
this soldier, before he enlisted, had been frequently
employed in his native country by factions, to fight
for them at fairs ; he took any side in their battles
for half-a-crown.   It may be supposed that this
champion was " large of limb and stout of frame ; "
the doctor was also of true grenadier proportions ;
therefore, when they sallied out together, and strode
along the ramparts, or about the esplanade, Fitzgibbon carrying the doctor's cloak, lined with scarlet,
on one arm, and shouldering his firelock and fixed
bayonet with the other, their appearance attracted

universal attention; and, to make the thing still
more ridiculous, Fitzgibbon completely mistook his
orders, for he fancied that he had been placed over
the doctor to protect him from danger, and, full of
this notion, he would say to his charge, by way of
keeping up his spirits, " Never fear, doctor, the d—l
a hair of your head will they touch while I'm here."
The kindness of Dr. B——'s disposition had made
him so great a favourite with the officers' children,
that, when they saw him, they all scampered off to
meet him, and it therefore required much vigilance
on the part of their parents and attendants to restrain
them from an infringement of this unsociable order,
which, however, was itself considered a gross infringement of the principles of British law. Would
such an excommunication of any individual, similarly circumstanced, have been tolerated in England?
And, if not, why should it have been practised at
Corfu?

The discontent of the soldiers in garrison at Corfu
was also very great, owing in part to their being substituted for horses at the government works, and
compelled to draw stone and rubbish-carts; they
had, besides, to discharge the stone, both by day and
night, from the vessels, according as they arrived
with it from Malta. Such duty should never have
been imposed on them; the climate itself was sufficiently unhealthy to keep the military hospitals tolerably well filled for half the year, and did not require
the aid of this system of constantly employing fatigue-
parties at such hard labour. Mules and carts were
kept for the commissariat, and there could have been

no great difficulty in procuring more, to draw the materials for the palace and other public buildings, instead of leaving to soldiers the work of beasts of burden ; and, besides, there were numbers of the natives, labourers inured to the climate, who wanted employment, and would have been satisfied with low wages. Such treatment has a manifest tendency to degrade soldiers in their own estimation, and to break that spirit which it should be a commanding officer's care to foster and encourage. I recollect a speech made by the present Duke of Richmond in his place in Parliament, in which he loudly lamented the degradation and hardships now so often the lot of the English labourer, and declared what a shock his feelings had received from a sight which he had witnessed a few days before, namely, a party of workmen tackled to a cart that was laden with stones. What, then, would have been the gallant Duke's pain, had he beheld, as I have, British soldiers, and many of them men who had fought in the same field with him at Waterloo, employed in a similar manner ? Another source of dissatisfaction was the fact, that even on Sundays the men were not permitted to enjoy Sabbath rest ; for, if Spiridione did not take the air, the chaplain read prayers in the morning, and no sooner did the troops leave the church, than they had to assemble on the esplanade for a field-day—a practice truly reprehensible, in whatever light it be regarded.

Nothing can be more distressing to the feelings of one who has the interest of the service at heart, than to be made to witness occurrences naturally tending to destroy the mutual good understanding which ought to exist between all ranks in the army. But it is impossible to prevent discontent and murmurs among the men, when they find their officers indifferent to their comforts and general welfare, and ever ready to go as far as, if not absolutely beyond, the limits sanctioned by military law, in the exercise of their authority. Such is the conduct of some men in command that it must almost lead one to suppose their chief aim to be to render the life of the soldier miserable, to treat him as if he were a creature without feeling, and thus to inspire him with disgust for the service ; to impress him with the conviction, that no change of circumstances can be for the worse, and to induce him to seize the first favourable opportunity for desertion—a crime here of no uncommon occurrence. Yet, if the regulations of the British army, as they now stand, improved successively by different officers, and especially by his late Royal Highness the Duke of York, were only acted up to in their true spirit, they would not only make the soldier comfortable and happy, but also proud of the service into which he had entered, and devoted in the cause of his king and his country. The writer of this narrative, from his length of active service, has had ample means of bringing himself acquainted with every wish and expectation of the soldier, and can safely say that he has never found them extravagant, or exceeding those bounds which the rules and nature of his profession define. At times, during the Peninsular campaigns, the privations that fell to the soldier's lot were as much as

some and more than others could bear; yet I
cannot charge my memory with my having ever
heard the Duke of Wellington's name mentioned
with the slightest disrespect. They knew very well
that he would not harass them unnecessarily, and
that his system was quite opposed to anything of
the kind; so that when matters were at the worst
they still confined their threatenings to the enemy:
"Well!" they used to exclaim, "we will make the
French pay for this yet."

It is fortunate that instances of military despotism
rarely occur in our service; but when they do, it is
for the advantage of the public at large, as well as
of the army, that they should be made generally
known. However, as such acts would never be
attempted, unless abroad, and then by some member
of a family that had the ear of royalty, or at least
considerable influence at the Foreign Office or the
Horse Guards, the individual who has been sacrificed
to abused power, and, as a matter of great favour,
has been permitted to retire on the half-pay list,
cannot hazard his all by publishing his wrongs to
his fellow-countrymen. Thus it happens that cases
of tyranny and oppression are concealed from the
notice of the public. It is also to be deplored that,
in the noble and honourable profession of arms,
recourse has been had, at certain times and places,
to the meanest system of espionage. The moment
a victim was singled out to be hunted down, as our
officers used to term it, the employés were instantly
on the alert; no portion of time was suffered to
escape the keenness of their observation; the past

was reviewed in order to discover some former acts of the object of the chase that might lay him open to injurious charges ; the present was not neglected whenever it afforded an opportunity of " picking a hole in his coat "—a phrase of little elegance, but often employed, and readily understood in a certain latitude ; and toward the future the eye of the deepest plotter was directed—if second-sighted, so much the better—to see what prospects it promised for the successful issue of embryo plans, soon to be in operation for the taking of the proscribed in the toils. His late Royal Highness, then commander-in-chief, was perpetually tormented by "secret and confidential" reports concerning points in the conduct of the obnoxious, which had been already submitted to the ordeal of a former trial, and intended to eke out a list of complaints which were founded on some more recent sin, whether of omission or commission ; and at length he issued an order to the effect, that when once an officer had been brought to a court-martial, and a decision had been pronounced with regard to his guilt or innocence, no reference should ever be made again to the charges there preferred against him. By this very proper regulation the functions of the whippers-in were narrowed—they were precluded materially from reaping the full benefit of their ingenious tracings of the past, and therefore turned their thoughts chiefly to hole-picking ; and those who are conversant with military matters cannot but agree with me in the opinion that there are few officers in the service who, if their actions and

Z

conversation were narrowly watched by the malicious, would not be found, at some period of their army life, to have done or said something that might be tortured into a serious charge.

A field-officer, who had been more than twenty-four years in one of the regiments in garrison in a certain island, felt perfectly convinced that he was no favourite at the palace, and that the pack were thrown off, and ready to take him at some short turn. Until the day of his landing on the island in question he had never known that he bore the character of being a *mauvais sujet;* and after it he used to affirm, when discussing matters connected with the chase, that he was perfectly satisfied of the injustice of the attempt to run him down, and equally so of the absence of all danger that his reputation as an officer would suffer by the result of such machinations, although it were the loss of his commission—an event that might happen if he did not observe the utmost precaution. Soon after his arrival his turn to be field-officer of the day came round ; there were twenty-one guards to be visited, and some of them were in the country, and at a distance of two miles from the town ; a thunder-storm continued throughout the whole night, and no orderly was then allowed to point out the different guards. In such weather some field-officers have visited none of the guards ; but they knew how they stood at headquarters. The officer in question went the rounds that night, never doubted but that he had visited all the guards, and sent in his report accordingly at the proper time ; but to his utter astonishment he was informed that he had

forgotten to visit one of them, and that one happened
to be among the nearest to his own quarters. The
fact was, the sentry did not challenge as he passed,
and thus the guard was not turned out. As soon as
the commanding officer of his regiment heard one of
the pack, who had caught scent of this mistake, give
tongue, he galloped off to the major-general to tell
him that the game was up. The general searched
for the field-officer's report, but by some lucky
chance it was missing, and he was obliged to resort
to cool hunting. The field-officer was sent for. A
search for the report was again instituted, and,
although it lasted two hours, again failed; and one
of the whippers-in, with a countenance ludicrously
expressive of disappointment and vexation, announced
that it was useless to hunt any longer. While this
trailing was going on, the general and the accused
remained at opposite ends of the room. Not a
syllable escaped their lips. This solemn silence was
intended to manifest the general's anxiety for the
benefit of the service, and to strike the offender with
awe. But at Waterloo the field-officer had seen the
soldier-like Picton on horseback, and now he felt no
inclination to tremble before a corpulent general in
an easy-chair; still, in some respects a real uncle
Toby, he would now and then cast a glance on the
general, while a blush for the service suffused one
cheek, and one for human nature the other, as the
painful and humiliating reflection arose, that an
officer of such rank could be induced, for any
expected consideration, to lend himself to so
base and despicable a party. At length silence

was broken.   The whipper-in, looking like him
who—

> " Drew Priam's curtain in the dead of night,
>   And would have told him half his Troy was burn'd,"

was directed to take his seat.   It must be acknowledged that an excellent hunt was foiled—prime
sport lost—by his inability to find the report.
According to the best authority, the conversation
was pretty nearly as follows :—" Major," said the
general, " you mistake me very much if you suppose that I can pass over so great an injury to the
service as you——" " I never injured the service,"
said the major.   " Don't interrupt me, sir !" exclaimed the general, " you have given in a report,
that you performed all the duties of a field-officer of
the day without having done so."   " If," rejoined
the major, " it had been my wish to save myself
trouble, I should not have visited all the distant
guards, and have omitted one so close to my own
quarters."   " No matter," said the general, " I must
issue a strong order in consequence of it."   And so
he did, and in such a spirit that, when these orders
reached the Horse Guards (for there they were invariably sent), it must have been supposed that the
major was totally unfit for the service ; and a very
small hole in his coat, coupled with this order,
would have been quite sufficient to cause his removal from the army, especially as strong suspicions existed that, in the secret and confidential
reports, his name had not been passed over without some invidious remarks.   However, he was too

wary, or too fortunate, ever to become again the object of even an attempted chase.

It has afforded matter of astonishment to many enlightened officers that the late Duke of York, who, in most respects, was undoubtedly an excellent commander-in-chief, should have countenanced those secret and confidential reports, utterly repugnant as they are to all true British feeling ; and that, in days like the present, anything so inquisitorial could be suffered to exist. Why is not the subject brought before the House of Commons ? Why is the free press asleep to the interests of the army ? Is it not unfair and unjust in the extreme, that a commanding-officer, who may be possessed of many of the worst feelings of our nature, should have it in his power, through underhand and secretly-working means, wantonly and undeservedly to inflict serious injury on men who may be every way his superiors, except in military rank, and this merely to gratify private pique or irreconcilable antipathies? In general, persons accused of an offence are, by the laws of England, allowed liberty to vindicate themselves ; this is supposed also to hold good in the army ; but a practice so just is suspended by an order from the Horse Guards. Hence, not only may the professional prospects of a military man be blasted for ever, but his reputation also may receive a stab in the dark, while he is unable to discover how, or by whom, the blow has been struck. Both he who in power sanctions, and he who for calumnious purposes avails himself of, such a system, may well be accused of injustice of the basest and most dishonourable cast. Every voice should be raised against it, and every able pen employed to write it down.

.   .   .   .

After spending some time in the Islands, I got leave of absence, and crossing the south of France, arrived at Bordeaux. Here I heard from a king's cutter, which had been sent from England for claret for the Marquis of Londonderry, that one of the Dublin packets was coming up the river. A few days after I took my departure from Bordeaux on board this packet. We had a most agreeable set of passengers, among whom was the Rev. Charles Wolfe ; this exemplary clergyman preached us an excellent sermon, extempore, in the middle of the Bay of Biscay. He appeared to be about twenty-six years of age ; but he was in a most delicate state of health, and had taken this trip thinking that sea-sickness might prove in some degree beneficial ; however, that unbidden and unwelcome companion to so many unseasoned sailors did not come to his relief. In person he was tall and slight, light-haired, pale-visaged, and freckled ; his countenance indicated benevolence, and his disposition was truly amiable. He is well known as the author of the admirable ode on the burial of Sir John Moore. Very soon after his arrival at Dublin he himself also paid the debt of nature, leaving to him who should undertake to write his epitaph, and to do justice to his virtues, a task of no ordinary difficulty.

When the packet put into Kingstown, the custom-house officer that came on board informed us of the fate of the Marquis of Londonderry, who was destined never to taste the wine for which he had despatched the cutter to Bordeaux.

My narrative now draws very near to its conclusion. Domestic interest, coupled with disgust at certain transactions of which I was an unwilling witness in the Ionian Islands, induced me to retire from the army ; for a revolution had been effected in my sentiments, of which at one time I could never have contemplated the possibility. It is true that I was little indebted to the service; but I was born in it, I had long learned to regard it with the strongest attachment, and in it I had hoped to end my earthly career. Feeling bound to the service, and not to the person who might have the command of the regiment, I always performed my duties with cheerfulness and attention, although it sometimes happened that we were placed under an officer whom it was impossible to respect. With regard to the soldiers, I may say that it was with me an invariable rule to suffer no irregularity, however slight, to pass without an intimation that it had not escaped my notice ; and the consequence was my being relieved from the necessity of resorting to courts-martial. It was ever my wish to maintain true discipline, but to avoid the imposition of all unnecessary restraint; and in endeavouring to promote the interests of the soldier I always thought that I best consulted the interests of the service.

With those remarks I might conclude ; but before I take my leave of the reader who has had patience to accompany me so far, I cannot refrain from

making a few more with reference to the treatment
experienced by many deserving officers of the old
army. After I had retired from the service, two field-
officers of my acquaintance were run down to half-
pay : one of them commanded a regiment of the
line, and had been repeatedly engaged with the
enemy ; and the other,[1] as senior officer present, led
his corps in three general actions, and was covered
with crosses and medals—tokens of distinction which
he must have prized, but which could not have been
more flattering, than his being compelled to retire
on half-pay, as unfit for service, was hurtful to his
feelings. Here cool hunting in secret, and confidential reports, were well calculated to have proved
efficacious ; yet the last-mentioned officer was so
indifferent to danger that, when the regiment he
commanded was much reduced at Waterloo, and
ordered to lie down in square to avoid in some
measure the enemy's very heavy fire, he, not being
just then required to remain on the alert, availed
himself of what he considered a lull, and took a nap
on horseback in the middle of the square, while his
men were constantly killed and wounded on all sides.
Perhaps, at that moment, some of those mighty
hunters who were instrumental in bringing about
his compulsory retirement, might not have felt very
comfortable had they been directed to go and awake
him. At length a spent ball hit him on the forehead,
and made him open his eyes ; he took off his hat,

---

[1] Colonel John Hicks, C.B., Knight of St. Anne of Russia, received the
Gold Cross for four general actions. Quitted the Service, 1828. Dalton,
Waterloo Roll Call.

rubbed the part affected, and then resumed his
former composure ; but, when an order to form line
was issued, his drowsiness vanished, and he put himself in motion, like a giant refreshed. Nearly at the
same time that his rest was broken by the bullet, his
horse was wounded by another ; but the animal,
standing fire like his master, only shook his tail. I
may here observe that, since the demise of the
master of a celebrated hunt, the pack have been
almost totally broken up ; for I am informed, on
excellent authority, that only one couple of old
hounds and a terrier remain at the once well
furnished kennel.

My strictures will probably obtain for me from
some persons the title of an old grumbler ; but, notwithstanding, I must fire another shot, although I
speak less on my own account than on that of others,
my retirement having been entirely my own voluntary
act ; indeed, it would have been a tolerable stretch of
fancy, to assert that an officer, who is at this present
moment [1] of a strong constitution, inured to hardships
and fatigue, in the perfect enjoyment, thank God, of
all his faculties, and in age nearer fifty than sixty,
should have been superannuated ten years ago.

The general treatment of old officers at the Horse
Guards cannot but be considered harsh and unjust.
It was intimated to applicants there for any promotion, that, unless their names had appeared in a
despatch, no attention could be paid to their claims.
This was an ungracious manner of closing the doors
against all who had not had sufficient interest to get

[1] 1833.

placed on the staff, or who were not otherwise in such a position that their services could be sufficiently conspicuous to force them into notice. The number of those who by separate commands were enabled to distinguish themselves, so as to attract a general's attention, when there existed no private reasons why such attention should be directed to them, was necessarily limited ; but this should be an additional reason why the faithful services of officers who had been actively employed during so protracted a war, and had contributed to the accomplishment of a series of the most decisive and desirable results, should be taken fairly and fully into consideration ; yet so far were they from being met in this manner, that no means of placing old officers on the shelf were left untried ; and of those individuals, such as had obtained, from length of service, the rank of Brevet-Major, and consequently were the most experienced officers in the army, seemed to be marked out as especially deserving of removal from their profession.

The first inducement held out was the raising of the price of a company from fifteen hundred to eighteen hundred pounds, with permission to sell the commissions after a certain length of service ; but this was a very poor remuneration, and few took advantage of it. It was, therefore, found necessary for the more successful prosecution of this unwise measure of making room for inexperience, to devise some other project, and offers of land in distant settlements were generously tendered to the brevets, to induce them to turn their swords into ploughshares ; but neither had this piece of kindness the desired effect. As the half-pay list is convenient for patronage, everything was tried before a general movement to it from full pay was encouraged ; but finally recourse was had to this expedient, and it was decreed that the obnoxious individuals might retire on the half-pay of Major, or sell out, receiving the regulated price of a majority. It is impossible for any one to feel comfortable in a situation where he knows that his presence can readily be dispensed with, and this was the case with a meritorious class of officers ; their pride was wounded, and the greater number felt that they had met with ingratitude in that quarter where they had least reason to expect it. Accordingly, many of them retired from a profession which they had chosen for itself, and not for amusement, to the benefit of which they had devoted their best exertions, and in which they had spent so great a part of their lives.

It was now industriously put forth, that, unless the old officers were removed, regiments would soon have field-officers unable to mount their horses ; but the fact is, that, up to the present time, had they continued in the service, the average of the ages of brevet field-officers in the British army would be between forty-five and fifty years ; and I should be glad to know when a man, enjoying a good constitution, and possessing the advantage of a familiarity with every species of warfare, however contracted or however extended the scale of operations, is fit to command a regiment, if not at the time of life just mentioned ? It is impossible to say how soon this country, in the present unsettled state of the civilised world, may be forced into a war, either owing to our ready interference in the squabbles of the lesser European powers, or to the aggressions of the greater ones upon ourselves. We know not when we may be called on to fight, if not absolutely *pro aris et focis*, at least for the integrity of our colonial and foreign possessions, especially when we reflect on the insatiable ambition of Russia, the great and important accessions of territory that she loses no opportunity of acquiring on her southern borders, and the danger of her eagle yet taking a bolder and a longer flight, and pouncing on our conquests in India. On the supposition, then, that we be drawn into a war of any magnitude, who will have the hardihood to assert that our present army, though making a more showy appearance than that of 1814, would undergo equally well the hardships and privations of campaigns like the Peninsular? Or would our men act, on trying occasions, with as much confidence under their present officers, as under those tried and experienced veterans whose removal from the service has been so sedulously effected? Were I to form an opinion from the present state of the corps in which I had the honour to serve, and which has only three officers who have ever seen a shot fired, and that only at Quatre Bras and Waterloo, I would say that, in the armies of the five great European powers, the most inexperienced regimental officers at this moment are the British.

There are persons certainly who will agree that an army ought to be officered entirely by young men, because certain great generals have been distinguished at an early age for their military abilities and warlike achievements; but armies are not composed of extraordinary men. We must take into consideration the capabilities of the generality of officers, and, as we have no reason to suppose that in the long run the talents and application of the young hands exceed those of the old, I think, when we throw experience into the scale with the merits of the latter, that the balance must inevitably turn in their favour. It is true that during the French revolution some men rose rapidly to high military rank, and commanded successfully; but, if there were among them officers who were young in years, it must be recollected that they were comparatively old in experience, while our young gentlemen in red coats are now wholly inexperienced. It is amusing to hear persons instance Napoleon, in the earlier part of his military career, as a specimen of young officers in general. His conduct not being preternatural, it is of course possible that our times may furnish a parallel to him, but it is not very probable; much less is it probable that the British army of the present day will produce many like him. He was endowed by nature with an extraordinary genius; he had the advantage of an excellent military education; he entered the army at an early age; he then saw active service, and was not slow to learn the practice of that which he knew in theory; the times in which he first commanded also were without a parallel; the enthusiasm and martial ardour of the French were at their height; the system of moving large masses on weak and partial points was introduced by them at that period; and its novelty, together with the uncommon impetuosity and fury of the republican soldiers, enabled them for some time to vanquish repeatedly the best troops

on the Continent. What grounds then do we here
find for the assertion, that it is preferable to have
an army officered by young men rather than by
veterans ?   It may also well be asked, whether any
one will venture to assert that equal reliance may
be placed on our militia regiments and on those
of the line ?   And in what does the superiority of
regular troops, compared with militia, consist, if not
in their greater experience ?   Besides, does not history
abound with instances of most dreadful reverses sustained by armies in consequence of the inexperience
of those in command, and of the most unhoped-for
successes obtained through the judgment and presence
of mind of experienced warriors ?   But I will not
insult the understanding of the reader by pursuing any
further the refutation of such ill-founded opinions.

I am aware that such comments as I have hazarded
may be supposed by many to proceed from a prejudiced *laudator temporis acti ;* but let the friends of such
a supposition know, that none are so ready to attri-
bute prejudice to those who differ from them in
opinion, as are the very persons whose own minds
an improper bias affects.   From the truly liberal
and unbiassed I do not apprehend a sneer at my
assertion of the superiority of the veteran to the
youth in his military noviciate, and at my slowness
to be convinced that the Imperial old guard at
Waterloo were not more to be depended upon than
a body of conscripts ; and I trust that I am not so
dead to all feelings of patriotism, or so indifferent to
the interests of that service from which I have retired
after many years spent in it, as not to desire to see
our present army excelling in all respects the old.

But as yet, whether it be through excess of prejudice or lack of penetration, I have not seen sufficient cause to give, not the preference, but even the credit of equality with the soldiers of 1814 to the British land force of 1834. The officers now in our army are very different from their predecessors—a difference upon which not a few of them may pique themselves. They are more showy in dress generally speaking, but less manly in appearance, and certainly not so fit to endure the fatigues and hardships of a military life. Well cultivated mustachios, a pinched-up waist, and a padded uniform—the lip of a terrier, and the figure of a wasp—may become, but do not make their possessor a soldier ; and I feel confidence when I say that the British army of the present day is inferior, both as regards officers and men, to that which served under the Duke of Wellington, not only in point of experience, but of hardiness and strength of constitution ; and I very much fear that the zeal and soldier-like sense of duty exhibited by so many of the old class would be too frequently wanting among certain of their more dandified successors. How many colonels of regiments do we not now see, who, having been pushed on rapidly from step to step over the heads of meritorious officers, are most excellent army tailors, but know as much of the military profession as their predecessors in command did of making inexpressibles. Since the war I have known a lieutenant-colonel, commanding a regiment, who would take more notice of any raw recruit who had the sagacity to sport a watch-ribbon than of the bravest old soldier in the corps.

But I must not be understood as considering the

dress of the men a matter of no consequence ; on the contrary, I think it very deserving of attention, both with regard to comfort and appearance ; a soldier should always appear clean and well clad, as this tends in no slight degree to increase his self-respect ; but *est modus in rebus,* and there is no necessity that the whole time which a commanding officer thinks proper to devote to his regiment should be spent in the master-tailor's shop.   The clothing of soldiers, too, should always be made with an eye to service, and should be calculated to allow them the freest use of their limbs and the greatest possible comfort.   Some officers find an inexhaustible source of torment for their men in the affair of clothing, and, besides, often compel them to lay out their pay on what I must beg leave to call " unnecessary neces- saries " ; this is done sometimes with a view of pre- venting the men from drinking, but it really is a piece of glaring injustice, and it would be much better if the officers themselves would set an example of temperance.

But now my grey-goose quill is worn to a stump, and warns me of the extent to which I have already indulged the *cacoëthes scribendi.*   Gentle readers, there- fore, I take my leave ; but, although this is my first, and probably will be my last, appearance before the public, I cannot venture to imitate the Cartha- ginian poet, and add a " plaudite," when I have said " valete."

THE END